New Angle on Writing

11 Universal Sentence Forms With Model Student Compositions

"Good sentences promise nothing less than lessons
and practice in the organization of the world."

Stanley Fish

Richard Dowling   Stephen Watson

Two Hands Approach Publishing

ISBN 9780973382259

Teachers and others are free to use all the charts and selections from the book for educational purposes, but not for commercial purposes or profit of any kind.

If you have any questions or suggestions, please email us at
2ha_sa@excite.com

Visit us also at our websites at

http://newangleonwriting.org
http://symphonicassemblage.org

Large portions of this book are excerpted from Dowling and Watson's 2 volumes *The Two Hands Approach to the English Language: A Symphonic Assemblage* published in Feb. 2010

Unless otherwise noted, over design and interior layout and additional graphics and photos by stedawa

Contents

 Semester 1

The Introduction

The Teacher Section

Part 1 – Grammar

Part 2 – Punctuation

Part 3 – Sentence Forms

The Student Section

Opening Note to Teachers, Students, and the General Public

With this book *New Angle on Writing,* we are presenting an innovative conception and methodology for teaching beginning students to write effectively within one year. This book is a reduced, abridged version of our comprehensive 2 volume survey of the English language entitled *The Two Hands Approach to the English Language: A Symphonic Assemblage* (totally more than 1600 pages). The original 2 volumes cover every aspect of the English language (grammar, vocabulary acquisition, reading, poetry, etc) and include a complete 1-year course in teaching writing to beginning students. However, this abridged book presents only the **first semester course** in writing from the first volume, omitting other material in that volume not related to writing. We present in this book an adequate number of model student compositions for beginning students to emulate in their assignments, but the model compositions are fewer in number and there are no essays by professional writers which both can be found in Volume I of the larger book.

We publish this abridged version because it is cheaper and adequate to present the essential elements of our innovative conception and methodology for teaching writing. If you are interested in the other aspects of the English language covered in Volume I as well as the philosophical background, underlying assumptions, and principles that guided our writing of the 2 volumes, then you should purchase Volume I. If you wish to present a full 1-year course in writing, covering the writing of expository, narrative, descriptive, and comparative essays (along with autobiographical

1

writing) with many accompanying model professional and student examples of those essay forms, then you should purchase Volume II. Or you may purchase the abridged version of Volume II, *New Angle On Writing (Semester 2)*, which has adequate but fewer student essays than the *Two Hands* (Vol.II).

Readers should know in advance that this book is divided into 3 sections. The first section, the Introduction, presents the **Historical Context, Rationale, and Unique Features of our Approach to Writing.** The second section, the teacher section, includes materials primarily useful for teachers who will use the book for a 1-semester course. The section opens with an brief descriptions of the 12 Turns of the English Language, the Twelve Kinds of Words, the Five Jobs of the Twelve Kinds of Words in Sentences, and the Twelve Punctuation Marks as well as additional guidance for instructors to implement in the class. In addition, this section starts with a series of lesson plans for the entire course, which is placed at the beginning of this section for easy access by teachers.

The second section of the book contains the actual lessons for students, including all Sentence Forms, examples of Sentence Forms, and successive writing assignments accompanied with models done by previous students of this course.

We trust that you will all enjoy and profit from this shorter version of our original first volume of *Two Hands Approach to the English Language: A Symphonic Assemblage.*

The Introduction

The Historical Context, Rationale, and Unique Features of our Approach to Writing

Our title announces and proposes a new angle, perspective, and approach to teaching writing. While it includes and incorporates earlier prevailing approaches to writing, it introduces for the first time a dynamic conception and methodology of teaching Writing that **possesses multiple distinctive features which guarantee that it can solve the most longstanding and vexing problem confronting contemporary education**.

And what is that problem? For over a hundred years, educators at both the secondary and university levels have disputed the best way to teach beginning students how to write competent, reasonably coherent, graceful prose. This is not a task that can be eliminated or left to chance; after all, no one can be called educated who lacks the ability to write consistently clear prose since most subsequent jobs and careers after college require one to write well. Indeed, almost all college classes themselves demand that students be capable of producing readable writing. So why have educators and theorists failed to find a way – consistently and universally – to enable beginning students to write passable, even stylistically memorable, prose?

It is a national scandal that the problem has not been solved, and no one claims or pretends that they have found a way to do so. Obviously, it is not for lack of trying. At least four prevailing pedagogies for teaching Writing (with their multiple variations) have appeared over the span of the hundred or more years since the first required college class in writing was introduced at Harvard in 1885 to address the perceived grievous lack of writing proficiency displayed by incoming freshmen.

4

Indeed, the two most recent of the four prevailing pedagogies of Writing only emerged in contemporary times from 1960 to 2000 as part of the growth of a fully fledged Discipline of Learning called *Composition Studies*, now with a formidable array of distinguished Doctoral Programs around the nation and its own set of noteworthy independent journals and Professional organizations.

The Progress has been impressive, but recently the discipline of Composition Studies itself has reached an impasse – entering into one of those periodic morasses that seem to regularly engulf academic disciplines when people become too introspective, career obsessed, and more interested in nitpicking quarrels and mutual fault finding than in ways to make learning relevant and serviceable for the life of the mind and the common public good.

While Post-Modernism has its virtues, extreme versions of it have infected, afflicted, and increasingly monopolized the ongoing public and academic conversation about teaching writing to the point of shutting out all voices not deemed "correct or sufficiently respectful" of certain canons of contemporary scholarship which have hardly stood the test of time.[1]

We ask educators, theorists of Writing pedagogies, and ordinary people in the general public, therefore, to listen with an open mind to what we advocate here: **namely, the actual solution to this longstanding problem of teaching all beginning students to write reasonably well within a year.**

However, we first have to know why the earlier pedagogies failed to be consistently and universally successful before we can understand why the distinctive features of our New

---

[1] For a fuller background on the growing complexity and narrowness of Composition Studies, in some quarters, see the article by Robert J. Connors *Composition History and Disciplinarity* in *Selected Essays by Robert J. Connors* and see Sondra Perl's introduction entitled *Writing Process: A Shining Moment* in *Landmark Essays on Writing Process* edited by Sondra Perl.

<u>Angle on Writing</u> will not fail in a similar fashion, why and how it can make up for their deficiencies – complementing, completing, and bringing to a successful conclusion what they so admirably started but could not finish. In short, we are not engaged in a quarrel with anyone nor do we intend to demean the accomplishments of earlier pedagogies of Writing. We wish only to complete and bring to fruition the endeavors and contributions of those before us.

The previous four prevailing pedagogies did not fail to make valuable and indispensable contributions to the solution of the problem; however, they failed to fully solve it. Why?

Some historical perspective is necessary here. Throughout history, some people have learned to be superb writers without any classroom instruction. And as long as colleges and universities remained largely restricted to an elite and privileged upper class who had a relatively sound secondary education as background preparation before entering college, most students learned to write reasonably well, especially with small classes and a low student class size to teacher ratio. However, with the coming of the Industrial Revolution, Democracy, and large land grant colleges and universities in the mid-19th century, the number of students entering college increased considerably. The sheer number of the new students, coupled with their less privileged educational background and preparation, placed a permanent and increasing strain upon the resources of colleges and universities. The new students had a weaker reading and writing preparation while the universities lacked an adequate supply of trained, capable teachers who could instruct the new students.

The colleges – partly out of ignorance, partly due to greed, and partly due simply to a lack of coherent vision and organization – harbored the pleasing delusion that anybody who had graduated from college must be able to teach writing to beginning students, so they adopted the practice (which soon became the established and unquestioned habit) of assigning aspiring graduate students in English or newly hired English faculty to teach large sections of English composition to incoming freshmen. The ratio of students to instructors rose to absurd proportions, and inevitably overworked, burned out instructors found it impossible to teach writing on a one to one basis and were reduced to handing out mechanical exercises and assignments that lent themselves to mass testing and grading. Since the graduate students and newly hired English teachers themselves had received little or no training and instruction in how to actually teach writing, they relied on standard textbooks for their own teaching of beginning students but with little comprehension of why, what, or how the textbooks were reliable guides for teaching writing. So the lowly Writing Teachers of beginning students struggled simply to survive and escape as fast as they could from the low esteem, overwork, and low pay deemed appropriate for their job, hoping to advance their monetary prospects and careers by being promoted to teaching literature classes.[2]

Given this practice, system, and structure for teaching writing, it was inevitable that it would be both a partial success and a partial failure – the perennial glass that is half full or half empty depending on the underlying intentions, aims, and perspectives of the beholder. Some students learned to write well as some always have learned due to native talent or hard work or the instruction of some dedicated teachers or the increasingly more relevant and efficient methods of instruction developed over time, but an equal number failed rather consistently to write well. If you held the underlying conviction that some people – either because of their inherent mental, racial, ethnic, class,

---

[2] This summary history is a capsule condensation of a brilliant history of the subject by Robert J. Connors in several brilliant articles in *Selected Essays of Robert J. Connors*, notably among them *Overwork, Underpay: Labor and Status of Composition Teachers Since 1880, Writing the History of Our Discipline*, and *Composition History and Disciplinarity*.

gender, or moral inferiority – were simply constitutionally and permanently unable to learn the complicated task of writing well, then you accepted the results as proof and validation of your realistic viewpoint, and you let the cards fall as they must, with no need to bemoan or second guess the final outcome.

On the other hand, if you held the contrary view that every student – regardless of their mental, racial, ethnic, class, gender, or moral background – could learn to write with proper instruction, then you deplored the results as an unacceptable violation and unjust outcome offensive to your idealistic viewpoint, requiring you to criticize, condemn, correct, and improve the pedagogy and practices responsible for such a consequence.

Meanwhile, the problem only got worse, much worse. Due to the increasing wealth of the growing middle class and perhaps even more to the social criticisms, convulsions, and reforms of the 1960s, many universities, starting in the early 1970s and later, adopted an open door policy of admitting all students with a high school degree regardless of their grades or preliminary test scores. Thus, there began a mass influx of students in numbers dwarfing all earlier expansions of student populations, and the new students entered with educational backgrounds far more grievously deficient than at any earlier time in American education. How could so many students so ill prepared by their previous schooling possibly be taught to write intelligible, competent prose by a system of instruction already overtaxed and manifestly failing half the time as it was?

In response, the two contemporary pedagogies of teaching writing emerged (the two contemporary pedagogies are explained below along with the two traditional pedagogies) – partly as a consequence of their own inherent growth and partly as a sorely needed response to the new requirements for more profound, efficient, and workable ways of teaching writing.

So, where are we now, and in what ways have the two contemporary pedagogies helped us advance toward solving the problem yet proved ultimately unable to solve it? Well, the two contemporary pedagogies between them did make enormous advances in four respects: (1) they provided the first reasonably systematic and coherent curriculum that assured the adequate training of competent professional teachers of writing; (2) they revolutionized the understanding of writing as both a process and interactive pursuit that must be taught and appreciated by writing instructors from the point of view and perspectives of students with their diverse cultural, cognitive, and rhetorical skill sets; (3) they recovered and integrated the ancient, medieval, and early modern insights and methods of teaching writing with ongoing research in composition studies both in classrooms and academic studies; and (4) they and their post-modern successors established Composition Studies as a permanent Discipline of Learning with accredited doctoral programs and creditable academic journals. In sum, the quantity, and even more the quality, of excellent scholarly examinations of the history, theory, and practice of teaching writing have proliferated and are now approaching a classic synthesis and maturity of attainment.

Yet, the four root obstacles preventing solution of the problem remained both unaddressed and unresolved by the two contemporary theories: namely, (1) the tremendous, indeed universal, expansion of the student population needing to be taught and needing to learn to write; (2) the lack of sufficient teachers to provide the required instruction as well as the lack of a simpler, more practical training course for such teachers; (3) the lack of an initial instruction course in composition that could be used with maximum effectiveness by both teachers and students in aptly organized lesson plans that are focused,

9

clear, and practically doable in manageably sized units which are incremental, progressive, cumulative, assessable, and enduring in their ability to improve the skills and capacities of students to write well; and (4) the conception and realization of a systematic core of Knowledge and Skills in Writing that could form the basis for a program of Writing Across the Curriculum that would insure a minimal level of assessable and continuous achievement.

First, the rise of the student population has now become universal because we live in a Global Age – the time of what Peter Drucker has called the Knowledge Society – where the basic skills to work in the New Global Economy require that everyone be able to compute, read, and write effectively. However, just when we need a course that will be universally effective for everyone, recent discussions in Composition Studies and Journals have begun to question both the possibility and viability of the previously basic required course in college composition. The present courses, they emphasize, fail too consistently, so despite all the advances that have been made, some theorists now rather dogmatically assert that all attempts to teach a core body of Knowledge and skills in Writing is impossible because earlier courses with a professed skills approach were found to be too reductionistic and mechanical, violating the personal, organic, and social nature of writing. This distinctly hopeless approach betokens at once a defeatist attitude, a lack of imagination, a refusal to invent a practical and useable method of teaching writing, and a pronounced failure in common sense in prevailing views of writing.

Second, the failure to teach everyone has always been partly due, and remains partly due, to the lack of adequately trained teachers. However, the lack of adequately trained teachers, who can teach an effective introductory course in writing, has everything to do with the excessively vague, abstract prevailing theories of writing that insure only a limited cadre of competent writing instructors are found at the university level, but especially at the high school level. Students come terribly unprepared to write well when they arrive at universities, and they don't always encounter even there a knowledgeable writing instructor.

However, even if the writing instructor at the university level is a competent instructor, aware of the latest contemporary as well as traditional pedagogies, his class is invariably too large for him to teach everyone using his prevailing methods only. Because he lacks the **conception and realization of a Systematic Core of Knowledge and Skills about Writing**, he or she cannot convey that Systematic Core of Knowledge and Skills about Writing to his or her students. **The Systematic Core of Knowledge and Skills about Writing** would teach most of the students what they needed to know and do provided they assisted and helped one another, and the teacher would be free to work more closely with the few students who needed extra attention and assistance. However, lacking a coherent, focused Systematic Core of Knowledge and Skills about Writing the teacher has to do the impossible and teach everyone in a continuously close, attentive, and time consuming manner.

So, we come to the Third and deepest Obstacle to solving the ongoing Problem: namely a one year course of instruction that would teach a Systematic Core of Knowledge and Skills about writing that would teach most students what they needed to know and do provided they assisted and helped one another, and would free teachers to give special attention to a few students. As stated above, such a course in composition would be used with maximum effectiveness by both teachers and students in aptly organized lesson plans which are focused, clear, and practically doable in manageably sized units that are incremental, progressive, cumulative, assessable, and enduring in their ability to improve the skills and capacities of students to write well. Such a course would also improve greatly the facility of teachers to edit and rewrite with ease, swiftness, and confidence the compositions of their students.

Fourth, and finally, the Systematic Core of Knowledge and Skills about writing in the initial instruction course in college (or even high school) would provide the basis for a writing course across the curriculum that would insure a minimal level of assessable and continuous achievement.

This book presents a course of instruction that teaches the needed Systematic Core of Knowledge and Skills about writing. The course possesses 17 or more distinctive features which are not sufficiently present in the prevailing four pedagogies of teaching writing. These 17 distinctive features correct the deficiencies in the four prevailing theories of writing, especially with respect to the initial course of instruction for students just beginning to write. When the initial course of instruction we advocate is widely adopted and used in conjunction with the insights and respective emphasis of the four prevailing pedagogies of writing, then the problem of teaching all beginning students to write well within a year will be solved.

We identify below the 14 Unique and Distinctive Features of our <u>New Angle on Writing</u> and briefly describe how each feature corrects previous deficiencies in teaching Writing as well as the nature of its particular contribution to solving the long standing problem of teaching beginning students to write effectively.

The 17 Distinctive Features of the

New Angle on Writing

The 1st Distinctive Feature

The First Distinctive Feature of the <u>New Angle on Writing</u> is its **Comprehensive** character. It is comprehensive in 4 respects: (1) it is holistic and not partial; (2) it is inclusive and not exclusive; (3) for the first time it identifies, provides excellent examples, and gives guidance for the effective employment of all sentences in the English language; and (4) it promotes a deep understanding of the teaching and learning of writing while imparting a feeling of closure and confidence in knowing henceforth how to steadily improve one's writing skills and style.

With regard to the first point, our initial course covers – at least briefly but with a fresh, novel presentation – all parts of language instruction, including an initial overview, grammar, the kinds of Words and their functions in the sentence, the Architecture of the Sentence, The Systematic Analysis of Sentences, Punctuation, Sentence Construction, Paragraph Development, and Essay Organization. For each Writing Assignment, we provide a representative cross-section of student compositions that serve as models and representations of the variety and caliber of writing that other students can do.

With regard to the second point, we introduce both teachers and students to an in-depth analysis of the 4 Prevailing Pedagogies of Writing, extolling the benefits of each Approach to Writing and encouraging both teachers and students to incorporate and integrate the insights and skills stressed in those pedagogies. We mention and promote various teaching practices associated with the 4 pedagogies and encourage their adoption in conjunction with our own approach. Thus, we are **inclusive and not exclusive in our coverage** and recommendation of the many approaches and practices that have proven helpful to various teachers and students over the years.

With regard to the third point, we identify, provide examples, and promote practicing (as individual examples and as incorporated into increasingly larger and varied compositions) all the 127 most frequent sentence forms in the English language, so students receive a comprehensive overview of the repertoire of sentence tools available for them to select in writing. Previous pedagogies have never provided this service for students.

With regard to the fourth point, when students have examined the history of teaching and learning about language and writing and when they have been presented with all the sentences employed in writing and practiced them, they feel confident and assured in their knowledge and use of language and feel they can progressively teach themselves to improve their writing daily because they have a proven method for doing so.

The 2nd Distinctive Feature

The Second Distinctive Feature of the <u>New Angle On Writing</u> is its **Systematic** character. It is systematic in four respects: (1) it identifies and defines the **Few Parts** that constitute the **Whole of the language** or **the Few Parts** that constitute **the lesser Whole of an individual Constituent Part of the larger Whole** ; (2) it delineates and demonstrates **the Forms** that the various few parts employ for clear expression; and (3) it describes **the Functions**, which each of the various parts of language (with their respective expressive Forms) play or perform in language usage; (4) it describes how each of the various few parts (with their expressive forms and functions) connect, interact, reinforce, and support one another in a proportionate and visual structure and configuration.

Thus, the book in <u>The Twelve Turns of English</u> identifies and describes the twelve parts of English, namely the 5 Skills, 5 Tasks, and 2 Crowning Achievements of language acquisition. Regarding **the lesser Whole that comprises all sentences**, we identify the 11 Parts or types and categories of sentences. With regard to the **lesser Whole of the single individual sentence**, we identify 5 Parts or Levels of the Sentence. And likewise with other aspects of the language. In contrast, the four prevailing pedagogies of Writing are notorious for their vague, abstract, and altogether too broad and unfocused presentation of their respective approaches. They are admirably philosophical, inspirational, and encouraging but hard to reduce to digestible, manageable, and practical lessons and exercises for assimilation. They lack completely a comprehensive scope, systematic structure, and effective visual representations of their teaching.

The 3rd Distinctive Feature

The Third Distinctive Feature of the <u>New Angle On Writing</u> is that it is **Visual.** All the vital core knowledge and skills described in the comprehensive, systematic course of instruction are presented in visual graphics and charts which enable students to use the Right Hemispheres of their brains to integrate and realize.an **integral**, **holistic** understanding of the language. Over time, they acquire an **intuitive vision, feel, and grasp** of the language. In contrast, most books on grammar and writing are notably lacking in visual graphics and charts to assist the comprehension and retention of language knowledge and skills.

The 4th Distinctive Feature

The Fourth Distinctive Feature of the <u>New Angle On Writing</u> consists of its **Focused** quality or characteristic. Visual graphics and charts automatically **focus** and concentrate the mind's attention on specific and clearly distinct parts and pieces of information. In general, learning without both intense attention and concentration is impossible, so focus is essential and indispensable for both effective teaching and learning. The identification and definition of only a Few Parts in a Systematic Structural Whole also promotes and facilitates **a clearer and more concentrated Focus in learning**. The Grouping of the 127 sentence forms into only eleven common categories also promotes and facilitates the **Focused and Concentrated Attention and Memory of students for learning and remembering the various Sentence Forms.** In contrast, the four prevailing pedagogies are altogether too indistinct and vague in their specific delineation of the major parts of their respective approaches.

The 5th Distinctive Feature

The Fifth Distinctive Feature of the <u>New Angle On Writing</u> is its **Lesson Learnable** character or ease of Acquisition. This characteristic reinforces the Distinctive Feature or Quality of Focus just discussed because the entire course is divided into distinctly manageable, clearly targeted, and focused lessons which can be presented and learned in individual and profitable segments, or even more profitably presented in successive and progressive order. Each lesson can be completed in various time frames from an hour to two or more hours. The lessons covered constitute individual and coherently comprehensive instruction in one aspect of writing, and the successive lessons lend themselves to fruitful periodic reviews where the aspect of writing covered can be examined, reinforced, and practiced more than once as needed by single individuals or a whole class. In sharp contrast, there are no clearly demarcated lesson units for the four prevailing pedagogies which reduces their ability to be accessed and usefully organized by teachers and students alike.

The 6th Distinctive Feature

The Sixth Distinctive Feature of the <u>New Angle On Writing</u> is its **Progressive** Character. It is Progressive in four respects: (1) **it proceeds from the simple and easy level of difficulty to increasingly harder and more complicated levels**, insuring that weaker, less capable students are not left behind and that all students gradually can adjust and acclimate themselves to the mastery of more difficult material; (2) the lessons are presented in **gradual, incremental stages** that provide sufficient focus and time for mastery; (3) the lessons are **cumulative** with the mastery of later lessons dependent upon the mastery of earlier lessons; (4) the lessons are **continuously confirming and reinforcing** since later lessons require the continued apt use and mastery of earlier lessons. Students constantly experience the ongoing relevance of the lessons they learn. In contrast, all four of the aspects of the Progressive Feature are largely absent from the four prevailing pedagogies.

The 7th Distinctive Feature

The Seventh Distinctive Feature of the <u>New Angle On Writing</u> is its **Modeling** Characteristic. Students are provided with excellent models for all the sentences as well as excellent student models for all the composition assignments and for the two examinations. This affords students another strong focus on what they should do and considerable confidence and examples to emulate in their own writing. In contrast, there are few or no models available with the other four pedagogies, or if they are available, there are only a few professional models which students find difficult to relate to and emulate as opposed to the models of fellow students.[3]

---

[3] See *The Two Hands Approach to the English Language: a Symphonic Assemblage* (Vol. i) for a much larger collection of Student Compositions for

The 8th Distinctive Feature

The Eighth Distinctive Feature of the <u>New Angle On Writing</u> is that it is **Practice Driven**. Writing is a Skill and cannot be learned just by theoretical study and understanding, but has to be primarily learned and perfected through continual practice leading to the gradual mastery of the craft of writing. Thus, students must immediately write two examples of every sentence form learned and then share and analyze their sentences with one another at the blackboard. They must practice reading their sentences out loud with the proper intonation and dramatic emphasis; otherwise, they will never develop a feel for the musical and rhythmic qualities of language or discover their own voice in expressing themselves in writing. Furthermore, students must practice writing notated and footnoted examples of the various Sentence Forms in longer writing assignments and then again share their compositions with follow students, editing and rewriting them into final, finished papers. The sentences that students must write are varied, specific, and targeted – distinctive in their form and excellence and resonant with the context of the surrounding language in which they are embedded. In contrast, the four prevailing pedagogies mostly just explain good writing and exhort students to somehow imitate what they enjoin rather like taking students to a professional ballet production and then coming home and telling students to put on their own ballet performance. There are no specific moves or forms of action to practice imitating or emulating, so it is quite difficult for students to focus and concentrate on what to learn and above all practice doing to demonstrate an adequate level of performance.

---

each assignment as well as excellent and powerful compositions by professional writers who put our Sentence Forms to good use.

The 9th Distinctive Feature

The Ninth Distinctive Feature of the <u>New Angle On Writing</u> it that it is **Performance Based.** Thus, the writing compositions of students are rendered real, because they must always be read aloud and presented publicly to fellow students and the teacher. Students invest and involve themselves more in their writing if they know it will be read, reviewed, analyzed, and edited by their peers as well as the instructor. Moreover, with an audience always present and responding to what they write, they tend automatically to become more aware of the content and coherence of their writing as well as to realize that all writing must appeal to and persuade an audience of readers with telling rhetorical expressions and a graceful style. The two contemporary pedagogies of writing have understood the necessity of this distinctive feature rather well, but the two traditional pedagogies have displayed little awareness or implementation of it in their approaches to writing.

The 10th Distinctive Feature

The Tenth Distinctive Feature of the <u>New Angle On Writing</u> is its **Peer Referenced and Collaborative** character. The content of everything students write is derived from their personal life experience, a life experience which is shared and at once familiar and interesting to all the members of their particular generation of peers. The students are regularly required to read aloud and share their writing assignments with their peers and to collaborate with these peers in editing and rewriting their papers and the papers of one another. Peer interaction and the pressure to perform well publicly before peers both provide added incentive and stimulation to students to write with greater care, attention, thoughtfulness, and imagination than if they were writing only to please or impress a teacher. And some students because of their temperament or more social disposition learn new knowledge and skills best in interaction with other students rather than from either books or the teacher. In contrast, only the rhetorical pedagogy of writing gives sufficient attention to this distinctive feature of how beginning students learn to write effectively.

The 11th Distinctive Feature

The Eleventh Distinctive Feature of the <u>New Angle On Writing</u> is its **Body Based** character. The book uses the **metaphor of Two Hands** and innumerable tangible physical graphics and charts to teach writing to students and to enable them to remember what they learn forever. **The recurring metaphor of Two Hands** to organize the Kinds of Words, The Functions of the Sentence, the 11 Sentence Forms, the opposed stylistic characteristics of an effective writing style, the Key faculties of the mind and heart, and many other aspects of language and language acquisition serve to integrate, connect, and interrelate whatever is learned as an integral whole – a whole ever accessible to memory by reference to one's own two hands. No book or computer is necessary to refresh one's memory, just the instrument and symbolic structure of the universe suggested by the structure and configuration of the two hands. In contrast, the four prevailing pedagogies of writing fail completely to ground their knowledge and skills in reference and relation to any aspect of daily physical or tangible reality, much less to the continuous presence, impact, and pervasive influence of the human body.

The 12th Distinctive Feature

The Twelfth Distinctive Feature of the <u>New Angle On Writing</u> is it **Assessment Accountable** character. The practice and incorporation of the 11 Sentence Forms in ever more complex notated and footnoted paragraphs and essays affords teachers a specific and measureable criteria for determining the level and degree of student mastery (1) of the various 127 sentence forms; and (2) and of the overall integration of varied sentence forms into a larger, integral composition. If students are found to be notably deficient in the mastery of any of the particular forms, they can instruct students to review those forms and practice them with more care and attention in additional papers. If students are found to be too artificial in their use of Sentence forms and to be missing a natural feeling for the flow, style, and grace of writing, they can be encouraged to write more freely and spontaneously with less regard for the specific use of required sentence forms. Any and all practices and methods can be employed from the four pedagogies of writing including free writing, sentence combining, and more intensive one on one consultation and interaction between the teacher and student about their actual, particular writing assignments. Whatever the ongoing individual problems appearing in student papers, all students will have achieved a more or less profound appreciation for the principle of form in their writing so their prose will be clearer, less sprawling and wildly proliferating, more focused and more effective in the use of varied sentence types. In contrast, the four prevailing pedagogies demonstrate few specific and consistent ways to control and structure the flow of prose and little useable criteria for assessing and evaluating writing.

The 13th Distinctive Feature

The Thirteenth Distinctive Feature of the <u>New Angle On Writing</u> is that it is both **Student and Teacher Friendly**. Because all the Writing Lessons and Assignments are clearly laid out, both the students and teacher always know what has been done, is being done, and will be done in successive classes. Students don't have to ask what content and assignments they missed during absences, and teachers don't have to remind them since the sequence and assignments are all in the book.

Students find the course especially helpful because they are given multiple examples as models for writing their own sentences and likewise numerous models, both professional and student models, to emulate in their longer writing assignments.

Since students are required to notate and footnote specific required sentence forms in their writing assignments, students don't even attempt to make lame excuses of why they could not do the writing assignments as stipulated, especially when other students are managing to complete the assignments. So, teachers are spared listening to the lame excuses and responding to them. And teachers can quickly review papers to see if the sentence forms are completed. Because the entire course is laid out for teachers, they do not suffer from burnout and exhaustion, and they therefore have the time and energy to develop creative lesson plans of their own to complement those in the book.

Moreover, the more teachers instruct students in the 11 Sentence Forms and the 127 sub-forms and the more they read and edit student papers, the more proficient their own mastery of writing will become. Before long, their skill and ease in editing and rewriting student papers will improve enormously. In contrast, the four prevailing pedagogies of writing lack a focused structure, clear lesson plans progressively developed, and few models to assist teachers in their instruction and students in their writing of assignments.

The 14th Distinctive Feature

The Fourteenth Distinctive Feature of the <u>New Angle On Writing</u> is that it is **Teacher Trainable, Globally Deployable**. Because the system and method for teaching Writing is clear, focused, progressive, and cumulative, and the entire course is presented in lesson learnable units with an entire master plan of classes to guide both teachers and students, **new and previously untrained teachers can easily learn and practice the system as they teach it to students**. By the end of the year, they will possess a comprehensive understanding of the essential, indispensable knowledge and skills necessary for teaching an effective beginning class in writing.

The fact that new teachers can acquire the system and method (or knowledge and skills) they need as they teach the class for the first time eliminates the need for directly training them to teach writing. While it would certainly be preferable that they have an initial training course in writing before teaching it, the reality is that most teachers have never had such a training, and the present training courses fail to provide the indispensable system and method that they require for teaching effective beginning courses in writing.

Because teachers can acquire the system and method they require to teach an effective writing course with this book, it means that there will now – **for the first time** – be a **sufficient number of competent teachers of writing** to insure that effective Beginning Courses in Writing can be **Globally or Universally Available**. As we enter the Global Age of what Peter Drücker designated the Knowledge Society, learning to write with a reasonable degree of competence has now become indispensable for most human beings , and it is therefore imperative that we have a sufficient supply of capable and trained teachers of writing.

The 15th, 16th, and 17th Features

We explain the last three features together because they bear directly upon the most **noteworthy and central contribution of this book**: namely, that **this book restores the sentence to its venerable place as the beginning foundation of effective writing instruction.** In support of the foregoing statement, we refer readers to the last published essay *The Erasure of the Sentence (College Composition and Communication, 2000)* by Robert J. Connors whom we regard as a mentor and as the foremost figure in the establishment of Composition Studies as a recognized discipline of learning.

In the *The Erasure of the Sentence*, Connors demonstrated that traditionally the sentence was at the center of all instruction in writing; moreover, he noted that in the 1970s and early 1980s three developments – the cumulative sentence of Francis Christensen, Sentence Combining, and Imitation Exercises – were at the exciting forefront of writing instruction. **And he cites repeated studies which proved that all three developments increased not only the ability of students to write more varied sentences but also improved their overall style of writing.** Yet for some curious and rather disgraceful reason, all these improvements were ignored, and the three developments were called failures because they disagreed with certain ideological and excessively extreme criticisms of any practice that smacked of formalism, behaviorism, or empiricism in contrast to a humanistic perspective. While we share the humanistic perspective of Composition Studies in general and agree in rejecting extreme versions of formalism, behaviorism, and empiricism, the field of Composition Studies went to the other extreme. As Connors wrote insightfully near the end of *The Erasure of the Sentence*, **"The loss of all defense of formalism has**

24

left some curious vacuums in the middle of our teaching."[4]

Connors has an extremely telling summary near the end of the article:

> **"It really does seem that the current perception that somehow sentence rhetorics 'don't work' exists as a massive piece of wish-fulfillment**. Leaving aside the question of syntactic fluency or maturity entirely, the data from holistic and analytic general essay readings are unequivocal. George Hillocks, reviewing the research in 1986, looked closely into all the major sentence-combining research and found many lines of inquiry that needed to be followed up. But after his careful dissection, he still concluded his section on sentence rhetorics with a quote that recognized the value of the technique: "Even with so many questions left unanswered, **one is tempted to agree with Charles Cooper (1975c) that 'no other single teaching approach has ever consistently been shown to have a beneficial effect on syntactic maturity and writing quality'** (p.72)" (151). In other words, if people believe that research has shown that sentence rhetorics don't work, their belief exists not because the record bears it out but because it is what people want to believe.
>
> *Why* we want to believe it is the interesting part.
>
> **So what was it that erased the sentence**, wiped what had been the "forefront in composition research today…at the cutting edge of research design" in 1980 off the radar screen of composition studies? What reduced it from a vital, if unfinished, inquiry into why a popular stylistic method worked so well to a half-hidden and seldom-discussed classroom practice on the level of, say, vocabulary quizzes? It was not, as we have seen, that sentence rhetorics were proved useless.

---

[4] Robert J. Connors, *The Erasure of the* Sentence (2000) in *Selected Essays of Robert J. Connors*, ed. by Lise Ede & Andrea A. Lunsford, Bedford/St. Martin's, 2003. p.473

Neither was this erasure the simple playing out of a vein of material before the onslaughts of the normal scientists who followed the major researchers of sentence rhetorics. If the last important work in sentence-combining, Daiker, Keker, and Morenberg's *Rhetorical Perspective,* shows anything, it is that many of the most interesting questions about sentence rhetorics were still being raised and not answered.

I think that we have, to a large extent, already seen what it was. **The sentence was erased by the gradual but inevitable hardening into disciplinary form of the field of composition studies as a sub-field of English studies**. The anti-formalism, anti-behaviorism, and anti-empiricism that marked the criticism of sentence rhetorics can be found in some earlier writers and thinkers in the older field of composition, **but not with the hegemony they gradually achieved as disciplinary structures were formed after 1975. These three attitudinal strands are hallmarks of English studies** and not of works in the other fields – speech, psychology, education – from which composition grew after 1950."[5]

And so Connors concludes as follows: **"The loss of all defense of formalism has left some curious vacuums in the middle of our teaching. Rejection of all behaviorist ideas has left us with uncertainties about any methodology not completely rationalistic or any system of pedagogical rewards. Distrust of scientistic empiricism has left us with few proofs or certainties not ideologically based."[6]**

In other words, we are left with theories for teaching writing to beginning students **by novice, untrained teachers, theories which are devoid of any system or method and thus any way to implement or assess their**

---

[5] *Ibid.* p.472.
[6] *Ibid* p.473.

value. In contrast, our book acknowledges both the proven accomplishments of earlier attempts to focus on the sentence, but recognizes that they were inadequate as a whole. **We proceed to provide the first systematic and methodical analysis of the sentence – its levels, its forms, its coverage of phrase usage as well as clauses in writing, its names, its rhetorical uses, and its underlying thought structures**. We do not ignore and thereby discount the value of the last published essay of Robert J. Connors, but respond to the challenge posed by his article. We correct and reverse the Erasure of the Sentence and restore it to the center of attention for all foundational courses in teaching writing. We do not by any means assert that understanding the sentence is the only knowledge and skill required to write well, but we do claim that it is the logical and proper place to begin teaching writing. We do not deny that students need instruction in the skills required for academic research, in the varied genres of writing, in the diverse disciplines of learning as well as how to write in the varied, demanding situations of work related tasks. However, while such matters can be introduced in introductory courses in writing, they can only be adequately addressed in courses subsequent to the foundational course in writing which should be primarily based on mastering the nature and rhetorical uses of the sentence.

With the identification and invention of the Eleven Forms of the Sentence, we **provide – for the first time – a Systematic Framework for Understanding and Teaching Sentence Construction in paragraphs and essays – in a gradual, progressive, lesson learnable order easy for both students to learn and teachers to teach**. With the provision of student models for students to follow in writing sentences and above all with the requirement that students **Notate and Footnote their use of Specific, Focused Sentences** in paragraphs and essays, we have **invented a Method of Skill Application of Sentences** in context that require students **to exercise attention and discipline in their writing** while leaving them free to choose their own topics, thus encouraging them to discover their own voice in writing and to invest what they write with feeling; moreover their writing is directed to an audience of their peers in collaborative assessment and rewriting of one another's paragraphs and essays. Also, with our invention of the **Five Levels of the Architecture of the Sentence**, we have provided **a novel analytical tool** that enables student to more easily identify and understand the formative units of meaning involved in the construction of sentences. Finally, by providing a comprehensive identification of sentence forms and placing them in the understandable and manageable system of Eleven Forms, **we have invented a system of Writing Across the Curriculum that can be implemented on an ongoing basis.** People have talked a great deal about programs for writing across the curriculum, but have never managed to conceive a common core of required knowledge and skills as the workable foundation for such a program. We have now provided that necessary core foundation for such a program.

Our approach balances Discipline with Freedom. It is particularly noteworthy that our **Method of Requiring students to notate and footnote** their use of particular sentence forms **provides a degree of Oversight, Control, and Flexible Implementation and Variety of Targeted Instruction as well as Accountability and Assessment features** never available to teachers previous to our approach. **Oversight** is provided because the sentences are practiced and mastered by students in a gradual, regular, progressive , and cumulative manner. **Control** is provided because sentences can be specified for emulation and practice when students are seen to be deficient or weak in their mastery of specific forms. **Flexible Implementation and Variety of Targeted Instruction** is provided because teachers can tailor the sentences targeted for emulation according to the perceived individual needs and proficiencies of individual students. Finally, **Accountability and Assessment** are provided because mastery of the various sentences forms and their effective incorporation into overall writing ability can be monitored and measured by the degree to which the various sentence forms are applied correctly and with rhetorical force and style. Our Approach thus insures **progress in the both the variety and effective rhetorical construction of sentences as well as in the overall quality of Writing**. It establishes a solid foundation course for teaching all students to write competent prose within a year of instruction that novice teachers can implement effectively and without undue strain, even without an initial training course in teaching writing.

In addition to the **Novel System of Eleven Forms of the Sentence** and the **Novel Method of practicing sentences by Notating and Footnoting them** as described above, the **15th Distinctive Feature of our approach is that for the first time there is Complete Coverage of all Phrases used in writing.** While traditional methods of teaching writing have not been systematic in their coverage of clauses, they have at least tended to highlight their importance, especially for defining and understanding the grammatical types of the simple, compound, complex, and compound-complex sentences. However, they have virtually ignored giving **Prominence or Practice in identifying and writing the six types of Phrases**, failing in fact even to define the respective types. In contrast, **our Tenth Form of the Sentence provides extensive examples of how all six types of Phrases are employed as additions to the beginning, middle, and end of sentences.**

The **16th Distinctive Feature is our invention of Novel Names for Sentence Forms,** facilitating their understanding and more particularly their effective rhetorical application in writing. We have invented many arresting and memorable names for many of the sentence forms. When we name something, we increase our awareness of it, own it, and gain more focused control over its proper purpose and function. Indeed, it is strange that no one before us, with the possible exception of the cumulative sentence of Francis Christensen, has tried to find telling and memorable names for more of the commonly used sentence forms. Thus, the Series Form A, B, and C we designate as the **Standard Series** to indicate that it is the most widely used series employed in writing. We designate the Series A, B, C as the **Triple Force Series** to highlight that its pronounced staccato sound carries a dramatic effect that only the spoken voice can render. We designate the Series A and B and C as the **Lyrical Series** to stress its rhetorical use as a means of musical expression and stylistic flair. **The names we give highlight and dramatize the effective rhetorical uses of the respective forms in writing**.

The **17th and Final Distinctive Feature complements and brings to fruition the understanding and effective use of the sentence forms** by not only precisely naming them but more importantly by highlighting **the Sentence Forms as Thought Structures.** Thereby, our Approach to Writing **not only makes students better writers but also improves their Critical Thinking Skills**.

Indeed, stranger even than the failure of earlier writing theories to provide cogent and revealing names for commonly used sentence forms has been the even more astounding failure to stress how specific sentence forms express and embody definite thought functions and structures. Perhaps, one of the reasons that students think too little has to do with their having been taught not to reflect about the sentences they use as forms and functions of thought. Thus, as well as identifying the seven coordinating conjunctions, we also distinguish them by name according to the function of thought they perform: namely, designating **and** as the **Association Coordinating Conjunction**; **but** as the **Opposition Association Coordinating Conjunction**; **so** as the **Result or Consequence Coordinating Conjunction**, and so on. We rename Subordinate Conjunctions as Adverbial Conjunctions which is how they function, and we separate them into the four thought categories of **Cause**, **Condition**, **Concession** and **Qualification**, and **Time.** When we teach the semi-colon, we don't just lump all sentences using the semi-colon into one indiscriminate category, but identify the **Association Semi-Colon**, the **Opposition Semi-Colon**, the **Explanatory or Expansive Semi-Colon** which all highlight the varied functions of thought – **association, opposition, and explanation** – which the particular sentence using a semi-colon employs to achieve its desired effect.

With all the significant improvements in teaching the sentence above, once all the sentence forms are explained, modeled, and practiced by students as individual sentences of their own making and as incorporated into longer writing assignments, they arrive at a systematic overview of all the sentence forms at which point they perceive that they need only observe the various forms in their daily reading and then practice them continually in their writing to steadily improve and grow in mastering the craft of writing. **They have mastered a system that empowers them to observe, analyze, understand, appreciate, and creatively emulate all the sentences they will ever encounter in the English language.**

Having now concluded our examination of the 17 distinctive features, we provide below an extended presentation of four additional important themes:

(1) The Intention and Aim of our Angle On Writing;
(2) Analyzing the Four Prevailing Pedagogies of Writing;
(3) Briefly Presenting the Content and Methodology of our Approach; and
(4) Noting the Uniqueness of our Approach compared with the Four Prevailing Pedagogies

All the teachers, many of the students, and most of the general public reading this book have all produced a variety of medium to long papers in course requirements for high school or university classes. It is therefore safe to say that most people have at least some extensive personal experience with the Process as well as the chief ideas, practices, and techniques associated with learning to write.

We assure everyone that our intention and aim here is not in any way to demean or dismiss what everyone already knows and understands about writing. Rather, we aim to validate and incorporate the worth and efficacy of what people presently know; moreover, we aim – in definite, concrete ways – to refine, expand on, add to, complement, and innovatively improve the way writing is taught to beginning students.

Our book often employs and highlights visual representations of our Innovative Approach to Writing, so permit us – initially – to present a visual capsule portrait and summary for an Initial Version of the Complete Form of our New Angle on Writing – via a **unified vision of our innovative Approach To Writing in one single graphic** or image (with a fourfold configuration organized under the **Headings of the Four Great Directions)** as is shown on the following three pages. The charts are intended to be read numerically in conjunction with each other; thus, the *1s* should be viewed together but contrasted according to the cardinal direction where they are placed. Similarly, the *2s* should be viewed together but contrasted according to the cardinal direction where they are placed.

North

1. **Subject**
2. **What**
3. **Plan**
4. **Conception: a reflective, comprehensive System**
5. **Teacher**
6. **Traditional Theory 2:** A investigative and thesis focused argument – in impersonal clear prose – highlighting Rational thought, logical consistency, and accurate evidence about an issue or problem of public interest and concern. In short, Writing informed by critical thought and expression
7. **From the Top Down**
8. **Clarity of expression**
9. **Construction**
10. **Competing**
11. **Structure**
12. **Form**
13. **Mind**
14. **Reason**
15. **Cause**
16. **Idea**
17. **Conceptual**
18. **Theoretical and Detached**
19. **Principles**
20. **Civic**
21. **Scientific**
22. **Academically and Professionally Impressed**
23. **Distinction and Status**
24. **Objective**
25. **Reflection**
26. **Jung's Thinking Function**
27. **General**
28. **Truth**
29. **Intellectual**
30. **Connection and Coherence**

West	East
1. **Language**	*1. Author*
2. **How**	*2. Who and Why*
3. **Product**	*3. Process*
4. **Execution: practical, effective method**	*4. Intention: a Universal, Integral, Person-Centered Approach*
5. **Classroom Environment and Materials**	*5. Student*
6. **Traditional Theory 1:** Grammatically and Mechanically Correct Prose	*6. Contemporary Theory 1: Process Informed Writing à la Elbow, Murray*
7. **From the Outside In**	*7. From the Inside Out*
8. **Correctness and Brevity of Writing**	*8. Voice, Authenticity, and Integrity of Writing*
9. **Classification and Collection**	*9. Composition*
10. **Coordinating**	*10. Integrating*
11. **Material**	*11. Spirit*
12. **Matter**	*12. Meaning*
13. **Body**	*13. Soul and Will*
14. **Sense**	*14. Choice*
15. **Means**	*15. Origin*
16. **Object**	*16. Self*
17. **Mechanical**	*17. Personal*
18. **Skillfully Engaged**	*18. Interpersonally involved*
19. **Rules**	*19. Values*
20. **Technical**	*20. Moral*
21. **Technological**	*21. World View, Ideological, or Axiological*
22. **Society Mandated and Job Required**	*22. Personally Inspired and Freely Chosen*
23. **Profit and Gain**	*23. Integral Identity*
24. **Outer**	*24. Inner*
25. **Behavior**	*25. Responsibility and Character*
26. **Jung's Sensing Function**	*26. Jung's Intuiting Function*
27. **Factual and Detailed**	*27. Concrete and Universal*
28. **Utility**	*28. Goodness*
29. **Physical**	*29. Spiritual*
30. **Stimulation**	*30. Inspiration*

South

1. *Audience*
2. *To Whom, Where, and When*
3. *Procedure*
4. *Motivation: Culturally Peer Referenced, Participation, and Performance Based*
5. *Class*
6. *Contemporary Theory 2:* Oriented and Informed by Rhetorical Tradition, especially contemporary novel theories and practices à la I.A.Richards, Burke, Corbett, Connors, and others
7. *From the Bottom Up*
8. *Style of Expression*
9. *Organization*
10. *Cooperation*
11. *Substance*
12. *Content*
13. *Heart*
14. *Imagination*
15. *Effect*
16. *Other*
17. *Organic*
18. *Socially Attached and Interactive*
19. *Cultural*
20. *Norms, Traditions, and Customs*
21. *Artistic*
22. *Class necessitated and culturally approved*
23. *Security, Approval, and Convenience*
24. *Subjective*
25. *Conduct*
26. *Jung's Feeling Function*
27. *Particular and Specific*
28. *Beauty*
29. *Emotional*
30. *Motivation*

The Ultimate Outcome of the realized integration of the fourfold configuration above may be condensed – with greater decisive brevity and compact precision of expression – in the visual graphic below:

	Thoughtful Connection, Clear Conception, and Comprehensive System	
Common Sense, Ordinary Language, and Practical Application	***Mature, Balanced Awareness***	*Person Centered, Responsible, Spiritual Perception and Integral Consciousness*
	Cultural Appreciation and Emotional Equilibrium	

The remainder of this presentation will be devoted to the Explication and Explanation of the Process by which we arrived at this Final Form along with its manifold meanings and implications for our Innovative Approach to Teaching Writing.

At the outset, as a provisional matter, permit us to characterize the prevailing knowledge about the Process, chief ideas, practices, and techniques of Writing as falling into two broad categories – the Traditional and Contemporary Theories of Writing – and further to designate these two categories together as the Right Hand Approach to Writing in contrast to our Innovative Approach which we will call the Left Hand Approach to Writing.

What are the principal distinctions between the Traditional and Contemporary Theories of Writing? And why do we lump the two categories together as possessing marked similarities, despite their differences, which set them apart as the Right Hand Approach to Writing as opposed to our Innovative Left Hand Approach to Writing?

Well, for starters, the Traditional Theories of Writing are derived from and Oriented toward the Past while the Contemporary Theories of Writing, as their name implies, were created in Contemporary circumstances and are Oriented toward the Present.

In contrast to both of these, our Innovative Pedagogy of Writing is Oriented toward the Future.

Generally speaking, there are two Traditional theories or schools of Writing – located respectively in the **North** and **West** and preceded by the number **6** – in our chart above. The oldest and most traditional of these theories or schools of teaching Writing is the one that stresses the achievement of <u>Grammatically and Mechanically Correct Prose</u>. Externally driven, from the outside in, students according to this theory should learn to write by observing and absorbing various examples of what good writers do and imitating their accomplishments through some process of osmosis never clearly described or explicated but nonetheless demanded of them.

Above all else, students should avoid errors and mistakes of any kind that violate various lists of rules which they are given and which presumably they should use to avoid errors. Many hours are devoted to innumerable exercises aimed at correcting mistakes in spelling, punctuation, and capitalization. Students are then graded by how few or many errors show up in their prose. Inevitably, incessantly and relentlessly, multiple errors persist in student writing, yet teachers doggedly persist in grading students mostly on the frequency of errors in papers, without much regard for the thought, style, or intended meaning of what students write or much effort invested to improve the thought, style, and content of their writing by close analysis and revision.

Class time is devoted also to endless hours of instruction in grammar – with extensive written exercises in and repeated discussions of grammar – but without any appreciable effect on student competence in writing, as numerous repeated studies have demonstrated. Students are told the importance of having an apt and telling title for their paragraphs and essays; they are informed of the obvious necessity of having a Beginning or Enticing Introduction, as well as a solid, informative Middle or Body, and fitting End or Conclusion to their essays; they are shown how to outline and notified of the value and necessity of a central idea, supporting ideas, and accurate evidence, facts, examples, and illustrations to prove their themes. This instruction helps for some, but fails for many. Between the atomized dissection of grammar, syntax, and punctuation and the broad, rather obvious abstract generalizations and instructions describing the grand profile and successive stages of essay writing, students don't have much to inform either the confidence and fluency of their writing or to focus their recognition and mastery of a variety of sentence constructions. Their writing is stilted, mechanical, awkward; they are stalked and bewildered, worried and bedeviled by their internalized critical voices mocking them for their errors and stumbling, labored prose.

The Second Traditional Theory of Writing insists with Robert Frost that *clear thinking makes for clear writing*. Good ideas make for good writing, and prose is judged by its clarity more than its correctness though correctness retains a subsidiary significance. Students are taught to search, evaluate, summarize, and incorporate outside research from multiple public and academic sources into thesis-driven papers that argue with rational cogency, logical consistency, and clear expression how to illuminate or solve problems and issues of public or academic concern. Some teachers succeed admirably in this endeavor with some students, but many other students never demonstrate much real power of thought or fluency and clarity of expression, perhaps because, for all the talk about it, they never get much instruction, explanation, or practical advice regarding how to think critically, or how to express themselves thoughtfully in a variety of sentence constructions.

Both Traditional theories are driven from the outside and stress the primacy of external products or models to teach writing, one by the minute analysis and dissection of innumerable pieces of prose explained by isolated, forlorn, and boring rules and the other by rather generalized exhortations to think, close readings of literary texts, and a few abstract strategies for organizing both thought and the construction of longer essays.

In contrast, the two Contemporary theories of Writing – located respectively in the **East** and **South** and preceded by the number 6 in our graph above – are driven and inspired *from the Inside Out (Process Writing)* and *From the Bottom Up (Rhetorically informed Writing)*. When students (in Process writing) choose their own topics and write seeking to express their own intended meanings, trusting their own voices and decisions about varied writing options and alternatives rather than fretfully worrying about grammatical errors and mechanical mistakes in punctuation and capitalization, their writing becomes vital, alive, invested with feeling and heart. Increased student interest and investment in writing leads to greater attention and concentration which almost automatically solves the correction problem of eliminating unsightly errors and mistakes.

Rhetorically Informed Writing (From the Bottom Up) is concerned with the reader of Writing and the audience for it – motivating students to collaboratively participate in writing with others, to read aloud their writing to others in a performative venue, and to discuss, evaluate, and revise writing assignments with their peers. Socially aware, motivated by and interactive with their peers as well as the cultural traditions and sensibilities of their immediate classmates, their native cultures, and their time and place in history, writers in the rhetorical tradition are inevitably sensitive to the emotional, dramatic, and connotative sense of words and to all the varied devices, strategies, and techniques that contribute to a striking style which can move others and persuade them to share the writer's own values and convictions. If writing does not attain its aim and have an effect upon the reader, then why write at all? The Rhetorical pedagogy of writing never forgets to concern itself with the effective impact of writing on others.

Now that we have briefly explored and summarized these four prevailing yet often competing theories of composition – two Traditional theories and two Contemporary theories – why do we yet lump them together, despite their differences, as sharing enough similarities to call them together the Right Hand Approach To Writing as opposed to our Innovative Left Hand Approach To Writing?

In yet another graphic chart, let us summarize the decisive distinctions between our Left Hand Approach to Writing and the Right Hand Approach to Writing.

Left Hand Approach	Right Hand Approach
Future Oriented	**Past and Present Oriented**
Integral	**Fragmented**
Wholistic	**Partial**
Mature Closure	**Arrested Development**
Universal	**Limited and Confined**
Values Freedom of Choice	**Either unduly Restricts or Exalts Freedom of Choice**
Freedom Married with structured system	**Excessive Freedom while being either too obsessive about Structure or too suspicious of system**

To say that the Left Hand Approach is *Integral* means that all the factors, aspects, parts, and components of the Approach harmoniously interweave, interact, support, and reinforce one another. Every component of the Approach is integrally arranged, developed, realized, and applied. The Approach, therefore, constitutes a *unified Whole* which is *inclusive* and not exclusive, continuous with the Past, conversant with the Present, and open to the Future. In other words, the Left Hand Approach incorporates the Right Hand Approach into itself but expands and goes beyond it into still unknown possibilities and territory. It accepts the relevant and relative value of all four prevailing theories of writing – the two Traditional theories and the two Contemporary theories – but innovatively arranges, complements, expands, and adds new ideas, practices, and techniques which lend Writing a dynamic new energy, coherence, and efficacy.

To say that the Right Hand Approach is **Fragmented** means that the various theories are isolated, disconnected, frequently in conflict and competition with one another, unable or unwilling to see or appreciate the respective merits of other theories because they remain too individualistically and obsessively focused on their own preferred version of writing to the exclusion of any and all others. In short, they are not Wholistic but **Partial – in the double sense of taking their own part of the Writing Puzzle for the Whole and in the sense of being egotistically Partial to their own theory of one segment of the Puzzle**. The Right Hand Approach to Writing shows itself to be in an **Arrested State of Development** while the Left Hand Approach to Writing attains a *Mature Closure of Inclusive Incorporation and Personal Appropriation of the entire history of Writing*.

To say the Left Hand Approach to Writing is *Universal* is to say that the Historical Assumption that underlies and grounds it (that this is the Age of Human Maturity on this planet), the Vision of Possibilities that informs it, and the Intention that impels it – all demand the universal achievement of competent self-expressive writing by all people on earth by the first year of university-level education if not well before that grade level. One of the characters in Shakespeare's play *Coriolanus* declares "Our virtues lie in the interpretation of the Time." That is one humdinger of a line, seldom if ever adequately appreciated and realized in its full bearing on human development and History.

We live in the Age of a complete and comprehensive psychological theory of human development which clearly and definitively distinguishes the powers, capacities, challenges, tasks, and talents that distinguish youth as a stage of human life from maturity. The possibilities and prospective achievements of the two stages can't conceivably be equated or mistaken as similar in content and effect. The one stage, Youth, is confined and limited, constricted and hampered in its conception and estimate of human capacity; the other, Maturity, is marked by confidence in the future with a sense of the enhanced possibilities and opportunities available to all human beings. And we know from Hologram theory, that what is true of the individual part is true of the whole, so the whole of Humanity is clearly now crossing the threshold of the Maturity of Human life of this planet just as individual human beings pass from Youth to Maturity in their development. Accordingly, the Left Hand Approach to Writing, informed and inspired by the vision of the Impending Maturity of Humanity as a Whole on this planet, expects and works for universal attainment of Writing Proficiency for all human beings. In contrast, the Right Hand Approach to Writing, mired in the Youthful Modern and Post-Modern view of human history, congratulates itself on a glass half empty – satisfied to teach limited segments of humanity to write but convinced the full glass of writing mastery for all is impossible to attain.

Every Master, or even competent, teacher knows that the Expectations you harbor, the Vision you have of the possibilities and talents of your students, determines the results you get. If you expect little, you get little. If you nurse high expectations, you work and find a way to bring them to fruition.

To say that the Left Hand Approach to Writing *values Freedom of Choice but marries it with structured system* means that, as an Integral Approach, it always tries to Balance Freedom with Structure, Feeling with Form, Rational Coherence, and Systematic development. It is always about providing for latitude and play for creativity, spontaneity, and initiative yet also insuring clear thought, comprehensive understanding, and stable, progressive development.

In contrast, the Right Hand Approach to Writing in Traditional theories either unduly restricts freedom and adheres with too much conformity to a mindless structure with little flexibility, or alternately in contemporary theories excessively experiments with fun filled activities that absorb interest for the moment but have little connection with one another or allow for little systematic development of writing.

The task that faces us at this juncture of our talk is actually to explain in both broad outline and in some detail *what* the Plan of our Innovative Theory is; *how* it is practically implemented, its proven Products, and its method of application and operation; and its overall Procedure of daily work in a given class. Once we have accomplished that task, we will then list 35 features of our Approach to Writing which are innovative, explaining why they are so novel and effective by referring to the previous detailed description we have given of the systematic conception and multiple practices of the theory in operation.

The master key to our innovative approach to writing is our discovery of **11 Sentence Forms** which in turn can be subdivided into 127 sub-forms. Please turn now to pages 134 and 135 and you will find there the 11 Sentence Forms, along with the mnemonic codes for each Form with the number of sub-forms for each Form on page 135. *In the charts, the Forms range from the most basic and simple on the left hand to increasingly complex and stylistically difficult sentences on the right hand.*

Each of the 11 Sentence Forms is a Mini-Lesson in itself. We will examine The Procedure for teaching the 11 Forms by using the **Series Forms** on page 143 as an example. Thus, we first present the students with the 7 sub-forms of the Series Form on page 143 and read aloud to them the names for each of the sub-forms and the clear examples there of each of the 7 sub-forms. We then instruct them to write two of their own examples of each of the 7 sub-forms for the next class, consulting for assistance the models and excellent examples of each of the 7 sub-forms that start on page 144.

On the next day in class, we ask for volunteers to place one example of the first sub-form on the board followed successively by most or all of the remaining students. At the board, students are asked to read aloud their sentences with sufficient loudness and some dramatic emphasis, highlighting adverbs with extra loudness and driving adjectives with extra loudness into nouns so that they hear as well as see adverbs and adjectives. If students have problems enunciating with sufficient clarity and volume, we show them how to identify and initially exaggerate the consonants of the English language, underlining the consonants and then exaggerating them, at first saying them extra loudly and then saying the words at normal pitch when all of a sudden they will become much clearer and louder automatically and effortlessly. In short, at the board students practice speaking aloud clearly and distinctly the English language, using the very sentences that they themselves have written.

Referring to the chart on page 87 where we identify the **Five Jobs or Functions of the Twelve Kinds of Words** (an innovative feature of our book) which we have earlier presented and explained to students and referring also to the three charts on **The Architecture of the English Sentence** (another innovative feature of our book) on pages 105-106 which we have also earlier presented and explained to students, we ask students at the board to identify the Heart, Essence, Core, and Base of their respective sentences, to determine the Kind of Word and the Job or Role that each word in the sentence is doing. At first, this is difficult for students, but assistance from the teacher and continued practice makes them more confident; moreover, students must pay attention to this practice because they know they themselves will soon have to perform this analysis in front of their peers. When and as this procedure of analysis becomes too boring or taxing for students, cut it off and then resume doing it again in a subsequent class with other sentences at the board.

Finally, assess the various sentences posted on the board by students in the most positive light possible without being overly critical. Remind the students that they are just practicing writing the sentences for the first time and that, therefore, the sentences at this point do not have to be perfect. We are just interested in seeing what is done well and learning from mistakes. Therefore, when a sentence is interesting, funny, clear, or wonderfully expressive in itself, say so and praise the student. When the form that is being practiced is correct, say so and commend the student. When the sentence itself is grammatically or mechanically flawed, ask other students to correct it or assist them to do so yourself if necessary. If the attempted form of the sentence is incorrect, point out how to put it into the right form if possible or declare that the sentence does not fit well with that particular form and move on.

We proceed in similar fashion with the remaining 10 Sentence Forms with their various sub-forms just as we did with the Form 2S Series Sentence Form and its sub-forms, except that we spend increasingly less time on the grammatical analysis of the various sentence forms and more on the quality and stylistic merits of the individual sentences. Thereby, we inform students, by both precept and practice, that grammatical and mechanical correctness are significant but hardly of overwhelming or paramount importance in teaching anyone how to write effectively. They are matters to which steady attention, discipline, and organization must be devoted, but their importance is subsidiary in determining the meaning, thoughtfulness, clarity, and style of written prose.

After students have posted two examples of all the sub-forms of the first Five Sentence Forms, we then require them to write a single paragraph (with a title) in which they employ at least five instances of the first Five Sentence Forms in their paragraphs, notating and footnoting the forms they use. We provide them with earlier models of completed student examples of such notated and footnoted paragraphs (page 178+) which they can study and emulate in their own paragraphs. After students have posted two examples of all the sub-forms of Sentence Forms 6, 7, 8, we then require them to write two paragraphs (with a title) in which they employ several instances of the first Five Sentence Forms in their paragraphs but now also several instances of Forms 6, 7, and 8, notating and footnoting the forms they use in their two paragraphs. Again, we provide them with earlier models of completed student examples of such notated and footnoted paragraphs (page 215) which they can study and emulate in their own paragraphs. After students have posted two examples of all the sub-forms of Sentence 9 which deals with colons, semi-colons, and dashes (what we call the **Power Punctuation Marks**), we then require them to write 3 to 4 paragraphs (with a title) in which they employ multiple instances of the first 8 Sentence Forms plus five sub-forms of Form 9, notating and footnoting all the forms they use. Again, we provide them with earlier models of completed student examples of such notated and footnoted paragraphs (page 72+) which they can study and emulate in their own paragraphs. Finally, in the same fashion, after introducing Forms 10 and 11, we ask students to write four paragraphs (with a title) incorporating all earlier forms, but now adding several sub-forms of Sentence Forms 10 and 11. Again, we provide them with earlier excellent student models of this assignment (page 359+).

The two examples for each sub-form that the student must write for each sub-form can be kept in a notebook.

On each occasion that students complete one of the four assignments above, they must type their assignments and make typed copies of their assignment for the instructor and for each of their fellow classmates. All the students then read aloud their assignments, and the entire class, with the help of the instructor, proceeds to revise and rewrite the assignments. Students then submit a re-typed copy of their assignment as revised in class and submit it again to the instructor. The students in the class thus have extensive experience revising their assignments as well as helping to revise the assignments of their classmates.

If you will now turn to page 378 in this book, you will see the first of several examples by students of a 4 to 6 paragraph essay, employing many of the 11 Sentences forms, duly notated and footnoted. With practice, students will start unveiling outstanding instances of Form after Form, again and again, with startling ease and rapidity.

At the end of the **first semester** of a year-long course, students take two examinations. In the first exam, they are given a choice of five topics to write about in two hours. They are required to write four paragraphs employing 15-20 designated sentence forms, notating and footnoting the required sentence forms in the paper. In the final exam, they are again given a choice of five topics to write about in two hours, but they can now write freely without any specified required sentence forms to notate and footnote.

At the end of the **second semester**, students would be required to write longer expository, narrative, descriptive, and comparative essays as well as a character sketch and an autobiographical essay.

Multiple students models of all these types of essays are available in the second volume of our two volume survey of English (but not in this abridged version of only the writing material in the first volume) along with extensive poetry selections and extended examinations of both the Process of Reading in general as well as some of the best ways to pursue the Interpretation of literary selections. Look at the end of the book for more information about this second volume and where you can purchase it.

Now that we have provided a rough sketch of our overall program for teaching students to write, we expand our original list of 14 primary distinctive characteristics into a longer list of 35 distinctive features of the Process, writing Plan, Products, and Procedure of our innovative writing theory and pedagogy.

Distinctive Features of this Writing Theory and Pedagogy:

1. Person and Student centered;
2. Integrally arranged, developed, realized, and applied;
3. Wholistically appreciative and inclusive of all previous writing theories and pedagogies;
4. Process Oriented;
5. Product Proven and Confirmed with over 200 student models;
6. Practice Driven;
7. Participation Based;
8. Performance Assessed;
9. Systematically Structured;
10. Peer Referenced and Interactive;
11. Form Focused;
12. Sentence Forms specifically targeted;
13. Model emulated;
14. Thoughtfully connected with sentences explained via Association, Opposition, Elaboration etc.;
15. Conceptually Clear with Definitions employing ordinary language with memorable names;
16. Culturally Appreciative and Conversant as well as Rhetorically Inventive, Sensitive, and Sophisticated;
17. Extensive employment of Metaphor, Analogy, Alliteration, Irony and other figurative uses of language;
18. Teacher Empowering and Liberating;
19. Cumulatively, Incrementally, and Progressively Developmental;
20. Universally Aimed and Empowering for everyone in the Global Age of Human Maturity;
21. Adaptable for use by both native and EFL/ESL students;
22. Provides a source of cultural and cross-cultural education regarding the interests and discourse usage of youth;
23. Body Referenced and Interactive;
24. Effectively and Efficiently Organized in 30 Manageable Unit Lessons;
25. Memory Friendly and Enhancing;
26. Theoretically Comprehensive and Illuminating;

27. Pedagogically validated in repeated class courses;

28. Flexible, supportive, and open to other proven English pedagogies such as the Sentence Combining of William Strong, the Free Writing of Peter Elbow and Donald Murray, the Cumulative Sentence of Francis Christensen, and other pedagogies;

29. Scholarly supported and validated, especially by the superb historical studies of Robert Connors, most especially his superb and authoritative article *"The Erasure of the Sentence"* (2000) in the volume *Selected Essays of Robert J. Connors* edited by Liza Ede and Andrea A. Lunsford.

30. Dramatically revised and revamped essentials of grammar and punctuation presented in just a few lessons, but cumulatively and successively incorporated and integrated with Writing Instruction;

31. Inventing The Architecture of the Sentence and a new term The Descriptor as one of the Five Functions performed by words in any Sentence;

32. Providing a Set of Rubrics to guide students in their writing and evaluation of essays;

33. Describing a balanced style with a set of Alliterative Nouns and a set of Alliterative Adjectives along with two other sets of Characteristics for an effective writing style;

34. Marked improvement in reading ability engendered by increased recognition of the incidence and rhetorical effect of Sentence Forms learned from the practice of writing with prescribed sentence forms;

35. This theory of writing provides the long sought basis for a program of Writing across the Curriculum.

Still Another Look at the 4 Prevailing Approaches to Writing

There are Four Competing Approaches to Writing, the older <u>Traditional</u> and **Modern** Approaches and the newer, more recent *Rhetorical* and *Process* theories.

We will place the Four Competing Approaches to Writing at the top of several Charts below which will then list the varied content and implications of each of the Four Approaches in a series of **Foursomes**. We will designate an identifying name for the Foursomes or else list them as a **Clarifying Foursome** because they make clearer the Foursomes before and after them in the Charts. All of the Foursomes are more or less clarified or coined by us, though many are based on known standard fourfold distinctions. While and as we present the Charts, we will describe the Four Approaches to Composition at greater length at various points in our exposition. We will then **apply our Mature and Balanced Integration of all Four theories to the Innovative System of Writing that we propose**.

Name	West	*South*	North	*East*
Composition Theories	<u>Traditional</u>	*Rhetorical*	**Modern**	*Process*
Aspects of Writing Situation	<u>Language</u>	*Audience*	**Subject**	*Writer*
Domain Referrals	<u>Thing</u>	*Other*	**Idea**	*Self*

4 Purposes of Writing

The Purpose of Writing in the Traditional Theory is Accuracy and correctness of Usage, Grammar, Syntax, and Punctuation; *the Purpose of Writing in Rhetorical Theory is the effective deployment of invention, arrangement, and style to make a persuasive, powerful impact on the reader or audience for writing*; **the Purpose of Writing in the Modern Period is to represent, analyze, or synthesize part of reality and the world through focused thinking, logical and consistent reasoning, comprehensive conception, and clear expression**; *the Purpose of Writing in Process Theory is self-expression and growth as a person through trusting oneself and developing confidence in one's own authentic voice, authenticity, and integrity as a writer and human being.*

Teaching Situation	Materials	*Class*	**Teacher**	*Student*
Clarifying Foursome	Environment	*Effect*	**Cause**	*Origin*
Clarifying Foursome	Order	*Content*	**Form**	*Energy*
Clarifying Foursome	Matter	*Substance*	**Structure**	*Essence*
Aristotle's Causes	Material	*Final*	**Formal**	Efficient
Aims for Writing	Efficient	*Effective*	**Thoughtful**	*Authentic*
Qualities of Writing	Cohesion	*Texture*	**Coherence**	*Unity*
Questions of Writing	How	*To Whom, Where, When*	**What**	*Who and Why*
Criteria of Writing	Brevity	*Style*	**Clarity**	*Integrity*

Salient Features of Writing	Craft	*Strategy*	**System**	*Intention*
Aspects of Writing	Technical	*Artistic*	**Scientific**	*Personal*
Values of Writing	Useful	*Beautiful*	**True**	*Good*
Communication	Communi-cation	*Impact*	**Message**	*Meaning*
Learning Modes	Movement	*Speaking*	**Writing**	*Reading*
Organ Preferences	Hand	*Ear*	**Eye**	*Whole Body*

4 Goals of Writing

The Traditional Goal of Writing is to enable students to achieve Organization, Efficiency, and Mechanical Accuracy and Correctness in Usage, Grammar, Syntax, and Punctuation. Targeted and graduated exercises are employed to help students recognize and correct errors as well as to instill attention to detail, organization, and proper formatting and editing of written material.

The Rhetorical Goal of Writing is to enable students to emotionally understand and relate to their fellow students as well as learn more effectively through social interaction, collaborative invention and writing, and various kinds of peer reviewing of writing. The aim is to empower students to imagine prospective readers of their papers and to appreciate and deploy strategies and stylistic devices to dramatically and powerfully impact those readers.

The Modern Goal of Writing is to enable students to investigate and reflect about the objective world, to think and write clearly about its character, systematic laws, and problems, and then to convey in logical deductive reasoning, through structured and focused

expositions, their conclusions and discoveries about that world and how to improve it.

*The Process Goal of Writing is to enable students to discover their true selves and Living Authentic Voices as writers so they can write with fluency, confidence, feeling, heart, soul, imagination, and spirit – unafraid of failure but instead able, through awareness of their own writing process, to reflect on their writing and regularly and consistently improve it, because they have come to love and esteem writing. They do not use writing only to express what they already know, but also as a generative instrument for discovering what they don't yet know or understand. They have come to realize that writing is not only **reflective**, but **generative**, that language is the very medium and means by which we create, discover, build, and dwell in a common cultural and social community and world.*

Ideal Writing Forms	Description	Persuasion	Exposition & Argumentation	Narration
Mental Processes	Analysis	Evaluation	Synthesis & Comprehension	Integration
Psychology Domains	Psycho-Motor	Affective	Cognitive	Conative
Social Domains	Private	Social	Public	Communal
Kolbe's Action Modes	Implementor	Fact Finder	Quick Start	Follow Thru
Language Referents	Term	Idiom	Name	Word
Language Domains	Fact	Symbol	Concept	Allusion
Figurative Language	Simile	Personification	Analogy	Metaphor

52

Intended Outcomes of this Writing Course

The Intended Outcome is **the universal mastery of self-expression writing of competent paragraphs and essays by all students of the Global Age by the senior year of high school or first year of college** (in a English native-speaking context). Students will display the following characteristics in their writing as a result of this system of writing.

1	Feeling for and Trust in an **Authentic Writer's Voice**;
2	**Greatly increased Subjective Confidence in their language ability**, eliminating writer's block and distaste for writing and replacing it with a steadily growing appreciation for and knowledge of language in general; for grammar and punctuation; and for the speaking, writing, and reading of language;
3	**Demonstrated Objective Fluency in producing** – in a reasonably short period of time – **a marked improvement in the Volume, Focus, and Quality of writing**;
4	**An Initial Skill and Growing Mastery of a Repertoire of the entire variety and range of English sentences**;
5	Increased awareness and skill in employing the **Specific Varied Components of an Effective Writing Style**;
6	Increased awareness and skill in using the **Vocal and Dynamic Rhythms of English prose**;
7	**Knowledge and Skilled Use of Specific Criteria for producing effective compositions**;
8	**Significant Subsidiary Improvement of the Listening, Speaking, Thinking, and Reading Skills of Students.**
9	**Cultivation of an Awareness of the Creational and Generational Aspects of Language, with a Beginning Awareness as well of the role of Silence**

How To Master Writing

The Traditional Approach believes that Writing is learned by mastering the mechanics, rules, and details of language with attention to external correct examples of writing.

The Rhetorical Approach believes that Writing is mastered by observing the Consequences and Impact of Writing resulting from empathetic appreciation for diverse audiences of gender, race, ethnicity, nationality, class, and occupation, using alternative dramatic strategies and stylistic devices.

The Modern Approach believes that Writing is mastered through studying writing and through critical reflection; rational, objective, detached thought; logical reasoning; clear conceptions; structured exposition; solid organization; and clear writing.

The Process Approach believes that writing is mastered, well, by writing – often, regularly, and incessantly – and with deep awareness of one's own unique writing process, writing with personal purpose, intention, passion, and an enduring desire (1) to learn who one is by writing and (2) to share with others whatever one might have learned that could lead to a more universal and deeper communion and community with others, nature, and the Transcendent.

Ideal Writing Forms	Outside In	*Bottom Up*	**Top Down**	*Inside Out*
Relating Modes	Nurturing	*Cultivating*	**Reflecting, Criticizing & Constructing**	*Communing*
Four Methods	Body Movement	*Peer Cooperation & Collaboration*	**Models & Forms**	*Choices*
Four Perspectives	*Outer*	*Subjective*	**Objective**	*Inner*

More on the 4 Main Writing Outcomes

Writing confers four kinds of benefits and blessings: namely, Practical Applications; *Emotional Balance and Equilibrium;* **Intellectual Comprehension**; *and Spiritual Vision and Integration.*

As the many foursomes above make clear, the Modern Approach to Writing centers around Writing as Clear and Critical Thinking. A great deal of research and innumerable college symposiums and workshops have addressed the field of Critical Thinking over the past 20 or so years, but without much notable success or clear consensus. We submit that the **Five Forms of Thinking** that we have begun to provide in our two volume comprehensive survey of the English language entitled The Two Hands Approach to the English Language: A Symphonic Assemblage will finally provide the workable framework for a truly useful course in critical thinking that cuts across the curriculum. We will bring forth at least a 1000 **Three Threads** and many additional Two Twists and Foursomes in a subsequent book that follows this one. These abundant **Three Threads** and numerous **Foursomes** will provide a huge foundational fund of ordinary words whose philosophical meanings and systematic connections with one another will become transparent for the first time, thereby fulfilling the aspiration and convictions of ordinary language philosophers who tried but failed to accomplish that task.

The time has finally arrived to conclude this section by explaining the last three adjectives or sets of adjectives that describe our Proposal for an Innovative System of Writing: namely, the adjectives *Vital, Universally Modeled and Doable, and Imaginative.*

Our proposed System of Writing is *Vital* and not artificial because it addresses the Four aspects, functions, capacities and powers, and temperaments of human nature, because it roots and begins writing instruction in the natural Mother Tongue of everyday life and mutual conversation and not in the impersonal Father Tongue (see the first of our two larger volumes about English where we describe at great length what we mean by the Mother Tongue, The Father Tongue, and the Imaginative Tongue). It recognizes, while Writing inherently stops Speaking and requires structure and thought, it is always rooted, anchored, and thrives or dies by its umbilical cord to Speaking through the supreme necessity and virtue of Living Voice as the first requirement of all competent and great writing. Writing must begin with the student, their personal interests and concerns. They must be allowed to choose their own themes and topics for writing and to employ the language and idiom of their own cultures and peers to express their experiences.

The British philosopher Whitehead noted in his short book *The Aims of Education* that education had three aims corresponding to the three stages of elementary and middle school, high school, and university. Whitehead named the aims romantic, precise, and general (which we would here rename universal). Those three aims correspond perfectly with The Mother Tongue, The Father Tongue, and The Imaginative Tongue. Whitehead insisted the first stage of all instruction was <u>romantic</u> because it should aim to inspire and encourage the student to explore in a free, spontaneous, and constantly encouraged way all the possibilities, opportunities, and joys of learning a subject – inciting creativity, discovery, and the tolerance of mistakes while avoiding all premature discouraging criticism or restriction and narrowing of focus and concern.

However, he insisted that by late high school the student had to advance, leaving what we would call using only the Mother Tongue in writing, so as to engage with more reflection and criticism, so as to focus thought and reasoning powers on one precise field or area and thereby to develop the discipline, concentration, and persistence necessary for any progress and worthwhile product to result.

Then, once the concentrated power of thought and reflection had been developed (or what we would call the Father Tongue in writing or the Modern Pedagogy of Writing as described above), the student, leaving high school or the early years of the University, should expand their horizons and fields of study and begin to see connections between and among subjects, using, in other words, their Imaginations or Imaginative Tongue to produce work of enduring value and benefit to themselves and others.

You could rename these three aims (1) the open, expansive, and self-expressive stage; (2) the disciplined, restrictive, and publicly addressed stage; and (3) the imaginative, personally integrated, and universally accomplished stage: in short, the Mother Tongue, the Father Tongue, and the Imaginative Tongue. Our system is *Vital* because it follows the natural course and stages of Progress in learning to write and does not impose undue burdens and requirements on students and gives them immediate feedback on the degree, extent, and fruit of their progress as writers.

What then makes our System *Universally Modeled and Doable?* **This is indeed the most important and transformative feature of our proposed system of writing.** While Writing is rooted in Speaking and The Mother Tongue, it is inherently about structuring and expressing thought or clear ideas as a first requirement of necessary coherence. And here again, we go to figurative language for some profound metaphors, insight, and personal experiential clarity.

Speaking is Music, flowing and involving the primacy of sound, the ear, and voice; Writing is Architecture, structured in form and function, involving the eye and the Recognition and Cognition of Form; Reading is Sculpture, involving touch and the whole body in movement and gesture, pulling and pushing and handling the text to analyze, take it apart, and appropriate it before putting it back together again imaginatively or holistically.

Since Form is so essential, the Greeks and Romans invented the standard Forms of Discourse – narration, exposition, description etc – that are still the macro-forms used in university English composition classes. Students are given anthologies of the Forms and then asked to read and imitate them in their own writing. This works reasonably well for students who can already write competently, but tends to befuddle and intimidate students who are just learning to write or who have little confidence or facility in writing.

At the micro level of learning to write, students are exposed to phrases, clauses, and sentences as formative features of language along with the form or look of some of the traditional parts of speech, such as the adverb; otherwise, **language instruction is impoverished by the lack of forms that can be used to provide models for students to learn to write.**

Our System of Writing provides the huge Missing Link in composition instruction by its invention and classification of 11

Sentence Forms which provide the foundation for all sentences used in English. We provide excellent examples of all the sentences, so that students can use their own content and imagination to construct sentences that are similar in Form. Students are given a choice to use a variety of the Forms in paragraphs and longer essays, and they are initially required to identify and footnote the forms they use.

Students are allowed to choose their own themes and topics with their own content, but they must practice using the variety of forms in varied assignments. **This both encourages and disciplines them to employ a wide variety of sentences, ensuring that they will acquire over time a formidable repertoire of forms of sentences and with them options for expressing their thoughts, feelings, and experiences.** *It also overcomes quickly and thoroughly any initial lack of confidence or blocks to writing that students and others often experience. The requirement of concentrating initially on the Forms of Sentences focuses and directs attention to the accomplishment of small, incremental concrete tasks that require regular, systematic, yet manageable exertions of effort and accomplishment.* Moreover, others in any given class are doing the same tasks, though they must supply their own content reflecting their unique life experience and imagination. Students can read their paragraphs and essays aloud to the entire class or to one another, and they can cooperate and collaborate in reviewing, evaluating, and revising their assignments to improve their voice, thought, word and sentence choice, structure and organization, and mechanical correctness in usage, grammar, punctuation, spelling, and formatting.

In other words, the **Proposed System of Writing employs all Four Approaches to Writing.** However, **the 11 Sentence Forms provide, in addition and qualitatively, a Precision,** as well as **a Systematic Conception and Implementation of Learning to Write,** unavailable in any other prevailing theory.

The **Proposed System of Writing employs clear models (1) with the 11 diverse sentence forms, (2) with excellent examples of all the sentences, and (3) with excellent student models of paragraphs and longer**

essays employing all the varied sentences. Because it is so clearly modeled; because it is realized in gradual, clearly distinct, and manageable stages, reflecting Whitehead's three aims of education; and because it concentrates on teaching writing initially as primarily a process of self-expression and writing itself as a way not only of reflecting life but also of generating and discovering its purpose and meaning, this **Proposed System of Writing** is *Universally Modeled and Doable, but also inspiring, motivating, and empowering.*

Finally, it is *Imaginative* (1) by virtue of its calling on the students always to choose their own subjects, themes, and topics for writing, and (2) and always to supply their own content for papers from the substance of their own life experience.

Teacher Section

The Essential Wholistic
Structure of English

The Essential Wholistic		
Words	**Phrases**	**Clauses**
12 Kinds of Words	**9 Types of Phrases**	**2 Kinds of Clauses**
---RIGHT HAND FINGERS---	1. Prepositional Phrase	1. Independent
1. Verb	-------------------	2. Dependent
2. Noun	2. Verbal Phrase	
3. Pronoun	a. Noun Verbal Phrase	**4 Types of Dependent**
4. Adjective	[infinitive, gerund]	**Clauses**
5. Adverb	b. Adverb Verbal Phrase	
---LEFT HAND FINGERS---	[infinitive]	1. Adverbial Clause
6. Conjunction	c. Adjective Verbal	FORM 7AC movable
7. Preposition	Phrase [present & past	2. Noun Clause FORM 8RN
8. VERBAL Infinitive	participle]	3. Reference Clause
9. VERBAL Gerund	3. Noun Phrase	FORM 8RN immovable
10. VERBAL Participle	-------------------	4. Adjective Clause
(Past, Present)	4. Adverb Phrase	immovable
------RIGHT HAND------	5. Adjective Phrase	
11. Appositive	-------------------	
------LEFT HAND------	6. Absolute	
12. Other	Construction	
	These are fully explained and exemplified in FORM 10TP Three Places.	

Structure of English

	Sentences	Paragraphs

	11 Traditional Types of Sentences
	
	A. Grammatical Types
	  1) Simple (1 independent clause)
	  2) Compound (2 or more independent clauses)
	  3) Complex (1 independent clause + 1 or more dependent clause)
	  4) Compound Complex (2 or more independent clauses + 1 or more dependent clause)
	B. Expressive Types
	  1) Declarative
	  2) Interrogative
	  3) Imperative
	  4) Exclamatory
	C. Stylistic Types
	  1) Loose
	  2) Balanced
	  3) Periodic
	D. Improper Types
	  1) Run On
	  2) Fragment
		5 Types of Paragraphs
		
		1. Opening Paragraph
		2. Regular Paragraph
		3. Transitional Paragraph
		4. 1- or 2-Sentence Paragraph
		5. Closing Paragraph

5⁺ Jobs of 12 Kinds of Words in Sentences 1. Main verb 2. Subject 3. Descriptor 4. Object 5. Connector	**11 Forms of the Sentence with their 127 Sub-forms** --- LEFT HAND FINGERS --- 1. 1F Fundamental 2. 2S Series 3. 3V Verbals 4. 4C Correlatives 5. 5R Repetition --- RIGHT HAND FINGERS --- 6. 6CC Coordinating Conjunctions 7. 7AC Adverbial Clauses 8. 8RN Reference & Noun Clauses 9. 9PP Power Punctuation 10. 10TP Three Places --- RIGHT FOREFINGER --- 11. 11ADD Additional	**5-Level Architecture of the Sentence** 1. Core = verb 2. Heart = Core + subject 3. Essence = Heart + object or object descriptor 4. Base = Essence + attachments 5. Total = Base + additions

12 Punctuation Marks

--------[PRIMARY]------------

-----STOP----red light------

1. **Period** – the Terminator
2. **Colon** – the Dramatic Pointer
3. **Semi-colon** – the Equalizer, the Balancer

-----PAUSE---yellow light----

4. **Dash** – the Emphatic Commentator, Amplifier, and Afterthought
5. **Comma** – the Flow Manager

-------[SECONDARY]----------

6. **Question Mark**
7. **Parentheses**
8. **Exclamation Point**
9. **Apostrophe**
10. **Hyphen**

11. **Quotation Marks**
12. **Ellipses**

Lesson Plan Schedule for Writing Class

Sample Term Syllabus, Schedule of Lesson Plans and Evaluations

Sample Term Schedule: 15 week term, 2 classes /week = 30 classes
Each class is 1.5 hours

Requirements: Classroom with blackboards on 2 walls. In Korea and other countries, there is usually one whiteboard. In that case, say that you need a whiteboard on wheels brought into the class.

Permission: Students sign a paper giving T (teacher) permission to collect and use their essays in a publication as examples with Two Hands Approach Associates or for re-use by the T in other classes.

We, the undersigned, do hereby allow my instructor, _____
_____, the Two Hands Approach Associates, and Two Hands Approach Publishing 2HA Publishing to reprint (with attribution) any of my exceptionally good Sentences, Written Assignments, or Written Exams produced during this course for use, study, reference, and emulation by future students taking this *New Angle on Writing* composition course.

Date	Print Name	Signature	Course Location

Assessment: Grading Sample 1

Quiz on 12 Turns, 12 Kinds of Words, 5 Jobs, 12 Punctuation Marks 5%
   Sentence Examples (notebook) 18% (18 homework sets)
Assignments #1 5% #2 7% #3 9% #4 11%
First Exam 15%
Final Exam 22%
Participation, Attendance, Performance 8%

<u>Grading Sample 2</u>

Quiz on 12 Turns, 12 Kinds of Words, 5 Jobs, 12 Punctuation Marks <u>5%</u>
Sentence Examples (check periodically, but collect notebook at end of term for final grade)
   <u>10%</u> (18 homework sets)
Assignments #1 <u>5%</u> #2 <u>10%</u> #3 <u>15%</u> #4 <u>15%</u>
First Exam <u>20%</u>
Final Exam <u>20%</u>
Participation, Attendance, Performance (+or – 5 points as possible bonus
   or loss to final grade)

	T= teacher, **S** = student, **para**=paragraph **ex**=example, **'** = minutes, **hwk** = homework, **Ass.** = Assignment, **E.**=English, **exs** =examples	
1	1 hr – students write on topic of their own choice 30'. – present **12 Turns of English Language** with chart The skills are not totally isolated, but have to be learned in conjunction with each other, spirally and progressing from one to another	Students memorize 12 Turns with hand gestures Get a notebook.
2	30' – as many students as possible come to front of class and recite out loud 12 Turns using the 2 hands 60' – present **12 Kinds of Words** and their **5 Jobs** using charts and 2 hands If time permits do **12 Punctuation Marks** Tell students they will have to perform and recite these charts	Students memorize 12 Kinds, 5 Jobs, 12 Punctuation marks and recite using 2 hands
3	30-45' – students recite 12 kinds, 5 jobs, 12 punctuation marks using 2 hands 45' – present **12 Punctuation Marks** if not done previously – introduce **1F Fundamental Forms** – if time permits, have students write examples and share by reading out loud	Test on 12 Turns, 12 Kinds, 5 Jobs, 12 Punctuation Write 2 examples of all the 1F sub-forms in notebook
4	15' - review orally Test on 12 Turns, 12 Kinds, 5 Jobs, 12 Punctuation 30-45'or more – give test 30' – present Form **2S Series** Forms If time permits, have students put their **1F** hwk on the board	Write 2 examples for each of the 2S Series sub-forms
5	50' Put up examples of remaining sub-forms of 1F on the board (1 or 2 of every sub-form) by	Write 2 examples for

	different students – put up …. for sub-forms of **2S** (T gives praise or kindly corrects as needed) 40' – introduce **3V Verbals** sub-forms	each of the 3V Verbals sub-forms
6	45' Put up any examples of **2S** still not covered and examples of sub-forms for **3V** 45' Introduce sub-forms for **4C Correlative Forms**. If time remains have Ss review 12 Turns, 12 Kinds, 5 Jobs, 12 Punctuation Marks	Write 2 examples for each of the 4C Correlatives sub-forms
7	50' Ss put on board examples of sub-forms of **4C** (T gives praise or kindly corrects as needed) 40' – introduce **5R Repetition** sub-forms	Write 2 examples for each of the 5R Repetition sub-forms
8	50' – students put 2 examples of sub-forms of **5R** on board (option – if T wants to give sample passage for reading as a basis for a topic to write about, T may do so in this or the next class before S work on Ass.1. This option may just provide Ss to read and discuss material in conversation with one another using the language as a welcome relief from writing and a complementary way to learn a language). 50' - Give instructions for writing **Assignment 1**, plus examples, Paragraphs (read out loud, noting sub-forms) (start writing in class if time allows)	**Ass.#1** – Ss choose their own topic Must type their paragraph with proper notations and footnotes and make copies for T and every S
9	Ss distribute their **Ass. 1** paragraphs Divide into groups to edit and rewrite their group's member's paragraphs. S reads it, everyone edits and rewrites it. (40 min) Ask for group to read their original and revised paras in front of class. Students can edit their copies of each S's para. Repeat for all groups if time allows T or Ss can comments at any point along.	Ss must prepare a typed copy of their revised para with proper notation and footnoting
10	Ss submit 1 copy of revised para to T Complete unfinished paras from last class if not all done. Present form **6CC** with examples from charts. If free time, do Sentence Word Analytics or present a song or interesting poem or story for reading and discussion	2 ex. each sub-form of 6CC (2 x7)
11	40' Students put on board examples of sub-forms of 6CC (T gives praise or kindly corrects as needed)	2 ex. each sub-

	50' – introduce **7AC Adverbial Clause** sub-forms If time permits….	form of 7AC
12	40' Students put on board 2 examples of sub-forms of 7AC (T gives praise or kindly corrects as needed) 50' – introduce **8RN Reference & Noun Clause** sub-forms	2 ex. each sub-form of 8RN
13	40' Students put on board examples of sub-forms of 8RN (T gives praise or kindly corrects as needed) 50' – present **Assignment #2** – reading student example essays out loud and noting relevant use of sub-forms Optional – T may wish to precede the writing assignment with a reading selection to help students to get a topic for the assignment or just to alternate reading discussion with writing as a way to learn E.	**Ass. #2** - Ss choose their own topic Must type their 2 or 3 paragraphs with proper notations and footnotes and make copies for T and every S
14	Ss distribute their Ass. 2 several paragraphs Divide into groups to edit and rewrite their group's member's paragraphs. S reads it, everyone edits and rewrites it. (40') Ask for group to read their original and revised paras in front of class. Students can edit their copies of each S's paras. Repeat for all groups if time allows T or Ss can comment at any point along.	Ss must prepare a typed copy of their revised para with proper notation and footnoting
15	Ss submit 1 copy of revised para to T T introduces all 3 **9PP Colon 9PPc1 to 9PPc3 sub-forms** and the first 2 **9PP Semicolon 9PPsc1 to 9PPsc2 sub-forms**	2 ex. each sub-form for **9PPc1-9Pc3** and **9PPsc1-9PPsc2**
16	40' Students put on board 2 examples of sub-forms of **9PPc1-9Pc3** and **9PPsc1-9PPsc2** (T gives praise or kindly corrects as needed) 50' – T introduce **9PP 5 useful semicolons 9PPsc3-9PPsc7** and the **2 difficult semicolons 9PPsc8-9PPsc9**	2 ex. each sub-form for **9PPsc3-9PPsc7** and **9PPsc8-9PPsc9**
17	40' Students put on board 2 examples of sub-forms of **9PPsc3-9PPsc7** and **9PPsc8-9PPsc9** 50' – T introduce **9PP Dash B and M 9PPd1 to**	2 examples each **dash B and M 9PPd1 to 9PPd8**

	9PPd8	
18	40' Students put on board 2 examples of sub-forms of dash B and M 9PPd1 to 9PPd8 (T gives praise or kindly corrects as needed) 50' – T introduce **9PP Dash E 9PPd9 to 9PPd15**	2 examples each **dash E 9PPd9 to 9PPd15**
19	Ss put on board 2 examples each dash E 9PPd9 to 9PPd15 50'- T gives instructions for writing **Assignment 3** **Optional** reading passage as earlier explained before giving Ass. 3	**Ass.#3** Ss choose their own topic Must type their 2 or 3 paragraphs with proper notations and footnotes and make copies for T and every S
20	Ss distribute their Ass. 3 of 3 to 5 paragraphs Divide into groups to edit and rewrite their group's member's Ass.3. S reads it, everyone edits and rewrites it. (40') Ask for group to read their original and revised Ass3 in front of class. Students can edit their copies of each S's Ass3. Repeat for all groups if time allows T or Ss can comment at any point along.	Ss must prepare a typed copy of their *revised* Ass#3 with proper notation and footnoting
21	Ss submit 1 copy of revised Ass3. to T 50' – T introduces **10TP B 10.1 to 10.7**	2 ex each sub-form **10TP B 10.1 to 10.7**
22	Ss put on board 2 ex each sub-form 10TP B 10.1 to 10.7 T introduces **10TP M 10.8 to 10.14**	2 ex each sub-form **10TP M 10.8 to 10.14**
23	Ss put on board 2 ex each sub-form 10TP B 10.8 to 10.14 T introduces **10TP E 10.17 to 10.25**	2 ex each sub-form **10TP E 10.17 to 10.25**
24	Ss put on board 2 ex each sub-form 10TP B 10.17 to 10.25 T introduces Lone Rangers **11ADD11.1 to 11.5**	2 ex each sub-form **11ADD11.1 to 11.5**
25	Ss put on board 2 exs 11ADD11.1 to 11.5 T introduces Lone Rangers **11ADD11.6 to 11.10**	2 ex each sub-form **11ADD11.6 to**

			11.10
26	Ss put on board 2 exs sub-form **11ADD11.6 to 11.10** T gives writing **Ass.#4**	**Ass.#4** Ss choose their own topic Ss must type their 4 to 5 paras with proper notations and footnotes and make copies for T and every S	
27	Ss distribute their Ass. 4 of 3 to 5 paragraphs Divide into groups to edit and rewrite their group's member's Ass.4. S reads it, everyone edits and rewrites it. (40') Ask for group to read their original and revised Ass4 in front of class. Students can edit their copies of each S's Ass4. Repeat for all groups if time allows T or Ss can comment at any point along.	Ss must prepare a typed copy of their *revised* Ass.#4 with proper notation and footnoting	
28	Ss submit 1 copy of revised Ass4. to T T tells Ss exam with specified forms will be given next class. It is open book. They can bring their textbook to the exam if they want. T decides how topic(s) will be chosen, and will tell them the 20 specified Forms they must use for the essay. Have students study and review on their own or in groups. See **First Exam** in Vol.1 that T chooses with 20 specified forms or an alternative mix selected by the T	Study all forms	
29	**Forms-Specific Exam** T chooses final topic with or without input from the. Students need not comply with every specified form, but must do most of them. Ss should be given **1.5 to 2 hrs** to write this composition	Review Forms and don't forget to bring Imagination to final class	
30	**Final Free-Form Exam** – Ss nominate 5 topics, choose 1, write on it footnote free (no footnotes required) for **2 hours**		
	T can compare Class #1 composition with Class #30 composition. How much has the S improved?		

Supplemental Activities

Sentence Word Analytics:
At any time when reviewing a sentence, stop and have students do a word by word analysis, stating the Kind of Word and the Job it does for each word in a sentence.

Sentence Form Analytics:
T can bring in an article or story by a professional writer and try *formspotting* (identifying the Forms used throughout the article or story.

Group Take Home Assignment: Students can be put into groups according to interest, and told to find examples of good sentences that exemplify the forms in anything that they want to read (internet article, novel, non-fiction book, etc). Looking at all the groups, see which group can find the highest number of forms in total and the widest range of forms (the most number of different sub-forms out of the 127 different sub-form).

Teacher Tips

Work on Board
- If only 1 whiteboard, get a portable white board and roll it in
- If homework has 6 or more sub-forms, have students randomly pick which sub-forms to put on the board. ie each student puts 1 to 5 sub-forms on the board (2 sentences each)
- After that group has read and discussed their sentences, another group can go to the board.
- T can keep a checklist of who has been to the board in which class and make notes accordingly on their work and enthusiasm

Instruction for the Teaching of Sentence Forms in the Classroom

At this point, we will outline a typical day during the Sentence Forms part of the course.

On the first day a Sentence Form is taught, the teacher should give the **name of the new form** and explain **how it is used**. Several easy as well as a **few literary examples** should be given for the student to scrutinize and discern the exact features of each Sentence Form. The students are then given some time to write a **few samples of their own**, and then told to **put them on the board**. These examples are then reviewed by the teacher and students, with the teacher making comments on and checking the accuracy of each example as is appropriate.

By this method, right away the students are involved personally in the creative process in the classroom. <u>Students are next told to write</u> **several (2 or 3) examples for homework.** **Students and teachers may find that a notebook would serve well as the site for these sentences.** These sentences will be **put on the board and looked at by the whole class the next day**.

In class, the students may talk over questions they may have or discuss their concerns about their sentences with some classmates while other classmates put their sentences on the board. The atmosphere should be relaxed, and the students should feel comfortable comparing notes and observing what others are doing.

The teacher can move around the classroom talking to students at their seats, helping the students at the board, or commenting about the final sentences placed on the board. The teacher is a combination coach, facilitator, encourager, and monitor of the ongoing efforts at sentence construction.

Although the atmosphere is relaxed, students realize that they must eventually put their sentences on the board. No one likes to appear foolish and incompetent in public, so students will naturally want to perfect the sentences that they want to display to others on the board.

Furthermore, we see that the content of **this system** is not confined to a single printed book, but instead **will grow each time the course is given**. From new additions by new classes of students, **better samples of writing can be saved** by the teacher **and shared** with subsequent classes. Posting better sentences on the internet also provides a unique enriching resource for teachers and students practicing this method.

Grammar is explained "on the go". Praise is given more often than criticism. Corrections are made with little or no fanfare or derogatory comments. **More attention is paid when the sentence forms are rendered correctly, rather than incorrectly.**

Students will, of course, make mistakes on the board, but that is also one of the purposes of the exercise. The primary purpose is to furnish the students with excellent examples of sentence forms and to inspire students with confidence so that they can write such excellent sentences.

A secondary purpose of the exercise, however, is for students to discover by themselves, with some correction and assistance from the teacher, the typical kinds of errors and mistakes that everyone makes when they first try to develop their skill at writing these sentence forms.

"The mistakes of others are good teachers." says an Estonian proverb. Letting students experience in public their mistakes and errors in writing these sentence forms will enable them to acquire mastery over those mistakes and take full control of the form. **Students learn best by sharing their own writing publicly before others**. They

73

automatically pay greater attention to corrections of their errors when their classmates are watching them. Public sharing of sentences is a form of real-world accountability where one shines or realizes painfully but constructively that one needs to improve.

Rivers (1987), talking about students keeping *dialogue journals,* recommends that teachers *"rephrase awkward expressions while commenting on the content."* Rivers notes:

> *Learning grammar, however, is not listening to exposition of rules but rather inductively developing rules from **living language material** and then [the] **performing** [of the] **rules**.* [bold emphasis added]

Teachers should correct students, and students should correct one another in these exercises, in a kind way. The first half of a Scottish proverb rings true for this situation: **"Wink at small faults..."** . Students, however, should be tolerant and supportive when others make mistakes, and should not deride their classmates. The real focus of every student should be on themselves, their own here-and-now, their own sentences. Students should pay close attention, understand the form, then emulate them many times to master them – not once, not twice, but often. **Students should not let up until they understand the forms and can replicate them in their writing**.

Sources of Examples for Students to Emulate (Good Places to Notice the Forms)

Students should be told to hunt for these Forms in anything that they read. They have free choice on what they read, but what they should pay attention to while reading are the use of the same Forms that they have studied in class. They can be put into groups and work together, extracting sentences from novels, news stories, interview scripts, and so on.

It will help them, too, to see that the English sentence has been mastered by not only people whose first language is English. Many people have excelled at writing good sentences whose native language is not English.

The chart below is not an exhaustive chart, but it might help acquaint the students with various styles of English by exhibiting to them examples taken not from a single book, but from the following five sources:

5 RELIABLE SOURCES FOR GOOD EXAMPLES FOR STUDENTS	
1	Examples of sentences **by students themselves** (most important by far);
2	Examples of sentences **by the teacher**;
3	Examples of sentences **by published writers whose first language was/is only English** i.e. Emerson, Twain; Stowe; Austen; Shakespeare; Margaret Atwood; Maya Angelou; John Grisham; Susan Sontag; and many more
4	Examples of sentences **from sources of wisdom** (reliable translations): (a) *proverbs* and *folk wisdom* from all the nations (b) *divinely-inspired examples*, i.e. the *Bhagavad Gita*, the Vedas, the Psalms, the Beatitudes, the Hadiths, the *Hidden Words*, ...;
5	Examples of sentences **by published writers whose first language was/is not English** i.e. Chinua Achebe, Joseph Conrad, ChangRae Lee, Phillis Wheatley, Amy Lee, Rabindranath Tagore, Lin Yutang, Paolo Soleri, Ayi Kwei Armah, Sri Aurobindo, etc

75

Once the students latch on to the system, they too will become sources of excellent examples of the Eleven Sentence Forms. Beyond a doubt, they too will want to show off their latest flashy or witty, insightful or scholarly efforts.

The teacher functions as a *coach*, insisting on *moderate discipline, conscientious effort, and diligent practice* - coordinating, delegating, reviewing completed work, and giving students new relevant assignments.

The New Angle on Writing Charts should be displayed around the room, helping to inspire and reinforce in the minds of the students the key components of the language. The various components of all the charts can be repeated, memorized, and recited individually or together at various times when called upon by the teacher. In this way, the teacher has available a repertoire of both written work and oral recitation that can be used in an interactive and integral function according to the needs of the students and the disposition of the teacher on any given day. The teacher can vary at will the content of the classroom in an interesting, varied, and non-repetitive manner.

Learning to write by imitation and emulation is not a new concept. When we are young readers, we always are attracted to certain writers or genres, because of the special style that we find featured in such books. We should extend and refine this natural practice by **asking students to find examples of the sentence forms in their favorite books**.

"The imitation of other artists is one of the means by which a person enriches and finally establishes his own individuality." Lewis Mumford

The Centrality and Importance of Oral Recitation in the Method of Instruction

There is another practice that is important in the instruction of this approach. **Students must read their sentences when their turn comes**. Only by doing so will they have sufficient practice in oral recitation to understand how to take apart and properly read texts. Only by reciting out loud will they learn to emphasize by sound the adverbs and also to emphasize the adjectives by driving them into the nouns.

Effective punctuation is as much a matter of sound as of sight; punctuation informs and guides the pace and rhythm of reading. **Only oral recitation will enable students to really understand the power and potency of the three power punctuation marks**: the colon, the semi-colon, and the dash. It is hardly any accident that most students after more than 16 years in public schools and colleges seem unacquainted with any punctuation marks except the comma and the period. Extensive oral recitation will remedy this lapse forever.

The New Angle on Writing thus incorporates **public performance in front of the class,** and enables the teacher to quickly publicly grade them based on their language as well as participation or leadership in the class and in their group activities and recitals.

> **We should teach our children to read and to look for the recognizable features buried in the sentence. Those features are there, students should become aware of them, and recognize their force, function, and nuance.**

Twelve Turns of the English Language

5 Skills (proficient performance) (unconscious)	5 Tasks (attentive mastery) (conscious)
1 **Listening**	6 **Vocabulary**
2 **Speaking**	7 **Basic English**

For the Basic English section:

a	Usage
b	Grammar
c	Syntax & Mechanics (i) Pronunciation (speaking) (ii) Spelling (writing) (iii) Punctuation (reading)

3 **Thinking**	8 **Sentences**
4 **Writing**	9 **Paragraphs**
5 **Reading**	10 **Essays**

Left Hand   2 Crowning Achievements   Right Hand

11 **Long Paper**	12 **Book**

Clap!

11   1   2   3   4   5   10   9   8   7   6   12

The 12 Turns of the English Language:
an Overture, Overview, and Introductory Map of the Basics of the English Language

The *New Angle on Writing* begins with a presentation *called The Twelve Turns of the English Language,* which is called an *overture.* **As an *overture*, it suggests the importance of sound and the musical rhythms that underlie language**.

The overture also functions as an *introduction and an overview* of the English language. As an ***introduction***, the Twelve Turns of the English language provides an initial identification and acquaintance with the elements of English, and as an ***overview***, it affords an aerial survey of the English language as a whole.

The **Twelve Turns of the English Language** are not polarities, but consist of five interdependent skills and five tasks which must be successively, continuously, and interactively developed, plus two crowning achievements that signify the final goal and desired outcomes of all language instruction.

These *turns* can be looked at as sequential and proprietary (*it's your turn*), as in the fleeting ownership of someone engaged in a conversation, or it can be looked at as circular, rotational, winding, coiling, as in the subtle yet irrefutable connections that exist between successive phases of any process. These twelve turns involve a linear progression down each of the columns (see chart), yet have a returning arc back to the top, keeping one always in constant awareness of each of the parts separately and yet of the whole that informs the parts.

FIVE SKILLS

(1) **Listening** – From amid the tumult of sounds that fill our waking and sleeping ears, we pick out sets of significant sounds. The sounds are words, and they have significance. MacNeil (1988) points out that our human aural conditioning goes back to the *"remotest origins of our species"*, and that the *"aural pathways to the brain – to say nothing of the heart – must be very sophisticated."* **He emphatically maintains that we need to restore**

the importance of listening in our society. He says that *"even for the literate adult undervaluing the importance of the sound of the language shrivels the language sense....Words heard clearly form the earliest layers because children live in the oral tradition."* As children, we revel in the sound of words newly learned. As older learners of additional languages, we may *revel*, or we may occasionally *revile* – depending upon the degree of mastery of those sounds, the phonetic inventory, of the target language.

The word *revile* comes from the Old French word, *viler*, which meant *to humiliate*. As an intransitive verb, *revile* means *"to use abusive language"*. Certainly, a major reason for the use of abusive language by various sectors of society is because they feel humiliated, and they lack the resources to express this frustration or inadequacy, and therefore resort to the most expedient and least laborious of means – the limited use (sometimes unlimited use) of the widening set of coarse and vulgar language noticeably slowly percolating through all levels of the society and the media. A child who is surrounded by such language learns to habituate and position his or her thoughts using a very limited set of words, words which do not uplift or *accentuate the positive* (as songwriter Johnny Mercer once wrote), but are instead marginal words lacking beauty and depth and respect for self and others.

You have to listen before you can speak.

(2) <u>Speaking</u> – In speaking, we undertake the initial construction and expression of life in connected words, deployed first to hear ourselves think and hold our thoughts in mind, and second to communicate with others. Everyone observes that children talk out loud to themselves constantly, as if to ground and root themselves in the sounds and permanence of words from their own mute silence and lack of communicative ability. **We must talk to ourselves for a long time out loud before we can know and understand ourselves, and talk out loud to others much longer to communicate with them.** Speaking is a long process of trial and error where many failures precede success. <u>You have to speak a long time in a language before you can think in it.</u>

You have to speak frequently before you can stop speech by thought and reconfigure it to become structurally coherent and connected.

(3) <u>Thinking</u>

– We must learn to think in the target language. We begin to piece the words together. Thinking is perception of structure and order. **Thinking is visual and architectural, and can be powerfully represented by various maps, charts, and models worthy of imitation.** We sometimes create new words or phrases, jumping quickly, perhaps, to a conclusion on the structure of the language long before we are formally taught about the language. In our new language mindfulness, we start to relate to people and things and events. Word by word and phrase by phrase, the vernacular is heard, perceived, recognized, connected, and absorbed. Elated in the joy of recognition, we store, keep, and upon a not-too-distant occasion in the future, we usher the language out from its new habitat in our mind, reproduce it, and launch it with full confidence and optimism, pondering the success or failure of the operation, pending the sign or response that the intended connection was made with the receiver. Then, does our repertoire of reusable and ramped up resources develop, enlarge, and consolidate. Ideas are put into the most basic of sentences or fragments thereof, **and the mind becomes accustomed to the new, strange, and wonderful land where thoughts are clearly expressed in suitable forms in language. Thinking is structural and visual. You have to think in the language a long time before you can break speech apart, and then reconfigure it in the coherent, clear, and meaningful manner required by writing.**

(4) Writing

– Someone drew before someone wrote. Someone wrote before someone read. We had symbols before we had words and literature. Paleolithic art tells us we were artists before we were writers. But then <u>at about the time of</u>

81

the Sumerians, the symbols became the words. Initial writing was used to record mercantile transactions, but later developed into a higher level of complexity and capability by means of which we could record and convey thoughts and information. Some people maintain that writing is more complex than speech, but as Brown (1994) says:

> ...that would be difficult to demonstrate. Writing and speech represent different modes of complexity, and the most salient difference is in the nature of clauses. Spoken language tends to have shorter clauses connected by more coordinate conjunctions while writing has longer clauses and more subordination.

Written language is rooted in and derived from spoken language, but is more structural and hierarchical in its determination of different levels of complexity and subordination. Writing also clarifies and reinforces the usage of many of the most common sentence forms. It permits the assurance that someone far away can understand our thoughts, feelings, and ideas. Family or social records, religious scripture written on papyrus or mulberry paper or directly on palm leaves, business receipts made with impressions on wet clay, memories scratched on bones or treated animal hides, typeset or diaries written with quill pens have been with us since the times of the **Mahabharata**, the **New Testament**, and Sumerian clay tablets.

Even in this age of keyboards, taking pencil or pen in hand is still an act that can have huge implications and impact, and one that should never be lost or eliminated from the curriculum. With the ever-threatening possibility of hard drive failure or operating system freeze, hand-written copies acquire an even greater strategic importance for the survival of the spoken and the scripted word. The paper mode, like one's hands, is independent of technology and is therefore more in a timeframe of its own. **This system needs no other basic hardware than pencil and paper**.

But not only is a piece of paper in a timeframe of its own, so is the writer. **Preferring solitude and places far from maddening crowds, the writer attunes her or his mind to silence**, resets the background music to something unobtrusive, picaresque, or pastoral. One draws away from the dimensioned world, the dymaxion grid, and prepares for comprehensible and comprehensive intake from the unconscious and the webs of conscious thought. One slips from the cocoon of ego and self and time, shedding it like someone gracefully disrobing, whereupon the self flies freely to another level of consciousness, somewhere at the interface of the unconscious and the conscious, of self and the Greater Self, being and the Greater Being.

This *ex-stasis* (ecstasy) is a wonderful moment, an irreproducible interval of pleasure, a moment of real bliss. It is love; the moment is full of great portent, great potential, great power. Words surface from the unconscious, display themselves in their conspicuous and awesome and rare beauty, and we – as writer and judge – surmise and select and use them one at a time, or in small groups. For those not selected, we let them of their own accord slip silently back from whence they came, drifting down from our stage of consciousness whilst yet others clamor for fame and publicity – to be the next one, to be the next one to be remembered forever. The bevy, the array, those waiting in the wings – such strikingly suitable and beautiful candidates they are – but if they cannot appear now, they know their time will come, at the right place and the right time with the writer who has the right poise and the right keenness of mind. Time wavers or flies by or is no longer there, as the student-writer's mind – somewhere in that unknown untapped dimension – draws from that Infinite source, catching all the fallen stars, meteoric and rising stars, and putting them on paper, or in a pocket, perhaps, maybe, for later use. It is a moment of forgetfulness of self, a remembrance of the true nature of being human. **It is with words that we are drawn out from the realms of ordinariness and dreariness. Writing is a setting down, for now and for posterity, the results of that momentary brush with the Infinite, with newly mined or minted words that are set down with multi-skill mastery.**

You must write frequently and in a variety of grammatical forms and styles to read effectively whatever a writer places on the page.

(5) Reading – We decode the symbols. We grasp the word. We understand the meaning. Proper reading is as essential a skill as writing, and is inseparable from that skill. One must write before one can read well. Once you are aware of the structures of the language, you can perceive the form of the discourse, digest the meaning, and grasp the essence of what is written.

Reading aloud is essential for reading well, though the last 500 years of history has terribly neglected and maligned the oral tradition. Reading should not be a silent activity, devoid of the sound, color, and movement of speech. In the library, silent reading is suitable. But somewhere in the learning environs, there should be a space for students to read aloud. Actors learn by reading aloud. *When you say something out loud and combine it with action or movement or gesture, there is a higher probability that it will be retained, vividly experienced, and appreciated.* If we don't read aloud, we should at least *sub-vocalize*, and listen to our voice. This takes us back to the first skill.

You have to read frequently so that, only by internally detecting the clear forms, the layout, and the resting stops in the written landscape, will you almost imperceptibly be able to detect the writer's voice and the nuances of his or her language, and the underlying pulse and rhythm of the reading passage itself. Then does reading become the rich experience that it is, where one finds *"the most disinterested and deepest acceptance, the most memorable pathos, the most resilient and inexhaustible humor, joy, suffering, pleasure, and human laughter without letup or end."* (Dowling).

Integral Interdependence of the Five Skills

The skills are **independent, interdependent, and integral with one another**. Focusing on one skill entails aspects of some of the other skills. The skills may be learned individually one at a time, but they are cumulative and integral in their operation, constantly reinforcing and influencing one another. **To become fluent and literate in the target language, students must be made aware of the different factors involved in the skills and how they are interactive**.

Writing Before Reading

You will notice that we place writing before reading, a departure from the usual way in which the skills are listed. Usually, we read to increase our vocabulary, to understand ideas, to enjoy story narratives, and it is assumed that the framework of the passage being read is self-evident to all readers. To think this way, however, is wrong. We may have chapter titles for books, but **rarely do books display clearly for readers the paragraph formations and sentence forms that render the books clear and coherent**. It is automatically assumed that students will be able to recognize these noteworthy features (paragraph formation and sentence forms) in the books they read and be able to duplicate them in the essays they write. This is a false assumption, for unless they are taught to recognize and imitate these features themselves, they will fail to understand and appreciate them. *Having seen a building, are we to assume that a person can construct a building or appreciate in any way its structure and beauty, without any training in building techniques or experience in building? To think so is foolish.*

We insist that only by having the direct and personal experience of duplicating the numerous established sentence forms will students ever be able to better absorb and understand the written word. Sentences have recognizable features. Corpus research is trying to program computers to parse and dissect text to its meaningful constituents, and we have trillions of bytes of parsed and analyzed texts, all fully searchable. **Yet, lamentably, prior to the *New Angle on Writing*, no one has devised a system that will teach students to write and read with recognition the essential sentence forms in any type of text whatsoever**.

Another reason for the early emphasis on writing involves *focus*. Writing causes a person to concentrate. Focus is part of the Periphery/Focus polarity. **Michael Polyani** has emphasized this polarity. Pencil in hand or fingertips on the keyboard – with intensity – one drafts, edits, re-phrases, successively re-drafts until the intended meaning comes clear. **The students must be aware of the constant focus and concentrated attention that writing demands, if their writing is ever to be deeply felt and clearly articulated**.

(6) Vocabulary

The Natural Approach maintains that vocabulary is the heart of language. As such, it is the first and foremost task. The 2HA believes that focused listening to bite-sized repeatedly spoken lexical items is still a useful way to learn a language, both in self-study and even more in social settings where one hears a native speaker.

Slowly, very slowly, a native speaker repeats the words syllable by syllable. At the same time that the native speaker pronounces the vocabulary word slowly, an image of what the word names should be presented to the learner as well as a very large printed rendering of the word in the native script.

Thus, if a foreign language student were to learn the English word "classroom", the native English speaker would pronounce each of the two syllables of "classroom" very slowly with a pause of 1-2 seconds between each syllable. At the same time, a picture of a "classroom" would be presented to the student. An enlarged printed version of the word should be placed on the screen or presented via a card to the student (type size should be at least 48pt).

The student should repeat the word aloud slowly, syllable by syllable, and 4 to 5 seconds of silence should elapse before the student hears the next word. Then the next word should be presented in a similar fashion. When 5 words have been presented, the student is asked to repeat them using the fingers of one hand, one word at a time, with proper pronunciation.

The next 5 are presented. Students are then asked to repeat the 10 words.

Vocabulary will not only include words, but commonly spoken collocations, idioms, and other phrases or expressions of popular usage. Words are magnets, and words have wings. With some we soar, and with some we sing. This book realizes the importance of vocabulary as the foundation of the language. With the advent of the mp3 player and the iPhone that have the ability to store speech digitally in a very compact portable format, there is no doubt that such devices will become available to assist people to build up their foreign and native vocabularies. Such portability gives the learner the ability to experience and iterate words and phrases while moving or when in settings with varied backdrops.

(7) Basic English – Usage, Grammar, Syntax & Mechanics

Elements from each of these three must be taught, giving students adequate opportunity for practice and self-expression. Students must be taught that _**usage**_ _governs what to write in terms of what is acceptable at that time_. The rules and terms of reference as governed by grammar can never pin or strap down language. Language will wriggle free; new structures and forms will emerge over time. _Usage must be taught – inclusive of idioms, collocations, colloquialisms, and all._

Grammar _must be taught more as the need arises_ in the stream of events as students unveil their novel creations. In this book , the basic foundation of grammar has been stripped down and simplified greatly. The working parts are 10 + 2 kinds of words that perform only 5 functions or jobs.

Syntax refers to the proper order, location, position, and sequence of words in a sentence.

The **mechanics** of **pronunciation** and **spelling** also receive attention in this book. The sole exception to turning attention to this postponed area is that pronunciation of any new word, phrase or sentence must be heard clearly and precisely punctuated from the onset. The mechanics of **punctuation**, however, will be taught using a new descriptive nomenclature and analogies. Notice how the 3 skills given here proceed (in priority) from sound to sight.

(8) Sentences

As we see later in The Eleven Sentence Forms Chart, **an appreciation of sentence forms is *the most important* part of this method. The Sentence has a new and different focus in this book. This book looks at the outward appearance of the sentence – the distinguishing traits, the visible markers, and its discernible patterns.**

> The **form** is a part of the world over which we have control, and which we decide to shape while leaving the rest of the world as it is. The **context** is that part of the world which puts demands on this form; anything in the world that makes demands on the form is context. **Fitness** is a relation of mutual acceptability between these two. . . . it is only through the form that we can create order in the ensemble.
>
> Christopher Alexander *Notes on the Synthesis of Form* 1964
> British urban planner and architect

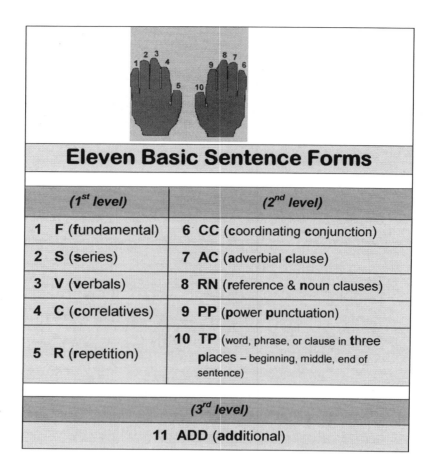

Eleven Basic Sentence Forms

(1st level)	(2nd level)
1 F (fundamental)	6 CC (coordinating conjunction)
2 S (series)	7 AC (adverbial clause)
3 V (verbals)	8 RN (reference & noun clauses)
4 C (correlatives)	9 PP (power punctuation)
5 R (repetition)	10 TP (word, phrase, or clause in three places – beginning, middle, end of sentence)

(3rd level)
11 ADD (additional)

Students will acquire the ability to recognize and recreate a multitude of *more than 100 sentence forms* – using an easy-to-recall and logical classification system. The topics in the sentences will reflect the important experiences and events in the actual lives and times of the students and their contemporaries. The *New Angle on Writing* provides a constantly renewing resource bank that will never fail to win and to keep the attention of the students.

(9) Paragraphs

Having mastered sentences, students will then be taught and learn the factors involved in the Writing Course, and especially how to develop paragraphs in a cohesive way. They will learn how to vary the sentence length and form to achieve balance, tone, effect, power, and subtlety. Rhetorical devices will be examined and mastered, so that the students will capture and hold the attention and concentration of their readers.

(10) Essays

Students will learn how to distinguish between, how to design and create, short essays in the 6 to 9 traditional rhetorical forms, on freely chosen topics. Although this might seem a prescription for teacher fatigue and early burn-out, it will be shown that by using **a novel footnoting system**, this book completely facilitates the task of checking and correcting the work of the students. Students must correctly use certain previously taught and specified forms in their essays, and they must footnote these forms properly. Then, the teacher can at a glance find the key sentences in the essay, and quickly determine whether the student has successfully shown mastery of the desired forms or not.

TWO CROWNING ACHIEVEMENTS

(11) Long Paper (long report or essay)
(12) Book

These are what you hope your students will achieve at some point in the future, having been adequately and rigorously instructed by you in all the key aspects of the language.

The system is meant to encourage a deep and lasting love of language. Students, inspired by the awesome potential of language and of their own deeper selves and creativity, will continue to read, appreciate, and produce good writing.

Twelve Kinds of Words

Little Five	Big Five
6 **Conjunction**	1 **Verb**
7 **Preposition**	2 **Noun**
8 **Verbal: infinitive**	3 **Pronoun**
9 **Verbal: gerund**	4 **Adjective**
10 **Verbal: participle** (a) *present participle* (b) *past participle*	5 **Adverb**
Two More	
12 **Other**	11 **Appositive**
Clap!	

12   10 9 8 7 **6**   **1** 2 3 4 5   11

The Two Exceptions in
The Twelve Kinds of Words

The **Ten Kinds of Words** have **two** exceptions that are so designated that way because of their importance and frequent usage in the language as fundamental building blocks.

The ***Appositive*** is the first of the two Exceptions, and it may initially appear not to really be a separate Kind of Word, but rather a sub-category of Noun, just as the articles (*the, a,* and *and*) are sub-categories of the Adjective, or personal, definite, and indefinite Pronouns are sub-categories of the Pronoun. However, *we single out the Appositive because of its importance and frequency of usage in language* which is undoubtedly why *traditional grammar gave it a special name without adequately highlighting its importance and frequency of usage.*

Finally, we mention the second Exception as an open Exception to include kinds of words such as interjections which have little importance or frequency of usage in written language, but abound in everyday spoken language. We call them the ***Other*** kind of word. They serve various functions such as conveying emotion (*gosh, crikey*) or getting someone's attention (*Hey! Yo!*). See *The Closing* (in Volume 2) for a more detailed explanation.

People should begin the study of grammar by concentrating on the Ten Main and the Eleventh Exception, and noticing the second Exception with limited attention or scrutiny.

The 12 Kinds of Words

The Two Hands Approach designates twelve *kinds of words* in the English language. The term *part of speech* is confusing and imprecise, since the entities to which it refers are used not only in speech, but also in writing. The constituents used in *both* speech and writing deserve a more exact and correct term for their collective reference, and a word that is less mechanical and more organic in its connotation. As replacement, we suggest the phrase *Kinds of Words*.

Traditional grammar designates the eight *parts of speech (Kinds of Words),* including the insignificant and seldom used *interjection*. This book removes the interjection from its place of primary importance, but retains the remaining seven. To the status of Kinds of Words, it nominates five additional kinds of words: the three *Verbals*, the *Appositive*, and a final kind called the *Other*. It is to the latter group that the lowly interjection is re-located.

It is not crucial to spend a lot of time trying to explain the abstruse differences between some of these older terms and their corollaries - such as *specifier, determiner, article* (which previous grammarians have kept in separate categories or classes). **They should not be part of a course outlining the foundation of language. These words can be explained when the occasion arises; they are of only marginal importance for this foundational approach to language**.

Five Primary Kinds of Words

The Two Hands Approach calls the **first five kinds of words** *primary* or *dominant*. They are used most of the time, and the right hand is used to remember them. With the fingers of **our right hand**, we can form a triangle with our fingertips. In the following diagram, the parentheses represent the fingertips of the right hand, **with the fingertips facing toward you, with the thumb to the far right and the little finger to the far left (palm inward)**

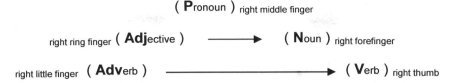

(Pronoun) right middle finger

right ring finger (**Adj**ective) ⟶ (**N**oun) right forefinger

right little finger (**Adv**erb) ⟶ (**V**erb) right thumb

The right thumb is the (1) <u>**Verb**</u>. The right pointer finger is the (2) <u>**Noun**</u>. The right index finger represents the (3) <u>**Pronoun**</u>. The index or middle finger often has a kind of axial or pivotal property. The Pronoun at the top stands for "I", **the first person singular, pivot and rivet of attention in everyone's mind's eye**. The right ring finger is the (4) <u>**Adjective.**</u> The Adjective is horizontally across from the Kind of Word it describes, the Noun. *Articles[7], determiners[8],* and *enumeratives[9]* are put in this group. The fifth right finger is the (5) <u>**Adverb**</u>. It is horizontally across from the Verb, which is one of the Kinds of words that the Adverb modifies or describes. *Intensifiers[10]* are put under adverbs.

This finger formation is an easy way to remember the relationship between the Kinds of words. Thus, Adjectives describe Nouns. Adverbs describe Verbs, but they also modify themselves (curl up the little finger), as well as Adjectives (the right ring finger).

You can also pinch the right thumb and forefinger together. **Placing these two fingers together designates that these two kinds of words, the Verb and the Noun, are the two most important of all kinds of words.**[11]

The other three right hand digits designate the other three kinds of words, and complete the set of the **5 dominant kinds of words** that have the <u>most meaning in English</u>, and which are **the most important, the most meaningful, and the most frequently used**.

---

[7] *the, an, a*
[8] *Determiner* is a general word that refers to articles, possessive pronouns, possessive nouns, demonstrative pronouns, and numbers.
[9] *first* customer, *second* day, *third, …*
[10] *very, more, less, somewhat, a bit,…*
[11] It is interesting to note that in some cultures, rubbing the thumb and first finger together is sign language for *money.* In the Information Age, it is the skilled use of Verbs (thumb) and Nouns (1st finger) in well-constructed sentences that will gain advantage and promotion in most work settings!

Five Secondary or Sub-Dominant Kinds of Words

The **second set of five**, called *secondary* or *subdominant* ones, are significant, but not as critical. (6) **Conjunctions** and (7) **Prepositions** (left thumb and forefinger) are both connectors and do not contribute as much to the meaning of a sentence as the five dominant Kinds of Words.

The remaining left hand fingers represent the three Verbals. The left index finger is the (8) **Infinitive**. This, in the *to-* form or stem form, represents the essence or basic form of the verb. The left ring finger is the (9) **Gerund**, and the last finger represents two types of (10) **Participles,** the Present Participle and the Past Participle.

Looking at the ends of our left fingers (palm inward), we have the following memory-aid diagram:

left middle **(V-inf)**

left forefinger **(Prep.)**   **(V-ger)** left ring finger

left thumb **(Conj.)**   **(V-part)** left little finger

The **Verbals are multi-functional Kinds of words**, performing the roles simultaneously in specific double combinations of verb, noun, adjective, and/or adverb (for example, verb + noun, verb +adjective, verb + adverb).

The Verbal Kinds of Words, together with the Verb, convey *the energy, the movement, and the dynamism* of the language. The inclusion of these three Verbals together with the Verb in our master list of Kinds of Words establishes the supremacy of the Verb over the Noun in all language.

Traditional grammar failed altogether in this respect, and violated both common sense and ignored the everyday usage of language, where Verbals occur with great frequency. Words that recur with such frequency cannot be consigned to the margins of language instruction. They are indeed in practice, with respect to their meaning and power, more important as Kinds of Words than Connectors and Prepositions (which follow). Traditional grammar undoubtedly viewed the Verbals as subcategories of the Verb, but thereby, unfortunately, minimalized and marginalized their pivotal role in language. This system now elevates Verbals to equal rank with the other seven primary and secondary Kinds of Words.

The Two Additional Kinds of Words

The eleventh category is the (11) **Appositive**. **An *appositive* is an additional name for another noun that usually precedes it in the sentence.** For example, in the sentence *Jenny, my best friend, lives down the street,* in our system, the appositive part is *friend.* Since it is the more important of the two additional Kinds of Words, we associate it with the ***right hand*** when teaching students to remember it.[12]

The (12) **Other** category is for the ever-present, non-conforming, idiosyncratic cases. You always have to expect the unexpected in English grammar; thus, the need for this coverall designation of "**Other**". We allocate to this category the short words previously called *expletives, interjections, fillers, invocative words, topic shifters, salutations, summons,* and (from discourse analysis) *pause and boundary markers.* Any additional items of this kind may simply be appropriately named and included in this category of *the* ***Other***[13]. Since the *Other* is the less important of the two additional Kinds of Words (it is used primarily in speech and not in written text), we associate it with the ***left hand*** when teaching students to remember it.

---

[12] The Appositive is a Noun that immediately follows another Noun or Pronoun and explains it further. Separated by a comma, it makes the antecedent Noun or Pronoun more definite or clear.

[13] Take an in-depth look our very comprehensive description and list of examples of *the Other* in *The Closing* in Volume 2 of the *Two Hands Approach to the English Language: A Symphonic Assemblage.*

The list of the 12 Kinds of Words is concise and gives priority to the kinds of words in the sequence of their importance. Inspect any passage from a novel or mainstream media, and it will be seen that no important kind of word has been left out.

Children want to write before they want to read. They are more fascinated by their own marks than by the marks of others. Young children leave their messages on refrigerators, wallpaper, moist windowpanes, sidewalks, and even on paper.

Joyce Armstrong Carroll *Acts of Teaching* 403

Five Jobs or Functions of the
Twelve Kinds of Words

Right Hand – Jobs that Words Do	
1 Main Verb	**MV**
2 Subject	**S**
3 Descriptor	**D**

4 Object [*left hand*]
 	
   1) direct
   2) indirect
   3) object descriptor
   4) object of preposition
   5) object of verbal
	O

5 Connector	**C**

Job or Function of the Twelfth Kind of Word, the Other

The twelfth Kind of Word performs the job of expressing a variety of emotions and speech expressions.

We call this job the **Emotive and Speech Modes.**

6 Emotive and Speech Modes	**SM**

5 4 3 2 1	1 2 3 4 5

The 5 Jobs of the 12 Kinds of Words

The functions that the 12 kinds of words play are 5 in number. The first three functions are placed in the above order to establish the primacy of the Verb over the Noun in learning and using language. It also emphasizes again the dual primacy of the Verb and the Noun. Finally, this order corresponds typically to the way people learn the various kinds of words, and employ them.

The word *Predicate* is not used at the outset, since it is not essential for understanding the foundations of the language, and since it is confusing. **Discussions about the Predicate should come much later in language instruction *after* the foundations have been laid with this approach.**[14]

The order has a simple logic:

⊕ **Main Verb** (*we first learn a language listening to our mother's verbal commands*);

⊕ **Subject** (*we then learn the word "I", since a baby's first emerging awareness is in response to the question "Who am I?" - probably as yet not existent in words, but perhaps there in spirit or another form in its memory*);

⊕ **Descriptor** (*we certainly know what happiness [smile], sadness, anxiety, and fear are right from the start of life (nice baby, good girl)*);

⊕ **Object** (*we learn that as agents we act upon, shape, and manipulate entities as objects (persons, things, ideas)*; and then we learn something about

⊕ **Connectors**, the putting together and joining of persons, ideas, and things, and the words which join, unite, and establish relationships between the persons, ideas, and things.
> *ie.* Bill *and* Jane, the boy *in* the home
> Conjunctions and prepositions, as in the examples above, are working as Connectors.

We learn that all reality is a connection and interplay of objects and motion, and words are the glue or links that we use to reference all

---
[14] To say it another way, familiar to us all: *Keep It Simple, Stupid.*

accountable and visible entities, and all the mental and invisible reality around us. (For those with an interest in physics, they should tackle reading Brian R. Greene's *The Elegant Universe* or his 2004 book *The Fabric of the Cosmos* whose culminating vision is of "a vibrant eleven-dimensional 'multiverse', pulsating with ever-changing textures, where space and time themselves may dissolve into subtler, more fundamental entities.")

Let's have a closer look at each of the 5 functions we listed above.

(1) <u>Main Verb</u>

We learn first about the **Main Verb.** Every human starts by responding to a simple imperative verb: *look, see, (don't) cry, smile.* It is accompanied with actions simultaneously. The whole body is involved; therefore, the mind easily remembers and uses verbal commands. **The learning of language begins with the Verb**[15].

The Verb is the only Kind of word that can legitimately stand on its own, and be considered a sentence.

There are 3 kinds of **Main Verbs** as are shown in the following 2 charts. In each case, the Constituent Verb is the part of the verb that indicates the action or process, and is not indicative of time (*I <u>have</u> <u>seen</u> the movie twice*) or volitional (*I <u>might go</u> there later*).

Phrasal verbs abound in spoken English and thus are a bugbear and burden for EFL and ESL students to learn. A phrasal verb can have a helping verb component as well as the basic verb and basic postposition components. For example, in *The child **is putting away** her toys*, we see all three possible components of the Main Verb (Helping Verb, Basic Verb, Preposition in post-position).

For native English speakers, the main verbs are read and can be identified with not much confusion; for EFL students, however, main verbs are not always easily noticed at first glance.

---

[15] This is why the learning of all vocabulary begins with verbal commands involving action. This is the merit of the TPR method, which works best and usually only effectively at the beginning of language instruction.

Five Kinds of Main Verbs I

	Five Kinds of Main Verbs	
1	**Linking Verb** MV = LV Main Verb = Linking Verb *is, was, were, are, look, seem, feel, taste, sound, get, become, remain*	She **is** smart. He **was** rich. There **are** students. They **became** weary. The food **tastes** good. You **look** great! That **sounds** good.
2	**Basic Verb (alone)** MV = BV Main Verb = Basic Verb	Jan **sings** very well. I **stand** alone. Betty **typed**. John **ran**. They **relaxed**. The news **spread**. Infants **cry**.
3	**Basic Verb (with Helping Verb)** MV = HV + BV Main Verb = Helping Verb + Basic Verb *be, do, have*	Dad **is watching** TV. I **have been waiting** for 20 minutes. He **didn't notice** the time. We**'ve been studying** this for two weeks. **Did** you **see** the movie? The clerk **had** already **left** by then.

Five Kinds of Main Verbs II

4	**Basic Verb (with Special Helping Verb)** MV = SHV + BV Main Verb = Basic Verb preceded by Special Helping Verb 1. that is Future-related; or 2. that indicates condition or limitation on action	**Future-Related** 1. Potentiality (or Ability) You **can** do it. (ability) [past form: *could* as in Last year I *couldn't* drive at all.] 2. Possibility I **might** go. I **may** be a bit late. 3. Suggestion You **should** get here on time. You**'d better** call first. We **should** renovate the house. 4. Preference I **would** stay here if I were you. 5. Proposition or Proposal We **should** raise the drinking age. We **should** update the highway system. You **could** look in the yellow pages. 6. Prediction I **will** be there soon. I think she **will** win the prize. **Condition or Limitation on Action** 7. Obligation You **must** see the film. They **have to** make monthly mortgage payments. You**'ve got to** try. 8. Permission You **may** leave now. You **can** go if you want. Last time, we **couldn't reach** the top because of rain. 9. Prohibition You **can't** do that.
5	**Phrasal Verb** MV = (HV) + BV + PiP Main Verb = (Helping Verb) + Basic Verb + Preposition-or-Adverb-in-Postposition	**Transitive: separable** **Turn on** the radio. **Turn** the radio **on**. **Hand in** your homework. **Hand** it **in**. **Turn down** the music. **Turn** it **down**. They all **put on** their boots. They all **put** their boots **on**. **Transitive: inseparable** She can't **get over** the breakup. **Get off** the bus at the third stop. You're **taking on** too much work. **Transitive: separated** You're **putting** me **on** (but not: You're putting on me.) That really **ticks** me **off**. **Intransitive** Many people **showed up** at the meeting. They are just **getting by** these days. I **woke up** at 6:00 am.

Descriptor

4 Types of Descriptor Functions	
Distant Descriptors	
Those that describe Nouns or Pronouns at a distance: (a) **Nouns** (b) **Adjectives**	Examples: [subject] [main verb] [distant descriptor] 	Subject	Main verb	**Distant descriptor**	 	---	---	---	 	noun or pronoun	verb	noun or adjective	 	I	am	a cyclist.	 	Jane	is	studious.	 The main verb (2nd sentence) is a linking verb, such as *become, appear, look, feel, grow.*
Descriptors	
Those that describe Nouns: (a) **Adjectives** (b) **Participles** (c) **Infinitives** (d) **other Nouns**[16]	Examples: <u>Adjectives can describe Nouns</u> (a) *hollow* feeling; *full* stomach; *green* eyes <u>Participles can describe Nouns</u> (d) *rhyming* verse; *spreading* virus; *paved* street; *powdered* milk <u>Infinitives can describe Nouns</u> (e) The need *to make peace* is very important. The will *to survive* is the law of the jungle. <u>Other Nouns can "describe" Nouns</u> (f) *brain* surgery, *news* stand, *corner* store.
Those that describe Verbs **(a) Adverbs** **(b) Infinitives**	<u>Adverbs can describe Verbs</u> (a) She left *quickly*. She dove *gracefully* from the diving board.

---

16   See discussion in Vol. 2 of *2HA SA* in *The Closing* on the property of Nouns performing the role or function as Descriptors. (ex. *roller suitcase, wheelchair access, etc*)

		Infinitives can describe Verbs (b) I went to the library *to study*. I bought a book *to help* me learn Korean.
	Those that describe other descriptors **(a) Adverbs** **(b) Adjectives**	Adverbs can describe Adverbs (a) The cars moved *very* slowly. Adverbs can describe Adjectives (b) This one is *more* expensive. That was *very* painful decision.

Just as grammatical roles of words depend on their context in the sentence, so too, in life, the perspective or content of a writer's contribution is always reflective and to a certain extent dependent on the community context, the times, and place. Many writers, however, such as Vietnamese-Australian Nam Le, are going beyond borders and cultural clinging, and are finding that details on almost *any* geographic location, local heritage and history are within reach, especially with those with access to the Internet, good libraries and bookstores.

> "Writing is always already writing for some purpose that can only be understood in its community context."
>
> Patricia Bizzell
>
> *Cognition, Convention, and Certainty: What We Need to Know About Writing*
> from *Cross Talk in Comp Theory*

Conjunctions

Types of Conjunctions						
COORDINATE CONJUNCTIONS join equal words, phrases, independent clauses. There are 7 coordinate conjunctions, and are dealt with in **Form 6**.						
and	for	or	yet	but	nor	so

| **CORRELATIVE CONJUNCTIONS** consists of two or more words that work in tandem, relating two ideas or events together in a variety of ways. An exhaustive list is not needed here now, as these conjunctions comprise form **4C The Correlatives.** |

ADVERBIAL CONJUNCTIONS function only as connectors of dependent clauses with other clauses that can be either dependent or independent. There are 18 adverbial conjunctions. The use of these comprises **Form 7**. Traditionally, they are called *subordinate conjunctions*.

Cause	Condition	Qualification	Time
because	if	though	when
since	whether	although	as
so that	once	even though	while
	whenever		since
	unless		before
	until		after
	in case		once
			as soon as

REFERENCE[17] CONJUNCTIONS function always as connectors, and sometimes as subjects or objects. There are 10 main RN conjunctions. This is **Form 8**.

	who	where	when
	why	what	how
	that	which	whose
	whom		

---

[17] What we here call *Reference Conjunctions* have traditionally been called *Relative Conjunctions*. We feel that this designation is confusing and should be replaced with *Reference Conjunction*. We explain this fully in **Form 8RN**.

Prepositions

Prepositions Sorted in Thought Categories

Time	Space	Logic
about	about	**.cause or reason**
after	above	according to
ahead of	across	against
along, alongside	against	as
around	ahead of	because of
at	along	on account of
before	amid	owing to
between	among	pertaining to
by	around	**.concession**
during	at	aside from
for	below	as well as
from	beneath	notwithstanding
in	beside	**.exception**
in the midst of	between	despite
on	beyond	except
over	down	**.addition**
past	in	in addition to
previous to	inside	**.specific instance**
since	into	in case of
throughout	near	**.comparison**
under	off	like
until	on	**.possession**
while	onto	of
within	out of	**.co-distinction**
	outside	apart from
	past	**.co-placement**
	previous to	up against
	through	with
	to	without
	toward	with regard to
	underneath	
	up	
	up against	
	upon	

107

Summary Chart of the
12 Kinds of Words and their 5 Jobs

12 Kinds of Word	5 Jobs					
	subject	main verb	descriptor	object	connector	emotive & speech modes
verb		●				
noun	●		●	●		
pronoun	●		●	●		
adjective			●			
adverb			●			
conjunction					●	
preposition					●	
verbal: infinitive	●		●	●		
verbal: gerund	●			●		
verbal: present participle past participle			●			
appositive			●			
other						●

108

12 Punctuation Marks I

Punctuation sets the pace for the reader, and assists the reader to determine the importance, association, and relationship of elements within the sentence.

Right Hand – The Big Five Punctuation Marks

	Traditional Name	Symbol	Nickname	Traffic Signal	Rhythm & Pace
1	**Period**	.	The Terminator	Red	Stop
2	**Colon**	:	Dramatic Pointer	Red	Stop
3	**Semi-Colon**	;	The Balancer The Equalizer	Red	Stop
4	**Dash**	—	The Highlighter The Commentator The Amplifier	Yellow	Pause
5	**Comma**	,	The Flow Manager	Yellow	Pause

1 2 3 4 5

12 Punctuation Marks II

Left Hand – The Little Five
Punctuation Marks

	Name	Symbol	Use & Effect
6	**Question Mark**	?	inquiry
7	**Parenthesis**	( )	addition of minor importance
8	**Exclamation Mark**	!	excitement, surprise, emphatic statement
9	**Apostrophe**	'	shows possession or contraction of two words
10	**Hyphen**	-	word joiner

Two Talkative Punctuation Marks
used to indicate direct speech or omitted speech

	Name	Symbol	Use & Effect
11	**Quotation Marks**	" "	marks off dialogue; citation of words of others; technical term; foreign word or phrase; notation of jargon; notation of ironic use of a word;
12	**Ellipses Dots**	...	indicates omitted words

12	10 9 8 7 6	11

Punctuation

Traditional instruction in punctuation has suffered from several shortcomings:

1. *Traditional instruction provides no clear distinction between the more important and the less important punctuation marks,* but instead they are all treated more or less equally. **This book distinguishes between the 5 punctuation marks that are <u>primary</u>, and the 5 punctuation marks that are <u>secondary</u>, plus 2 talkative ones, for a total of 12.**

2. *The names of traditional punctuation marks are not suggestive of what they do or how they function in the sentence.* The purpose of punctuation marks is to control the flow of movement within the sentence; they need names that clearly describe their function. **The 2HA gives new names for the punctuation marks, words that are more indicative of the functions they that they do in the sentence.**

3. *The traditional names for punctuation marks carry no powerful images descriptive of their functions* as traffic policeman and pace-setters, *controlling the flow of movement, the pauses, and stops within and between sentences.* **The 2HA provides analogies and images of punctuation marks as traffic signals, with pauses representing yellow lights and stops designated as red lights.**

4. *Traditional names fail miserably to capture and convey the inherent musical character of language with its qualities of rhythm and pacing, beat and measure, pitch and tonality.* It is the pauses and stops in language that enable the reader to invest the words with the tone, melody, and mood which together convey the full range of human feeling. **This book teaches the timing and pacing involved with each of the punctuation marks, and fully elucidates the proper and judicious use of the full use of such in one of the Sentence Forms as a means to establishing mood, and emphasis.**

Students, indeed, are seldom told the purpose or meaning of punctuation, so they never really understand, but simply memorize rules, which they soon forget. Having forgotten the rules, they then cannot reconstruct them by simply thinking about them, which they could do if they understood their meaning and purpose and had an image to guide their reconstruction of the rules. This book provides a simple memory-aid diagram for that purpose.

Five Primary Punctuation

There are *five primary punctuation marks*, symbolized by the **right hand**. This book uses new names and traffic signals to help students remember and differentiate between the diverse functions of punctuation marks. Below are the primary punctuation marks, so designated because of their primary importance over the other punctuation marks.

		TRADITIONAL NAME	NICKNAME	TRAFFIC SIGNAL	RHYTHM AND PACE
FIVE PRIMARY PUNCTUATION MARKS					
	1	**Period** .	the Terminator	red	Stop
		Colon :	the Dramatic Pointer	red	
		Semi-Colon ;	the Equalizer, the Balancer	red	
		Dash —	the Afterthought, the Commentator, the Amplifier	yellow	Pause
		Comma ,	the Flow Manager	yellow	

In this instance, we use the right hand and fingers to identify the most common and significant punctuation marks. The right hand is thus both a visual image and a tactile device for remembering the punctuation marks and their functions. **When the right thumb and the small finger (#1 and #5) are put together** (they represent the most common punctuation marks), **the middle three fingers** form a **side-by-side triple alliance. This is important, as these three punctuation marks will**

112

occupy an important rank in the formation of the Power Punctuation Sentence Forms, which will be discussed later. The three middle fingers symbolize respectively the **power punctuation** marks: the forefinger stands for the **colon**, the middle finger stands for the **semi-colon**, and the fourth finger, the **dash**.

The use of the traffic signals emphasizes the functions of the punctuation marks as speed control managers in the sentence. **The function of the comma and the dash is to make the reader _slow down_, and so commas and dashes are represented by the traffic signals of _yellow_ lights. The function of the period, semi-colon, and the colon is to make the reader _stop_ and _reflect_ at greater length; therefore, the period, the semi-colon, and the colon are designated as the traffic signals of _red_ lights.**

> In the eye method, you're told to put a period at the end of the sentence. In order to do this, you have to know what a sentence is. But no one knows. In the ear method I tell you put a period whenever your voice makes the sound of the period. That is, the voice slows down, the _tone_ falls, and the voice comes to a full, complete, solid stop. Like that. Did you hear the period? Read it aloud, and then you will.
>
> Robert C. Pinckert
> _The Truth about English_

Seven Secondary Punctuation Marks

There are *five secondary punctuation marks*, symbolized by the **left hand**. These are also significant, but do not rank in importance with the first five. **We indicate their secondary importance by not assigning them new names or traffic signals.**

SEVEN SECONDARY PUNCTUATION MARKS			
		TRADITIONAL NAME	
	6	**Question Mark**	**?**
	7	**Parentheses**	**( )**
	8	**Exclamation Point**	**!**
	9	**Apostrophe**	' or '
	10	**Hyphen**	-
	11	**Quotation Marks**	" " ' '
	12	**Ellipsis (Dots of Omission)**	. . .

6 The **Question Mark** goes at the end of question sentences.

7 **Parentheses** include all the four pairs of bracket symbols found on most computer keyboards { }, [ ], < >, ( ). The curved Parenthesis symbol will be discussed in Form 10.12 and 10.13 as parenthetical asides or further explanations.

8 The **Exclamation Point** goes at the end of sentences to indicate a stronger voice, an urgent intention or warning, or a surprising fact.

9 The **Apostrophe** indicates possession, and is also used to indicate that some letters are missing from a contracted word or phrase, as in *I'm, we're, etc.*

10 The **Hyphen** is used in many compound words, as in *vice-president, mother-in-law, X-ray*, and is also used to split up words that can't fit on a single line in a typeset setting such as a newspaper column.

Finally, there are *two additional punctuation marks* that are used in communicating directly the spoken or written words of others: **Quotation Marks** and **Ellipsis.**

11 **Quotation Marks** include both paired *single* and *double* quotation marks (' ' and " "), or less stylish hash marks (' ' and " "). They indicate the direct and exact words spoken or written by another person. They were used to quote special expressions, titles of books or magazines, and foreign words when typewriters were used (italics is often used to do that now).

12 **Ellipsis** (**Dots of Omission** ...) indicate that some part of someone's dialogue, written passage (beginning or end of a sentence, or paragraph), or list has been omitted or left out. We hereby designate the nickname *Dots of Omission* for *Ellipsis*, a coinage first invented and suggested by literary critic Stanley Cavell. There should be a single space before and after the ellipsis, but the spaces at both ends are omitted if the ellipsis is followed by a period, comma, question mark, or exclamation mark. Also, if you quote the latter part of a sentence, do not place an ellipsis at the beginning of a quotation to indicate the omission of material. Some typographic style guides advocate spaces between the dots (as you see above.)

For the **hand sign for Quotation Marks**, the student can slightly move the curved forefinger and middle fingers up and down to represent the hash mark style Quotation Marks. For the **hand sign for Ellipses**, the student can move the right or left hand in a slight chopping action three times from left to right. Or students can invent their own hand sign for the hand gestures for Punctuation Marks #11 and #12.

Quiz on Grammar Charts

based on the previous Grammar Charts

1) What are The Twelve Turns of the English Language? Specifically, (1) what are *The 5 Skills* that an English student must constantly master; (2) what are *The 5 Tasks* that an English student must successively accomplish; and (3) what are *The 2 Crowning Achievements* of English study? *Value: 24 pts.*

2) What are The Ten Plus Two Kinds of Words in the English language (otherwise called The Twelve Kinds of Words or The Twelve Parts of Speech of the English language)? Specifically, (1) What are The Big Five Kinds of Words; (2) What are The Little Five Kinds of Words; and (3) What are The Other Two Kinds of Words? *Value: 24 pts.*

3) What are The Five Functions or Jobs that the Twelve Kinds of Words Perform in the English Sentence (or) What are The Five Uses of the Twelve Kinds of Words in the English sentence? *Value: 20 pts.*

4) What are The Twelve Punctuation Marks in the English Language? Specifically, (1) What are The Big Five Punctuation Marks; (2) What are The Little Five Punctuation Marks; and (2) What are The Other Two Punctuation Marks of English? Value: *24 pts.*

This test gives 8 free points to the student to make the test out of 100.

5-Level Architecture
of the English Sentence

1 2 3 4 5

Five Architectural Levels or Analytical Stages of the Sentence		Subject	Main Verb	Direct Object or Distant Descriptor	Attachments to subject, verb, object	Additions
1	**Heart** = main verb		●			
2	**Essence** = heart + subject	●	●			
3	**Core** = essence + object or subject complement	●	●	●		
4	**Base** = core + attachments	●	●	●	●	
5	**Total** = essence + additions = core + additions = base + additions	●	●	(●)	(●)	●

Base Level: includes **attachments** which are words or phrases *attached* to one or more words in the Core (that is, the subject, main verb, and direct object or subject complement if there is one).

Total Level: includes **additions** which are words, phrases, or clauses placed in the beginning, middle, or end of the sentence as openers, interruptions, or closers of the sentence. They can be added to the Essence, Core or Base. They are separated by one or more punctuation marks.

The **Main Verb** earns the title for **Heart** of the sentence, because when we read we should initially locate the Main Verb and then find the other parts assembled around it. It is relevant to note here that the Main Verb is primary in Japanese, Korean, German, and several Amerindian languages, and it is placed at the end of the sentence to highlight its importance. Lastly, Verbs in general (especially the Main Verb) allow us to place ourselves and events in the perspective of time.

Samples That Illustrate the 5-Level Architecture of the English Sentence

	1 My mother, who made real corn bread almost every day of my growing up life, has a great pan, a square cast-iron skillet given by my great aunt. Ronni Lundy **Corn Bread with Character** in Sarah Skwire **Writing with a Thesis** 10th ed.	2 With the help of a basketball scholarship, Cassidy had attended junior college in his small hometown in Kentucky before laying out a year to work and raise enough money to attend a university. Sandra Brown **French Silk**
1 heart verb	has	had attended
2 essence + subject	<u>mother</u> has	<u>Cassidy</u> had attended
3 core + d. object or subject complement	mother has <u>pan</u>	Cassidy had attended <u>college</u>
4 base + **attachments** to core words	my mother has <u>a great pan</u>	Cassidy had attended <u>junior college in his small hometown in Kentucky before laying out a year to work and raise enough money to attend a university.</u>
5 total +other **additions** (side branching)	My mother, <u>who made real corn bread almost every day of my growing up life</u>, has a great pan, <u>a square cast-iron skillet given by my great aunt.</u>	<u>With the help of a basketball scholarship</u>, Cassidy had attended junior college in his small hometown in Kentucky before laying out a year to work and raise enough money to attend a university.

Another Graphic Representation of the 5-Level Architecture of the English Sentence

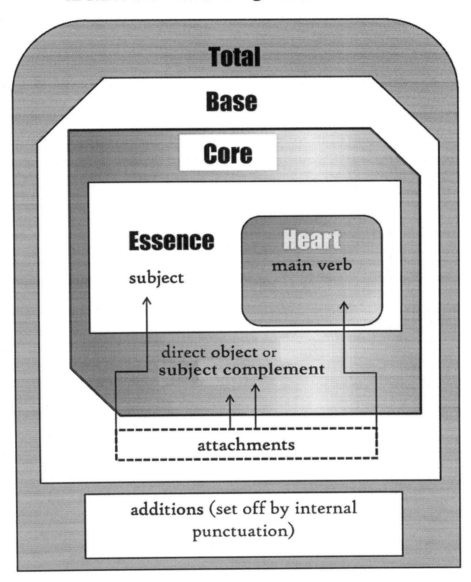

Traditional Names of Types of Sentences with a New Classification

A.   **Expressive Types of Sentences**
  1.   Declarative
  2.   Interrogative
  3.   Imperative
  4.   Exclamatory

B.   **Grammatical Types of Sentences**
  1.   Simple
  2.   Compound
  3.   Complex
  4.   Compound Complex

C.   **Stylistic Types of Sentences**
  1.   Loose
  2.   Balanced
  3.   Periodic

D.   **Improper Types of Sentences**
  1.   Run On
  2.   Fragment

"Traditional Types of Sentences"
in Tabular Format

Below is a table that summarizes the various combinations that the traditional ten types of sentences give rise to:

	Simple	Compound	Complex	Compound Complex
Declarative	✓	✓	✓	✓
Exclamatory	✓	✓	✓	✓
Imperative	✓	✓	✓	✓
Interrogative	✓	✓	✓	✓
Run-On	These types of sentences – for the most part – are not acceptable where good writing is valued. Unless your name is Gertrude Stein or James Joyce.			
Fragment				

We see that our "traditional ten types of sentences" (when presented in table form) can actually give rise to 18 types of sentences, of which 16 are considered acceptable. Examples of such **traditionally acceptable** sentences would be: *Sit up and shut up. We won, so we celebrated! After winning, we went drinking and got tanked. After winning, we went drinking and got tanked! Are you happy, or are you sad? The email that I received had taken 0.534 seconds to arrive at my computer. After studying, do you want to shoot some hoops? The farmer committed suicide. Life happens. Does life happen? Life happens!* Examples of **traditionally unacceptable** sentences would be: *No way! A bit later. Some sentences have the peculiar characteristic of going somewhere, but the reader is never quite sure, as it just kind of wends and winds its way to who knows where, and stops who knows when; such a sentence sentences the reader to continual torment and the added pressure of tracing the thrown line of thought throughout, with absolutely no guarantee of getting to the writer's main idea or purport.*

Occam's Razor, Life and Language

Area	Constituent Forms	Use, Range, Variation
1) Alphabet	26 letters	all words of the English dictionary
2) Genetics	4 nitrogen bases	DNA coding for all animal, plant, bacterial, viral, and fungal species
3) Proteins	20 amino acids	essential and active in all life forms (actually not 20, but 5 are enough to make a protein)
4) Music	8 tones	all melodies, tunes, symphonies, etc
5) Screen color	red-green-blue	16.8 million RGB colors
6) Digital Information	0 and 1 (*bits = binary digits*)	all digitized texts, websites, files, digital media, CDs
7) Sentences	11 basic forms	127 forms – infinite in variation and recombination, and found across the curriculum

Occam's Razor: the more elegant, economical, and simple the solution, the better it is.

Students Learn to Write During Class Time Even Without Doing Homework

The students are required to participate by writing fresh, original examples of every new form. They must then place their sentences on the board in class as already discussed. Social peer pressure induces them to participate. Students must learn in class, and will learn the forms even if they don't do the homework.

Inevitably, they will practice the forms so frequently in the classroom that they will master the forms even if they don't do all the homework. This fact is of major importance, because it is common knowledge that in innumerable American high schools, students do little or no homework. They must be taught to write during class time, but few present methods succeed in doing that.

Method of Assigning Compositions

Once several forms have been studied, the teacher should then assign a composition that must include a specified set of sentence forms, anywhere from 3 to 15 sentence forms, in whatever combination or frequency the teacher specifies. Obviously, the teacher should begin by assigning 1 or 2 paragraphs with 2 to 5 specified forms, then, gradually, increasing the number of paragraphs until they become essays, then varying the types of essays assigned. The students can mix in their own sentences written without attention to or without following the specified forms of the current assignment, but they must include at least those specified forms.

Whenever the student uses one of the assigned forms in their composition, that student *must specify by a footnote or endnote which sentence forms they used. In the footnote or endnote, they should designate the*

sentence form that was used by giving the form's short code. Thus, by just glancing at the footnotes or endnotes, the teacher can tell which forms were used and which ones were not used, and it is an easy task to see whether or not the student has done the assignment correctly. **The forms are a control on the student to pay attention to what they write, and the teacher can look below at the footnote or endnote to see the various forms used in the composition.** The teacher has manageable control over the output.

There are many advantages of this system. First, the student is given clear and concrete directions on how to vary their sentences; for another reason, the teacher has a running record of the sentence forms that a student has mastered or not mastered, and can make assignments to correct any shortcomings. Still another advantage of this system is that it eliminates the increasing problem of plagiarism.

We may echo the sentiments of Barry M. Maid when he wrote his book review of Barbara Danish's *Writing as a Second Language* in 1981, and hope that even young learners will write suitably sterling examples of these sentence forms:

"What's most impressive about most of the student responses, which are written by primary to junior high students, is that while some of the student pieces are better than others, all of them are real. All of them say something. It is clear the students are not merely giving the teacher pieces of writing intended to impress the teacher, but are writing about things which they consider important. There is no appropriation of the writing by the teacher. It clearly belongs to the students, and it is writing the student writers want to share with their readers. If only all student writers were that honest. Though the student examples come from the lower grades the assignments are workable at any level."

General Instructions to Students and Teachers regarding the Character and Sequence of Written Assignments

WRITTEN ASSIGNMENTS AFTER LEARNING A FEW FORMS

After students have identified, studied, and written practice examples of several Sentence Forms and shared those forms with their fellow classmates, they will be assigned the task of incorporating a number of the practiced forms into written assignments. The written assignments at first will be very simple, requiring students to incorporate some of the learned Sentence Forms into one, then two, and then three or more paragraphs.

Students will always be given the choice of incorporating about half of the sentence forms they examine, but the ones they do incorporate in their paragraphs and essays must be footnoted in the paper itself and then identified by number and name at the bottom or side of the page. If students feel some choice and latitude concerning which sentence forms they use (rather than be required to do every one), they will invest more actively in the writing process and feel less resistance to using specified Sentence Forms. Moreover, as students read and share their respective writing assignments with one another, they will eventually see the full display of all the Sentence Forms they studied and practiced, both the ones they employed in class practice and in their papers as well as the ones they chose not to use but others did. They will also see how well or how poorly other students employed the identical Sentence Forms that they used.

Reading the various student papers in class thus becomes a telling exercise in perceiving and realizing how and when certain Sentence Forms are graceful or awkward, obscure or clarifying, trite or compelling, commonplace or memorable. While the written assignments are precise and exacting, they are doable and not overwhelming. Moreover, whatever any student writes contributes to the learning of all the other students in the class. The Sentence Forms will be familiar from previous study and practice, yet novel and interesting in the variety of their usages in the context of similar writing assignments by diverse students. The class review of papers thus becomes an apt exercise in the familiar and novel – in stability and change, in the variety of language usage but also in the constancy and power of Sentence Forms as a structuring force of language.

Later, the written assignments will become more difficult, requiring students at the end of Semester I to be able to write a lengthy composition incorporating 15 to 20 Sentence Forms in them. The last test will challenge the student to draft and revise an in-class composition without the need for footnoting forms on a topic from a student-built list.

Students should thus be notified at the outset that they will not always be required to use specified Sentence Forms for the whole class and that greater freedom and options to write will be given to them as the class progresses. Hopefully, they will then **view the first six compositions** (4 assignments, 2 exams) **as useful experiments, rehearsals, and preparation for the next Semester** when they can write freely. They will be expected at that point, however, by the end of the class to display the mastery of a varied repertoire of Sentence Forms and constructions.

The purpose of requiring students to use specified Sentence Forms in the first six written assignments is to familiarize students with the variety of Sentence Forms available to them and to concentrate and focus their attention on the active employment of such forms in their writing. Students should be told that the instructor realizes that writing assignments which require the use of specified Sentence Forms might make writing papers more difficult at first and result in a prose that is more artificial and less natural than would normally be the case. **The aim of such assignments, however, is less a polished, finished product than a rehearsal or practice session in the use of varied Sentence Forms in writing**. The fact that one does not at first aim for a polished, finished sample of writing should encourage students to experiment and make mistakes, learning from their failures as well as successes. **Perfection, or a more finished and refined writing product, is not expected all at once, but it is to be achieved gradually and progressively in a continuous Process of steady development and improvement in the fluency and grace of one's writing style**.

A **form-specific** and a **free-form exam**, however, will be administered in which students will be required to complete a composition in class based on a choice of five topics. In the mid-term exam, they will be required to employ a number of specified Sentence Forms, but in the final exam they will be able to write freely without any stipulated forms. In both exams, students will be graded on the accuracy, fitness, and grace of the Sentence Forms they employ as well as on their grammar, spelling, organization, imagination, and thinking.

NOTATING AND FOOTNOTING

Regarding the **method of notating and footnoting the various Sentence Forms employed by the students**, a simplified *short code* is provided for each subform. The *short code* is the Form Number and the Form Letter Code plus its short nickname or descriptive phrase; for example, *2S Compact Duo*, or *4C rather than*, or *5R word*. We do not feel that the names of the forms should be reduced further to formulaic codes or technical abbreviations. Instead, the notations of the forms should be presented in clear, plain English that accurately and vividly describes the function and use of the form in the text, but in a shorthand that is memorable and easy to recognize.

While it is commendable if a student can remember the exact form number (such as *9.sc7*) for many forms, we feel **it is better to remember the name or nickname**. Although it may seem laborious at first, by writing this name (the one in the short code) out repeatedly in the footnote to identify a form, the student ineradicably fixes that form's name in the their long-term memory, thereby makes it easier for them to recall and use the various forms – rather like memorizing the multiplication tables for mathematical proficiency.

By checking the short codes at the bottom of each page for this or any given composition assignment, all will easily see how the system works with little effort and confusion. Minimally, the teacher just needs to find the footnoted sentences, check them for accuracy, and then make sure the student has written the required number of assigned forms.

You will also note that when there are two or more Sentence Forms displayed in one sentence, we **separate the individual short codes with a semicolon**.

Instructions for the 4 Written Assignments and Exams

ASSIGNMENT #1 1 PARAGRAPH WITH FORMS 2 TO 5

Students should be told to write one paragraph of five to seven sentences in which they incorporate, notate, and footnote at least 3 or 4 of the various subforms of the Forms 2, 3, 4, and 5. *Since the **Fundamental** Form is so basic, there is no need for them to write, notate, and footnote any of its subforms, though they will often employ simple **Fundamental** subforms in their prose.* However, they should write at least one Series, one Correlative, and one additional Form of the other first Five Forms.

Students should provide a **title** for their paragraph which identifies or suggests the main idea of the paragraph, and the paragraph should thereby be unified with all the sentences developing or revolving around the one main idea.

Students may be told to write either a paragraph based on a topic or theme of their own choice, or the teacher may ask them to write a paragraph about one of the 4 or 2 seasons of the year (spring, summer, fall, winter in temperate; rainy, dry in tropical climates).

The Student section starts with a student essay from China which shows in both content and style the merits of writing in a natural and conversational manner. The section then displays **model examples of 1 paragraph assignments written by students which show the required notations and footnotes that should accompany this assignment.** Students can survey these examples as models to emulate and adapt in a way that will give them guidance in writing their own assignments.

ASSIGNMENT #2 2 TO 3 PARAGRAPHS WITH
FORMS 1 TO 5 BUT NOW ALSO INCLUSIVE OF FORMS 6 TO 8

In the previous assignment, students were asked to incorporate several different examples of the First 5 Simple Sentence Forms into their paragraphs. In this second assignment, students should continue to incorporate 2 or 3 examples of the First 5 Simple Sentence Forms; however, in addition, they should also now incorporate 2 to 4 examples of the Compound and Complex Sentence Forms 6, 7, and 8 into a theme with a length of two or three paragraphs. Once again, **they should have a focused title, and they should notate and footnote the Sentence Forms that they choose to employ.**

Below are some examples of how earlier students completed this assignment to serve as models for students to follow who are doing this assignment for the first time.

The third assignment will deal exclusively with learning and incorporating various examples of Sentence Form 9.

ASSIGNMENT #3 2 TO 4 PARAGRAPHS WITH FORMS
2 TO 8 BUT NOW ALSO INCLUDE INSTANCES OF FORM 9

For this third assignment, students will concentrate on incorporating the all-important Form 9 Sentence Forms, using the punctuation marks of the colon, semicolon, and the dash in their sentences. What distinguishes excellent from only average writers is often the precise and effective use of the colon, semicolon, and dash, so the practice of writing and incorporating the various sub-forms of Form 9 into essays is critical to success in writing.

Students should write on a theme of 2 to 4 paragraphs with a **focused title**, and as before, should incorporate 3 or more different examples of Forms 2 to 8 in their paragraphs; however, they should now also incorporate 2 or 3 examples of Form 9 in their paragraphs, employing the colon, semicolon, and dash. As always, **they should notate and footnote all the various sentences that they choose to highlight**.

ASSIGNMENT #4 3 TO 4 PARAGRAPHS WITH FORMS 2 TO 9 BUT NOW ALSO INCLUDE INSTANCES OF FORMS 10 AND 11

When students have written and shared several individual examples of forms ten and eleven, they should incorporate three to four instances of Forms 10 and 11 in a three to four paragraph essay. They should also incorporate a varied selection of earlier sentence forms in the essay, especially one or more examples of Form 9. Once again as in the previous three assignments, they should have a **title** that suggests, focuses, and unifies the main theme of their essay, and they **should notate and footnote the sentence forms that they employ**.

In the Student section after these instructions are some essays by earlier students to serve as models for this assignment.

Exam #1:
FORM-SPECIFIC EXAM
(Specified Forms Used, Notated, Footnoted)

After students have finished the four required writing assignments, the time has arrived to give an in-class exam. However, this exam does not come at the midpoint of the course, but almost at the end.

In this exam, students will be given 1.5 to 2.5 hours to complete an essay with a focused title, using required, specified sentence forms. At the beginning of the exam class, the students may nominate 2 topics of their own choice and the teacher will nominate 3 other topics for a total of 5 topics. Students must choose 1 of the 5 topics as the theme of their composition, giving their essay a more focused, original title.

This form-specific exam requires students to use, notate, and footnote specified sentence forms. The teacher will give them the specified mix of required Sentence Forms to use in their composition. Students do not have to use every form required, but should use most of them.

The teacher may choose as their choice of topics for this exam the following ones: *Music, Family, Vacations, Work, Hobbies, Animals, Friends, Memories, Clothes, Movies, Travel, Entertainment, Food, Seasons, Holidays, Life Lessons, and Sports.* The subjects were chosen because of their general familiarity to most people and therefore the ease with which students could write about them.

Below is a sample list of required Sentence Forms that teachers might specify for this exam, followed by actual examples of essays written by students in class for the form-specific exam.

- 2 of 2S Series
- 3 of 3V Verbals
- 2 of 4C Correlative
- 1 of 5R Repetition
- 2 of 6CC Coordinating Conjunction
- 4 of 7AC Adverbial Conjunction
- 2 of 9PP Colon
- 2 of 9PP Dash
- 2 of 9PP Semicolon
- 2 of 10TP Three Places
- 1 of 11ADD Additional

Students may consult their charts, books, or notes to assist them in writing the essay as well as notating and footnoting the Sentence Forms.

Exam #2:
FREE-FORM EXAM
(No Specified Forms, No notation, At-Will Use of Forms)

In the Free-Form Exam, students are given 1.5 to 2.5 hours to write an essay on one of 5 possible subjects. **They are *not required* to use, notate, and footnote any specified Sentence Forms**. They are *not* given any specific mix of Forms to include and do *not* have to notate and footnote at all. Their use of the Forms learned is of their own choosing.

The aim of the examination is simply to see how effectively and gracefully they can write in a specified, reasonable period of time. The 5 subjects given to the students for the final exam can either be nominated by the students the night before the exam and then the final subject chosen on the day of the exam itself. Or, if the teacher prefers, the 5 initial topics may be chosen from the following list the night or class before the exam and then the actual final topic chosen by the students on the day of the exam itself: *Music, Family, Vacations, Work, Hobbies, Animals, Friends, Memories, Clothes, Movies, Travel, Entertainment, Food, Seasons, Holidays, Life Lessons, and Sports.* The subjects were chosen because of their general familiarity to most people and therefore the ease with which students could write about them.

The Student section follows with some examples of final examinations written by previous students.

Student Section

Twelve Turns of the English Language

5 Skills (proficient performance) (less conscious)	5 Tasks (attentive mastery) (more conscious)
1 **Listening**	6 **Vocabulary**
2 **Speaking**	7 **Basic English**
3 **Thinking**	8 **Sentences**
4 **Writing**	9 **Paragraphs**
5 **Reading**	10 **Essays**

7 Basic English

a	Usage
b	Grammar
c	Syntax & Mechanics (i) Pronunciation (speaking) (ii) Spelling (writing) (iii) Punctuation (reading)

Left Hand **2 Crowning Achievements** Right Hand

11 **Long Paper**   12 **Book**

Clap!

11   2 3 4   1   5   9 8 7   10   6   12

Twelve Kinds of Words

Little Five	Big Five
6 **Conjunction**	1 **Verb**
7 **Preposition**	2 **Noun**
8 **Verbal: infinitive**	3 **Pronoun**
9 **Verbal: gerund**	4 **Adjective**
10 **Verbal: participle** (a) *present participle* (b) *past participle*	5 **Adverb**
Two More	
12 **Other**	11 **Appositive**
Clap!	

12   10   9   8   7   **6**   **1**   2   3   4   5   11

Five Jobs or Functions of the Twelve Kinds of Words

Right Hand – Jobs that Words Do	
1 Main Verb	**MV**
2 Subject	**S**
3 Descriptor	**D**

4 Object [*left hand*]
 	
   1) direct
   2) indirect
   3) object descriptor
   4) object of preposition
   5) object of verbal
	O

5 Connector	**C**

Job or Function of the Twelfth Kind of Word, the Other

The twelfth Kind of Word performs the job of expressing a variety of emotions and speech expressions.

We call this job the **Emotive and Speech Modes.**

6 Emotive and Speech Modes	**SM**

5 4 3 2 1	1 2 3 4 5

12 Punctuation Marks I

Punctuation sets the pace for the reader, and assists the reader to determine the importance, association, and relationship of elements within the sentence.

Right Hand – The Big Five Punctuation Marks

	Traditional Name	Symbol	Nickname	Traffic Signal	Rhythm & Pace
1	**Period**	.	The Terminator	Red	Stop
2	**Colon**	:	Dramatic Pointer	Red	Stop
3	**Semi-Colon**	;	The Balancer The Equalizer	Red	Stop
4	**Dash**	—	The Highlighter The Commentator The Amplifier	Yellow	Pause
5	**Comma**	,	The Flow Manager	Yellow	Pause

1 2 3 4 5

12 Punctuation Marks II

Left Hand – The Little Five
Punctuation Marks

	Name	Symbol	Use & Effect
6	**Question Mark**	**?**	inquiry
7	**Parenthesis**	**( )**	addition of minor importance
8	**Exclamation Mark**	**!**	excitement, surprise, emphatic statement
9	**Apostrophe**	**'**	shows possession or contraction of two words
10	**Hyphen**	**-**	word joiner

Two Talkative Punctuation Marks
used to indicate direct speech or omitted speech

	Name	Symbol	Use & Effect
11	**Quotation Marks**	**"** **"**	marks off dialogue; citation of words of others; technical term; foreign word or phrase; notation of jargon; notation of ironic use of a word;
12	**Ellipses Dots**	**...**	indicates omitted words

12	10 9 8 7 6	11

Quiz on Grammar Charts
Based on the previous Grammar Charts

1) What are The Twelve Turns of the English Language? Specifically, (1) what are *The 5 Skills* that an English student must constantly master; (2) what are *The 5 Tasks* that an English student must successively accomplish; and (3) what are *The 2 Crowning Achievements* of English study? *Value: 24 pts.*

2) What are The Ten Plus Two Kinds of Words in the English language (otherwise called The Twelve Kinds of Words or The Twelve Parts of Speech of the English language)? Specifically, (1) What are The Big Five Kinds of Words; (2) What are The Little Five Kinds of Words; and (3) What are The Other Two Kinds of Words? *Value: 24 pts.*

3) What are The Five Functions or Jobs that the Twelve Kinds of Words Perform in the English Sentence (or) What are The Five Uses of the Twelve Kinds of Words in the English sentence? *Value: 20 pts.*

4) What are The Twelve Punctuation Marks in the English Language? Specifically, (1) What are The Big Five Punctuation Marks; (2) What are The Little Five Punctuation Marks; and (2) What are The Other Two Punctuation Marks of English? *Value: 24 pts.*

SENTENCE
FORMS

"The sentence has changed. Once I could not remember. Now I cannot forget."

Elly Danica

from *Don't: A Woman's Word* in *Stolen Life: The Journey of a Cree Woman* by Rudy Wiebe and Yvonne Johnston

> Picasso couldn't have been a cubist if he hadn't learned to draw figures.
> David Bartholomae *Writing with Teachers* from *Cross Talk in Comp Theory*

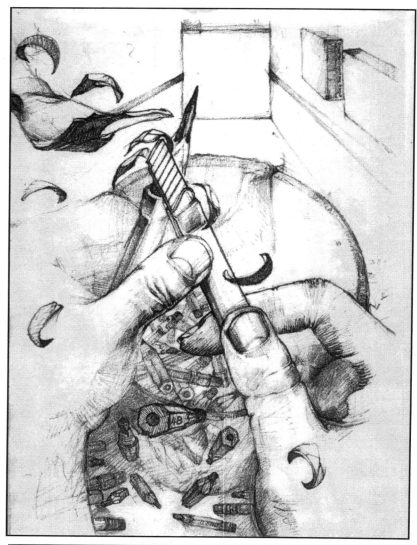

A pencil is an appropriate tool for both writing and drawing. Sketch by April.

The 11 Forms of Sentences

(simple level)	(compound & complex level)
1 Fundamental	6 Coordinating Conjunction
2 Series	7 Adverbial Clause
3 Verbals	8 Reference & Noun Clause
4 Correlatives	9 Power Punctuation
5 Repetition	10 Three Places
(third level – additional + new forms not in the above 10 groups)	
	11 ADDitional

1 2 3 4 5   10 9 8 7 6   11

from right fist,
flick forefinger
upwards twice

Sentence Forms Mastery Checklist

1F Fundamental 1 2 3 4 5 6 **6**	**6CC** Coordinating Conjunction 1 2 3 4 5 6 7 **7**
2S Series 1 2 3 4 5 6 7 **7**	**7AC** Adverbial Clause 1 2 3 4 5 6 7 8 9 10 11 12 13 14 15 16 **16**
3V Verbals 1 2 3 4 5 **5**	**8RN** Reference & Noun Clause 1 2 3 4 5 6 7 8 9 10 11 **11**

4C Correlatives
 	
1 2 3 4 5 6 7 8 9 10
     10
	9PP Power Punctuation
	colon 1 2 3
	semicolon 1 2 3 4 5 6 7 8 9
	dash 1 2 3 4 5 6 7 8
	        9 10 11 12 13 14 15
	     27

5R Repetition
1 2 3
     3
	10TP Three Places
	Beginning 1 2 3 4 5 6 7
	Middle 8 9 10 11 12 13 14 15 16
	End 17 18 19 20 21 22 23 24 25
	     25

	11ADD Additional 1 2 3 4 5 6 7 8 9 10 **11**
Grand Total	**128**

1 (F) Fundamental Forms

1.1	**F main verb**	F_{mv}
	Think. Smile. Write. Remember.	

1.2	**F subject**	F_s
	We went. **They** are eating. **Friends** are talking. The **rabbit** hopped. **Dad** is cooking. **Mom** is reading.	

1.3	**F descriptor**	F_d
	(distant noun) I am a **student**. Mom is an **engineer**. Jake is a **cook**.	
	(distant adjective) The ball is **round**. This course is **tough**. Jake is **studious**.	
	(adjective) **Red** leaves are falling. They built a **small** hut. **Tall** trees grow.	
	(adverb) You sang **beautifully**. The couple danced **effortlessly**.	
	(noun) The ball hit the **brick** wall. Let's go to the **bus** station.	

1.4	**F object**		F_o
	Direct	Dad cooked **spaghetti**. Juliet plays **harp**. Jan designs **pictures**.	
	Indirect	Ted made **her** a tea tray. She gave **him** the tickets.	
	After Object Descriptors (noun and adjective)	Noun: The company named Jane Smith **president**. The students elected Tom **treasurer**. Adjective: I pushed the window **open**. He painted the car **silver**. This is driving me **crazy**.	
	Object of Prep.	She sat in the **boat**. They played until **lunch**.	
	Object of Verbal	I really want to visit **you**. My sister likes baking **cookies**. I want to learn **physics**.	

1.5	**F connector**		F_c
	Conjunction	They are poor **but** optimistic. The food was good **but** salty. Can you sketch **or** paint?	
	Preposition	She grew up **in** the 70s. He dove **into** the water. The rocket went **into** space.	

1.6 s	**F there and it construction**	There **are** four people in the car. It **was** a cold day.	$F_{there\ or\ it}$

149

1 F Fundamental Forms

These simple forms are effective when used among longer sentences. They slow down the pace. They make us notice the simple beauty of words in a well-written short sentence.

1.1 F main verb

●Look! ●Hurry up! ●Don't go! ●Write! ●Speak! ⌘

1.2 F subject

●**We** went. ●**They** are eating. ●**Friends** are talking.

●The **rabbit** hopped. ●**People** gathered. ●**Politicians** promised. ●**People** believed. ●The **snow** came down.

●**They** whispered. ●**Hearts** pounded. ●**Birds** chirped.

●The **crowd** laughed. ⌘

1.3 F descriptor (4)

①distant noun ●I am a **student**. ●Mom is an **engineer**.

●Dad was a **fireman**. ●Tara is a **gardener**. ●She became a **dentist**. ●Our boss is not a **tyrant**. ⌘

②distant adjective ■Jake is **serious**. ■The ball is round. ■Sushi is **delicious**. ■The course is not **easy**.

■Jade is **witty**. ■Their company is **innovative**. ■Your idea is **creative**. ⌘

③adjective ●**Plum** trees blossomed. ●The **strong** wrestler will fight. ●**All** workers showed up. ●**fluffy** clouds drift. ●**Avid** groupies press forward. ⌘

④adverb ■The eagle soars **gracefully**. ■The couple danced **effortlessly**. ■The toddler walked **carefully**. ■They ate **quickly**. ■She sings **well**. ■The baby wailed **loudly**. ■The siren blared **noisily**. ■The business failed **miserably**. ■They prospered **moderately**. ⌘

⑤noun ■ I have **motion** sickness. ■ You need a **bread** knife. ■ They went to a **rock** concert. ●He made a **jump** shot. ■ They said goodbye at the **train** station. ■ I'll have a **cheese** sandwich. ■ I'm going to the **language** center. ⌘

1.4 F object (5 types)

DIRECT OBJECT
●Dad cooked **spaghetti**. ●Juliet plays **harp**. ●Jan designs **pictures**. ●Singleton cooks **breakfast**. ●Let's shoot some **hoops**. ●They built a **bridge**. ●I like **piano**. ●The clerk counted the **money**. ⌘

INDIRECT OBJECT

●Ted made **her** a bookcase. ■She gave **him** the concert tickets. ■I'll send **you** a postcard. ■Give **me** your homework. ●She lent **Julie** her book. ⌘

OBJECT DESCRIPTOR (ADJECTIVE)

●I made Mom **angry**. ●They painted their house **gray**.

●I found Canada **interesting**. ●Computers make life

easy. ●She made the food **spicy**. ⌘

OBJECT DESCRIPTOR (NOUN)

●Call it **fear**. ● We elected Sam **captain**. ● They

selected Betty **Chief Executive Officer**. ⌘

OBJECT OF PREPOSITION

■Put the book on the **table**. ■He sat on the **floor**.

■She drove her car through the small **village**. ■The

task was beyond his **ability**. ■She lives in the next

town. ■It rained until **noon**. ⌘

OBJECT OF VERBAL

To make five types of objects, we include this object here, but it should not be taught until after Forms 1 and 2 are finished. A few examples are given for brief illustration.

object of gerund: ●My brother likes fixing **bikes**.

●I went outside after doing my **homework**. ●Learning **English** takes time. ●After polishing my **shoes**, I put them on. ●Before submitting your **paper**, make sure your name and number are on it. ●The teacher praised the student for noticing the Form 1 **sentence** in the novel.

object of infinitive: ●I really want to visit **you**.

●I asked him to fill in the **form**. ●I want to learn oil **painting**. ●You went out to get a **newspaper**. ●I worked hard to pass the **test**.

object of present participle: ●The teacher caught the student copying the **answers** from his neighbor. ●The police saw the man opening the **door**. ● She saw him calling **someone** on his cell phone. ●I imagined myself giving a **speech** to a big group. ⌘

1.5 F connector (2)

<u>Conjunction</u> [*but, or, nor, yet, and*]
●A good hammer is cheap **but** durable. ●The food was good **but** too salty. ●Do you like vanilla **or** chocolate. ●Walk **or** take a cab. ●I won't buy you lasers **nor** trinkets for Christmas. ●I was curious **yet** cautious. ⌘

<u>Preposition</u>
■Think **about** it. ■Put the book **on** the table. ■ They drove on **through** the sunny morning fields. John Steinbeck *The Grapes of Wrath* ■She rollerbladed **along** the park path. ■I grew up **in** the '50s. ■I can park **between** those two cars **across** the street. ■She put her hat **on** the table. (Compare with: *She put her hat on.* (*put on* = phrasal verb) ■He froze **in** his tracks. ■There's a bug **in** the program. ■You're on **after** her. ■They sang **until** dawn. ■The news was **on** the radio. ■The woman wore a shawl **over** her hair. ⌘

1.6 F Starting there or it
●**There** **is** a reason for this. ●**There** **are** 60 or so people here on a good day. ● **It** **is** foolish to think that. ● '"**There's** no photograph of you on the walls."'

Ahdaf Soueif *The Map of Love*

154

Short Code Chart for Fundamental Forms

1 F Fundamental			
NUMBER	SENTENCE FORM LETTER CODE	DESCRIPTION OR FORMULA	SUBFORM NOTATION (NAME OR SHORT CODE)
1.1	F	Main verb	1F Main Verb
1.2		Subject	1F Subject
1.3		Distant and Regular Descriptor	1F Descriptor (distant, regular)
1.4		Five kinds of objects	1F Object
1.5		Conjunctions and prepositions as connectors	1F Connector
1.6		There is (there are, it is) construction	1F there is/are 1F it is

2 (S) Series Forms

2.1	## A and B The Pair
	● **Barney and Wilma** live down the street. ● The bag was **heavy and full**. ● I like **apples and bananas**.

2.2	## A, B Compact Duo
	● The soup was **creamy, chunky**. ● Korean trains are always **punctual, reliable**. ● The motorcycle ride was **fast, risky**.

2.3	## A, B, and C Standard Series
	● Chocolate is **sweet, yummy, and divine**. ● Fall is **cool, mellow, and colorful**. ● The triathlon consists of **running, swimming, and cycling**.

2.4	## A, B, C Triple Force
	● The apple was **red, crisp, delicious**. ● Chantel is **smart, talented, humble**. ● Mount Kilauea is a **majestic, powerful, active** volcano.

2.5	## A and B and C Lyrical Series
	● **Green and blue and gold** were the colors of the peacock's proud tail. ● The forest is **dark and deep and mysterious**.

2.6	## A and B, C and D Rhythmical Pairs
	● We need better **schools and hospitals, streets and playgrounds**. ● The new generation is **bold and inventive, idealistic and hopeful**.

2.7	## A, B, or C Choices Series
	● Rehema will move to **Turkey, India, or Chile**. ● Water can be a **solid or a liquid or a gas**.

2 S Series Forms

A *series* is two or more items (adjectives, nouns, adverbs, verbs, phrases) put together in a list. Commas or *and*s are used to separate the elements of the list. Omitting the *and* before the last item in the series (as in Forms 2.2 and 2.4) makes the sentence more forceful, punchy, and direct — an almost staccato effect that conveys thriftiness and seriousness in which every impressionable word counts. To a small extent, especially in The Triple Force, it slightly highlights the last item in the series.

2.1 The Pair Series A and B

●**Stop and think**. ●The food was **delicious and cheap**. ●Keep it **short and sweet**. ●She likes **diamonds and pearls**. ●He likes **jazz and soft rock**. ●My favorite colors are **red and green**. ⌘

2.2 Compact Duo Series A, B

■The new house was **spacious, luxurious**. ■The drummer was **young, talented**. ■I put cream on my **dry, sunburned** hands. ■The **confused, lost** traveler asked the police officer for help. ■The **black, striped** sweater belongs to Jill. ■Olympians are always **fit, confident**. ⌘

2.3 Standard Series Series A, B, and C

●In Canada fall is **cool, mellow, and colorful.** ●She is a **bright, educated, and wise** woman. ●Three forms of water are **solid, liquid, and gas.** ●That band can play **reggae, waltz, and calypso** dance styles. ●Korean food is always **nutritious, colorful, and delicious.** ⌘

2.4 Triple Force Series A, B, C

■She bought a **cute, little, red** sports car. ■The actor's performance **impressed, dazzled, electrified** the audience. ■The children played with **blocks, sand, a beachball.** ■The troops won the war with **courage, determination, faith.** ■The new father was **laughing, crying, whooping** with happiness. ■She described **the time, the place, the moment** that the murder occurred. ■A responsibility of literature is to make people **awake, present, alive.** (Natalie Goldberg *Writing Down Bones*) ⌘

2.5 Lyrical Series Series A and B and C

●Friendship is wrapped in **loyalty and trust and love.** ●She is tall **and beautiful and athletic.** ●Monique's talk was **informative and timely and uplifting**.

●Amidst the oppressive **heat and** the unquenchable **thirst and** the gnawing **hunger**, the people of Niger continue to search for a place that can sustain them.

●"He runs up a shadowed ramp and into a crossweave of **girders and pillars and spilling light**." (Don DeLillo *Underworld* describing part of a baseball stadium) ⌘

2.6 Rhythmical Pairs Series A and B, C and D

■**Bananas and cream, milk and cookies** are good late night snacks. ■Winter in Korea is **cold and frigid, dreary and lonely**. ■**Lennon and McCartney, Jagger and Richards** were popular singer-songwriter duos in the sixties. ■**Pam and Sam, Jill and Bill** were the best-dressed couples at the dance. ■**Books and notebooks, pens and pencils, cups and glasses** occupied the desk. ■**Blue and orange, red and green** are two pairs of complementary colors. ⌘

2.7 Choices
(a) Choices A or B
(b) Choices A or B or C
(c) Choices A, B, or C

●I'll have some **juice or green tea**, thanks. ●The answer is **A, B, or C**. ●The boy always had **rice, toast, or porridge** for breakfast. ●They could **flee, surrender, or continue to fight**. ●At The Captain's Table, a person may entertain himself by **playing** Trivial Pursuit **or** chess **or** backgammon. ●A popular game in Asia that uses black and white saucer-shaped pieces on a 19x19 grid is called *igo* **or** *go* in Japanese, *weiqi* **or** *wei ch'i* in Mandarin, **or** *baduk* in Korean. ●We will take a vacation in Florida **or** California **or** Mazatlan. ⌘

Short Code Chart for Series Forms

2S Series			

NUMBER	SENTENCE FORM LETTER CODE	DESCRIPTION OR FORMULA	SUBFORM NOTATION (NAME OR SHORT CODE)
2.1		A and B	2S The Pair
2.2		A, B	2S Compact Duo
2.3		A, B, and C	2S Standard Series
2.4	S	A, B, C	2S Triple Force
2.5		A and B and C	2S Lyrical Series
2.6		A and B, C and D	2S Rhythmical Pairs
2.7		A or B; A, B, or C	2S Choice(s) Series

3 (V) Verbal Forms

Verbals function like a verb (but never as Main Verb) plus →	Other duties
## Verbal **Infinitive** Vinf **3** **.1** • She wants **to travel**. • Remember **to call** me later. • **To learn** another language is not easy. • The plan **to restore** peace will cost millions. • She went to the store **to buy** bread. • Let me **help** you. Watch me **flip**. Help me **move**. [infinitive missing *to*]	Noun Adjective Adverb
## Verbal **Gerund** Vger **3** **.2** • I sometimes like **baking** bread. • I did my homework after **watching** TV. • Turn on the alarm before **sleeping**.	Noun
## Verbal **Present Participle** Vprp **3** **.3** • The **passing** ship blasted its horn. • The skater gave a **dazzling** show. • A **growing** toddler needs proper food. • Catch a **falling** star.	Adjective
## Verbal **Past Participle** Vpap **3** **.4** • I bought some **bottled** water. • See the **attached** file. • I drank some **chilled** juice. • The **damaged** goods were returned. • Shoppers enjoyed the **reduced** prices.	Adjective
## Verbal **Headlines** Vhl **3** **.5** • Green belt **to encircle** desert. • Pilots **to have** stun guns. • **Dying** words reveal secret. • **Kidnapped** girl found.	The above four forms help enliven headlines.

162

3 V Verbal Forms

For far too long, the importance of these forms has been overlooked and undervalued. They occur with high frequency in all good writing, and deserve and accordingly receive a higher recognition in our scheme of sentence forms.
Word of Caution: Do not confuse the Participle Verbals and Gerund Verbals with look-alike (*-ing, -ed*) Basic Verbs contained in the Main Verb of a sentence.

Verbals add action, life, and movement to sentences.

3.1 Verbal infinitive   Vinf

As noun

●Remember *to call* me later. ●I plan *to visit* Vietnam next year. ●The family desired *to travel* to the east coast. ●They wanted *to try* sailing a catamaran. ●The children started *to giggle*.

As adjective

●The goal *to travel* was always on his mind. ●A suggestion *to sing together* was put forth.

As adverb

. ●She went out *to play*. ●She went to the store *to buy* some moon cakes and yogurt. ●It's hard *to forget*. ●She is determined *to succeed*.

Omitted *to*: ●Could you help me [*to*] *push* my car? Just let him [*to*] *be*. The teacher made the students [*to*] *stay* after school.⌘

3.2 Verbal gerund

■I sometimes like *baking* bread. ■They fell asleep while *watching* the movie. ■Turn on the alarm before *sleeping*. ■*Writing* sentences demands full attention. ■After *swimming* I took the bus home. ■He started this business by *borrowing* money from his aunt. ■*Mastering* this form takes practice. ⌘

3.3 Verbal present participle

●A *rolling* stone gathers no moss. ●She likes to wear *twinkling* jewelry. ●I saw the man *giving* her a brown envelope. ●He bought a new *carving* knife. ●"Karl and I went through the children's room [at the local library] like word-*seeking* missiles. (Ursula LeGuin *The Wave in the Mind*) ●The *singing* waiter sang as he brought the food. ●"*Beginning* to consider the rhythms of writing, my mind wandered about among the world's beats: the clock, the heart, the interval between the last meal and the next meal, the alternation of day and night. (Ursula LeGuin *ibid*) ●They bought some *folding* chairs. ●His life was but a *fleeting* shadow in his family's history. ●The *gathering* clouds indicated imminent rain. ●They went to the **skating** rink. ●The **parking** lot was full. ●I bought a new **jogging** suit. ●She takes **dancing** lessons. ⌘

3.4 V past participle

■The **overjoyed** crowd clapped and yelled for more. ■The **smuggled** owls were put in apple boxes. ■The **broken** toy could not be fixed. ■**Loaded** weapons were gathered and exchanged for agricultural machinery after the truce. ■"We slept in a **bookwalled** room with creamy shelves and deep carpets and lighting that had a halftone density. . ." (Don DeLillo *Underworld*) ■He drove the **broken-down** car to the repair shop. ■The **buried** landmine blew the child's foot off. ■A **caged** bird never sings. ■The **endangered** pandas moved to a smaller patch of bamboo. ■The **abandoned** mine became home to a new year-round, thermally-**heated** greenhouse experiment. ■Two **lost** children emerged from the jungle mist. ■The post office will compensate for these **damaged** goods. ■The **flooded** plain looked like a vast lake. ⌘

3.5 Verbal headlines

Note: Actually, this is not a separate or novel sub-form, but rather is included so as to draw attention to the enlivening use of Verbals in headlines, as well as book titles, song titles, album titles, and movie titles.

●Seven *lost* in avalanche. ●Green belt *to encircle* desert. ●Pilots *to have* stun guns. ●Tax system *to get tough* on drinkers. ●New funds *to protect* against bio-terrorism. ●*Eradicating* poverty a **shared** duty. ●New laws *to protect* old-growth forests. ●History plentiful below *frozen* tundra. ●*Buried* treasure found in **sunken** wreck. ●Newly-*minted* Chinese coin features Zheng He. ●*Regulating* tourism in the Three Gorges. ●Traffic signals *to include* audible countdown timer. ●International trade fair *to benefit* Pacific Rim islands. ●Gumi bus routes *reassigned*. ●Young people gather *to cherish* peace. ●*Tapping* offshore oil to new depths. ●Under Rug *Swept*. *Jagged* Little Pill. *Tainted* Love. (album and song titles by Alanis Morissette) ⌘

Short Code Chart for Verbals Forms

	3 V Verbals		
NUMBER	SENTENCE FORM LETTER CODE	DESCRIPTION OR FORMULA	SUBFORM NOTATION (NAME OR SHORT CODE)
3.1	V	Infinitive	3V Infinitive
3.2		Gerund	3V Gerund
3.3		Present Participle	3V Present Participle
3.4		Past Participle	3V Past Participle
3.5		Headlines or Titles	3V Headline or 3V Title

SENTENCE WORD ANALYTICS, PART 1

Word analytics is a new term that is equivalent to the old term, **parsing**. Sentences are written in charts. The student analyzes each word individually, writing the word, its kind, and its function in the appropriate box. Sentences are written downwards on the left side, one word at a time. This is best done at the board.

There is a definite procedural order when doing word analytics. The student should follow this order exactly and not deviate from it in order to become efficient at taking a sentence apart and thereby discerning its architectural structure.

	SEQUENCE FOR DOING WORD ANALYTICS
1	Locate the **main verb** (with its auxiliary if present) and underline it twice.
2	By asking who performed the action of the verb, locate the **subject**, and underline it once.
3	Look to see if the main verb is a linking verb, and, if it is, look for a **distant descriptor.**
4	Look for the **direct object**, and if there is one, underline it three times.
5	Ask if there is an **indirect object**, by asking, To whom? or For whom? something was done.
6	Identify all **adverbs** and **adjectives** attached respectively to the previous five elements
7	Identify all **prepositions**, their **objects**, and their **attachments**
8	Identify all **verbal elements** (infinitives, present and past participles, gerunds)
9	Identify all **noun, adjective, adverb phrases**

For some sentences, the process of classification may tend to bog down and seem hazy or too difficult. In such instances, considerable time should not be spent wrangling over the correct analysis.

The practice of Analytics is intended to make students able to **confidently grasp at a glance the construction of the sentence,** and **to know which parts of the sentence are more important to understand** (the main verb and subject), and which parts may be less important. Analytics shows familiarity with the building materials of the sentence; it enables a student to deconstruct a sentence to its word level components.

SENTENCE WORD ANALYTICS OF SOME FIRST LEVEL SIMPLE SENTENCES		
Sentence 1: *Tina went to the store and bought some gouda cheese.*		
Word	**Kind**	**Job**
Tina	noun	subject
went	verb	main verb
to	preposition	connector
the	adjective	descriptor
store	noun	object of preposition
and	conjunction	connector
bought	verb	2nd main verb
some	adjective	descriptor
gouda	adjective	descriptor
cheese.	noun	direct object
Sentence 2: *Tired from her trip to Europe, Tammy rested all afternoon.*		
Word	**Kind**	**Job**
Tired	verbal past participle	descriptor [Tammy]
from	preposition	connector
her	adjective	descriptor
trip	noun	object of preposition
to	preposition	connector
Europe,	noun	object of preposition
Tammy	noun	subject
rested	verb	main verb
all	adjective	descriptor
afternoon.	noun	descriptor

...MORE SENTENCE WORD ANALYTICS ON FIRST LEVEL SIMPLE SENTENCES

Sentence 3:

Flashing her new engagement ring, Tina strolled triumphantly down the sunny street.

Word	Kind	Job
Flashing	verbal –present participle	descriptor [Tina]
her	adjective	descriptor
new	adjective	descriptor
engagement	noun	descriptor
ring,	noun	object of verbal
Tina	noun	subject
strolled	verb	main verb
triumphantly	adverb	descriptor
down	preposition	connector
the	adjective	descriptor
sunny	adjective	descriptor
street.	noun	object of preposition

Sentence 4:

After eating breakfast, the children went to school.

Word	Kind	Job
After	preposition	connector
eating	verbal - gerund	object of preposition
breakfast,	noun	object of verbal
the	adjective	descriptor
children	noun	subject
went	verb	main verb
to	preposition	connector
school	noun	object of preposition

SENTENCE WORD ANALYTICS, PART 2

The purpose of analytics is not to enable one to exhaustively and perfectly analyze every word in every sentence. Such an aim is a recipe for frustration, as there are many exceptions that will always elude the most brilliant teachers of grammar, not to mention the students.

When one encounters – as one often does – words or combinations of words that are difficult to analyze, one should simply guess at the best possible answer, and laugh at the difficulty of grammar. Students can be reminded about how difficult grammar is, but that it is not essential to know grammar perfectly when learning to write.

What they must understand is that they can analyze effectively 80% to 90% of what they read and write. That *does* matter a great deal. *Students must feel competent and confident that they can grammatically understand the overwhelming majority of the words of the sentences that they write and read*. Once they know that they can do this, they are not intimidated or frightened by the language, nor do they worry too much or take too seriously minor failures to understand difficult points of grammar that would challenge or even defeat a very gifted student or teacher of grammar.

It is a notorious commonplace that excessive attention on the fine points of grammar serves only to depress and frustrate students and afflict them with the conviction that they can never master the simplest forms of expression. At the outset, students need only to understand the basic fundamentals of grammar as we have set them forth in this book, and then practice some Sentence Word Analytics. This skill can be used sporadically as a change of pace without undue stress and emphasis, or it can become an in-depth lesson on how grammar can nail down functional labels most of the time, but not all, as some exceptions and puzzling phrases may stump even the teacher in trying to provide an explanation.

For the real understanding of sentences comes not with Sentence Word Analytics but with the mastery of the 11 Sentence Forms. Only after they have seen and used all the Forms and gained a sense that they have a fluid mastery of multiple options in self-expression should further attention be paid to more complex exercises in Word Analytics or Analysis.

Even then, only some attention (and never excessive attention) should be given to Sentence Word Analytics. Sentence Word Analytics will help some students, especially incipient linguists, and give some confidence to others. Some people, however, may always find word analytics unduly frustrating. In such cases, forget it, and concentrate on improving the student's mastery of the sentence forms.

In the following sentences, students have analyzed sentences taken from a Tongass National Park (Alaska) interview with a concerned forester at the National Geographic website at *nationalgeographic.com*. The article was about an old growth forest in Alaska. The last example is taken from a children's storybook.

Sentence Word Analytics.

STUDENT 1

And you look up and you see the ragged canopy of this forest.

Word	Kind	Job
And	conjunction	connector
you	pronoun	subject
look	verb	main verb
up	preposition (in postposition)	part of main verb (a phrasal verb) see p.76
and	conjunction	connector
you	pronoun	subject of second clause
see	verb	main verb of second clause
the	adjective	descriptor
ragged	verbal - past participle	descriptor
canopy	noun	direct object
of	preposition	connector
this	adjective	descriptor
forest.	noun	object of preposition

STUDENT 2

This is the forest duff, the organic soil in the forest, and it is very thin.

Word	Kind	Job
This	pronoun	subject
is	verb	main verb

the	adj.	descriptor
forest	noun	descriptor
duff,	noun	distant descriptor
the	adj.	descriptor
organic	adjective	descriptor
soil	appositive	descriptor
in	preposition	connector
the	adj.	descriptor
forest,	noun	object of preposition
and	conjunction	connector
it	pronoun	subject
is	verb	second main verb
very	adverb	descriptor
thin.	adjective	descriptor

STUDENT 3

Though maps of the Tongass show mostly green, less than half is forested.

Word	Kind	Job
Though	conjunction	connector
maps	noun	subject
of	preposition	connector
the	adjective	descriptor
Tongass	noun	object of preposition
show	verb	secondary main verb
mostly	adverb	descriptor
green,	adjective	descriptor
less	adverb	descriptor
than	conjunction	connector
half	noun	subject
is	verb	helping verb in main verb
forested.	verbal - past participle	basic verb in main verb

173

STUDENT 4		
Jenny calmly ate her breakfast and got ready for school.		
Word	**Kind**	**Job**
Jenny	noun	subject
calmly	adverb	descriptor
ate	verb	descriptor
her	adjective	descriptor
breakfast	noun	direct object
and	conjunction	connector
got	verb	(second) main verb
ready	adjective	descriptor
for	preposition	connector
school.	noun	object preposition
[from the book *I Am Not Jenny*]		

4 (C) Correlatives

Opposition or Contrast

4.1	*C* A, not B	●The car was <u>black, **not** red</u>. ● It's the <u>job experience</u> that counts, **not** <u>the money</u>.

Addition or Putting Together

4.2	*C* not only A, but (also) B	● My new bag is **not only** colorful, **but also** large. ● We **not only** laughed, **but also** cried.
4.3	*C* as well as	● Sam **as well as** <u>Sally</u> wanted to be a dentist. ● She can swim **as well as** ski.

Choice or Preference

4.4	*C* either A or B	● I'll get **either** the green **or** the blue one. ● **Either** you **or** I have to go.
4.5	*C* neither A nor B	● **Neither** Bob **nor** Sol enjoyed the movie. ● I can neither **dance** nor **sing**.
4.6	*C* A rather than B, rather A than B	● I'll have mineral water **rather than** lemonade. ● I'd **rather** jog **than** walk.

Pre-Condition, Consequence, or Result

4.7	*C* more, more less, less -er -er	● The **more** you try, the **more** you'll learn. ● The _faster_ you go, the _greater_ the chance for error. ●The **less** time you have, the **greater** the need for time management.
4.8	*C* no A, no B	● **No** trade, **no** wealth. ● **No** music, **no** life. Tower Records

Parallel Context, Analogy, or Comparison

4.9	*C* just as A, so (too) B	● <u>Just as</u> many Koreans enjoy eating pizza, <u>so</u> too Italians are discovering the taste of *kimchi*. ● **Just as** winter gives way to spring, **so too** will your problems soon be solved.

Range

4.10	*C* from A to B	● I like all music **from** classical **to** jazz. ● **From** Algeria **to** Zanzibar, the news spread worldwide.

175

4 C Correlative Forms

When writing or speaking, we often need to compare things, or say how things are similar, or add more information, or indicate a range or choice when describing events, things, people, or ideas. We use *paired connectors* called *correlatives* to do this. **They allow us to put the items together in a way that shows a certain logical relationship between those events, things, people, or ideas.**

OPPOSITION
4.1 C A, not B; not A, but B

●Go *left,* **not** *right.* ●We should *walk,* **not** *take* a taxi.

●The child was *calm,* **not** *excited.* ●These days we

don't need more *money,* **but** more *honesty.* ● "The

Christian God revealed himself as a man, **not** *as a*

coyote or a raven." (Robert V. Hine and John Mack Faragher in *The*

American West) ● "The salt was another matter, **not** *cheap*

like today." (Amy Tan in *The Hundred Secret Senses* 189) ⌘

ADDITION OR PUTTING TOGETHER
4.2 C not only A, but B

Note: Joseph M. Williams in his lucid and insightful book *Style: Ten Lessons in Grace and Clarity* (1997) posits that in the paired connectors we call *correlatives*, there is *a slight emphasize that goes to the "last element of the pair"*. He recommends that one should end the pair with the "positive half of the construction". So, instead of *"We must clarify these issues and develop trust."* can be rendered as *"We must not only clarify these issues, but also develop trust."*

●The trip was **not only** *relaxing,* **but also** *educational.*

- The new governor is **not only** *bi-racial*, **but also** *tri-lingual*. ● **Not only** *did* I *fall*, **but** I **also** *hurt* my knee. ● **Not only** *did* the trip *give* me a chance to relax, **but** it **also** *gave* me a chance to see the Rockies around Banff. ● The broadcast **not only** *was televised*, **but** *was* **also** *streamed* on the Internet. ⌘

4.3 C A as well as B

■ She took her sunglasses **as well as** her purse. ■ We will serve sushi **as well as** deep-fried shrimp. ■ Tom **as well as** Ursula went to the conference. ■ He gave her a ring **as well as** a necklace. ■ Tutorials, seminars, and group teaching are used **as well as** lecture methods. ⌘

CHOICE

4.4 C either A or B   A or else B

■ I'll have **either** a *Coke* **or** a *Pepsi*. ■ **Either** *you sink* **or** *you swim*. ■ We can play **either** *long ball* **or** *frisbee*. ■ We could go to **either** *Cyprus* **or** *Malta*. ■ I'd like to **either** *go* for a walk **or** *watch* a video. ■ (variant) We have to *increase* sales **or else** we will *go* bankrupt. ⌘

4.5 C neither A nor B

●**Neither** the little *boy* **nor** the little *girl* wanted to play outside in the rain. ●**Neither** *Bob* **nor** *Sandy* enjoyed the new movie. ●**Neither** *North* **nor** *South* Korea wants any more armed conflict. ●**Neither** *oxygen* **nor** heart *massage* could revive the landslide victim. ⌘

4.6 C rather A than B

■I'd **rather** catch an overnight bus **than** stay in that cheap hotel. ■Would you **rather** be there **than** here? ■She'd **rather** have water **than** milk. ■Would you **rather** have a veggie burger **than** a Caesar salad? ⌘

PRE-CONDITION, CONSEQUENCE, OR RESULT
4.7 C more -er

●The **more** you read, the **more** you will learn. ●The **more** I live here, the **less** I want to leave. ●The **further** you run, the **faster** your shoes will wear out. ●The **faster** we drive, the **sooner** we'll get there. ●The **sooner** I do my homework, the **quicker** I can go outside. ●The **richer** you get, the **more possessive** you become. ●The **longer** I wait for her, the **more upset** I become. ⌘

4.8 no A, no B

Note: This form usually implies a precondition that implies a certain consequence: that is, A is necessary before B can happen.

●**No** pain, **no** gain. ■**No** trade, **no** wealth. ■**No** music, **no** life. (Tower Records, Japan) ■**No** exercise, **no** fitness. ■**No** tries, **no** prize. ■**No** love, **no** laughter. ■**No** language, no country. (motto of Manx Language Society, Isle of Man) ■**No** music, **no** passengers. (local daladala buses, Tanzania) ■**No** scenery, **no** visitors. ■**No** money, **no** food. ■**No** rain, **no** grain. ⌘

COMPARISON OR ANALOGY
4.9 C just as A, so too B

Note: This correlative should not be confused with the preposition *just as* which has the meaning of *at the same time as*.

●**Just as** your parents were once young and met life's challenges, **so too** will you survive your youthful years.

●**Just as** East and West Germany took two political systems and made them one, **so too** North and South Korea may merge their differences and re-unite.

●**Just as** the sun shines for all that live on the earth, **so too** should a good leader listen to and give attention to each and every person in their region. ●**Just as** many are convinced that there is only one way to properly pronounce their language, **so** others are sure

179

that it is wrong for their language to change over time. *(Joel Davis Mother Tongue)* ●(variation) One word may lead to another, **just as** one topic of conversation may lead to another. ⌘

RANGE
4.10 C from A to B

■It's a 30-hour bus ride **from** Winnipeg **to** Toronto. ■**From** rock climbing **to** paragliding, extreme sports offer you many exciting challenges. ■**From** armadillos **to** zebras, humans enjoy confining animals in cages in unnatural man-made environments. ■She can count **from** 1 **to** 100 in six languages. ■The show will be on **from** 7:00 **to** 9:00 pm. ■**From** dawn **to** dusk the farmer worked outside. ■The city will stage 106 performances ranging **from** singing, dancing, drama, and symphonies, **to** traditional Chinese operas, acrobatics, and puppet plays. ■**From** baking cakes **to** grilling chicken, my mother has a recipe for every dish. ⌘

Short Code Chart for Correlative Forms

4 C Correlatives			
NUMBER	SENTENCE FORM LETTER CODE	DESCRIPTION OR FORMULA	SUBFORM NOTATION (NAME OR SHORT CODE)
4.1	C	A, not B	4C A, Not B
4.2		not only A, but B	4C Not only, but
4.3		A as well as B	4C As well as
4.4		either A or B	4C Either or
4.5		neither A nor B	4C Neither nor
4.6		A rather than B	4C Rather than
4.7		The more, the less	4C More less
4.8		No A, no B	4C No no
4.9		Just as A, so (too) B	4C Just as
4.10		From A to B	4C From to

5 (R) Repetition Forms

5.1	## Repetition of Key Word — **Rкw** ● Tammy dreamed of living a glamorous **life**, a comfortable **life**, a **life** full of luxury. ● If you want to be happy, then live in love – **love** for yourself, **love** for others, **love** for life. ● Your victory makes this a **time** for celebration, a **time** for elation, a **time** for action.
5.2	## Repetition of Word — **Rw** ● He had **no** fears, **no** questions, **no** worries. ● Graduation is a grand conclusion to **all** the hard work, **all** the sleepless nights, **all** the headaches. ● The school is **so** clean, **so** beautiful, **so** quiet. ● There was **no** pause, **no** pity, **no** peace, **no** interval of relenting rest, **no** measurement of time. Charles Dickens ● "...**no** limits, **no** frames, **no** boundaries" Rusty Schweickart (Apollo 9 space walker)
5.3	## Repetition of Adverbial Conjunction at Beginning of Sentence — **RAC** **Note**: Though this form technically should be classified as Form 7 because it is a complex sentence, we place it here because it is a stunning example of the valuable use of repetition. ● **If** it snows, **if** it hails, **if** it sleets, then you're definitely not on Guam. ● **Because** I thought it was difficult, **because** I was tired, **because** it baffled me, I almost gave up on Form 5.3.

5 R Repetition Forms

The echoing of a word or phrase deeply emphasizes it, and lets us take momentary delight in its sound and meaning. Repetition also is a form of parallelism between the parts of the sentence that share the repeated common word. It is a common thread as well as reinforcement.

In ancient Greek drama, the mix of dancing, poetry, and singing by the *chorus* included repetition. Pop songs have their verses, but more importantly, their memorable and repeated choruses that again and again strengthen the sentiment being conveyed.

Repetition also has its place in ritual and ceremony, where the evocative power and pace, timing and volume of the spoken and repeated word are all brought into play (or are all finely tuned to create the intended effect).

5.1 Repetition of key word or phrase

● This is a **moment** like no other, a **moment** to etch in our hearts, a **moment** to cherish forever. ● She wanted a comfortable **life**, a happy **life**, a **life** with him.

● There is **pollution** in the air, **pollution** in the water, **pollution** in ground, and **pollution** in the heart. ● There was **light** all around, **light** above, **light** below, and **light** on all sides. ● She is **in a hurry** to get ready, **in a hurry** to get there, and **in a hurry** to get down to work. ⌘

5.2 Repetition of word

● The feather is **very** small, **very** soft, **very** white.

● This school is **so** clean, **so** beautiful, **so** quiet. ● She was **tired** of his lies, **tired** of his laziness, **tired** of the struggle. ■ They had **no** fears, **no** worries, **no** questions. ■ The students were **against** large classes, **against** expensive fees, and **against** homework. ■ **All** muffins, **all** loaves of bread, and **all** bagels taste delicious if they were made at the Millstone Bakery. ⌘

5.3 Repetition of adverbial or reference conjunction in several clauses

Note: This form can be saved until Form 7 and 8 have been completed, or practiced in advance here if the teacher and students wish to do so. It's worth the try.

● **If** he studies hard, **if** he practices daily, **if** he checks previous tests, he will surely do well on this math exam. ● **After** she had come back from her trip, **after** she had recovered from jet lag, **after** she had all her film developed, she couldn't stop telling everyone about all the places she had visited in Switzerland and Scotland. ● **Because** my parents are going out, **because** my brothers are going to the movies, **because** my sisters are sleeping, I am going to enjoy the peace and quiet. ● **If** the lighting is dim, **if** the music is soft, **if** the air is fragrant, romance might set in. ⌘

Short Code Chart for Repetition Forms

	5 R Repetition		
NUMBER	SENTENCE FORM LETTER CODE	DESCRIPTION OR FORMULA	SUBFORM NOTATION (NAME OR SHORT CODE)
5.1	R	Repetition of key word or phrase	5R key word, 5R key phrase
5.2		Repetition of word	5R word
3.3		Repetition of adverbial or reference conjunction	5R adverbial conjunction, 5R reference conjunction

I believe ... that we can create a culturally inclusive curriculum in our writing classes by focusing on the experiences of our students.

Maxine Hairston *Diversity, Ideology, and Teaching*

Rubrics for Rating Student Compositions

Written work of a competent English writer

THESIS ☐ has a focused thesis or theme supported by compelling ideas that are backed by convincing and accurate details as proof or illustration

IDEAS ☐ there are a few key ideas which are coherent, well-developed, and adequately support the central thesis; ☐ some of the ideas may cross subject boundaries, but should be consistent with the thesis; ☐ hopefully, many of the ideas will be worth sharing with other students around the globe

VOICE ☐ has an authentic voice, a personal style (personality shows through), that suits the intended audience and represents the writer; ☐ vocabulary suits the intended audience; ☐ shows an enthusiasm for and about the topic and for how it is expressed

ORGANIZATION ☐ has an arresting opening and potent or powerful conclusion ☐ follows appropriate format for the type of composition that it is; ☐ sticks to one idea, and weaves together accurate and reliable evidence, or an adequate amount of significant and vivid detail; ☐ the logic and choice of the method or order of arranging the main ideas or events is clear and well-handled

SENTENCE FORMS AND FLUENCY ☐ sentences are coherent and adequately linked; ☐ a variety of sentence forms and lengths of sentences are used; ☐ paragraphs stick to their one idea or event, and are bridged; ☐ the whole piece stands as a complete, unified, integrated whole ☐ the piece is unique in its imaginative conception, and artistic in its composition

WORD CHOICE ☐ is intelligible ☐ shows proper and sufficient use of diction appropriate to the topic and the grade level of the student, along with the correct use of professional vocabulary and all lexical items while avoiding jargon and clichés ☐ contains precise, clear, powerful, and concise word expressions ☐ appeals to the reader's imagination and senses; ☐ does not have too many Greek or Latin words

CONVENTIONS ☐ contains no usage, grammar, capitalization, punctuation, or spelling mistakes; ☐ is properly formatted according to specifications, and is done within the required timeframe

Rubrics for Rating Student Compositions for non-native Writers

The rubrics or guidelines for non-native writers are identical as for native writers with the sole exception of the guidelines for Conventions. Below is the revised guideline for Conventions that should be used for non-native writers.

CONVENTIONS ☐ contains few instances of *interference* from mother tongue (Konglish, Chinglish, etc); ☐ has some, but not too many usage, grammar, capitalization, punctuation, or spelling errors

Written Assignments

ASSIGNMENT #1 1 PARAGRAPH WITH FORMS 2 TO 5

You will be told to write 1 paragraph of five to seven sentences in which you incorporate, notate, and footnote at least 3 or 4 of the various subforms of the Forms 2, 3, 4, and 5. *Since the **Fundamental** Form is so basic, there is no need for you to write, notate, and footnote any of its subforms, though you will often employ simple **Fundamental** subforms in your prose.* However, you should write at least one Series, one Correlative, and one additional Form of the other first Five Forms.

You should provide a title for your paragraph which identifies or suggests the main idea of the paragraph, and the paragraph should thereby be unified with all the sentences developing or revolving around the one main idea.

You may be told to write either a paragraph based on a topic or theme of their own choice, or your teacher may ask you to write a paragraph about one of the four seasons of the year: spring, summer, fall, and winter, or another relevant topic of a common experience.

What follows are some **examples of 1 paragraph assignments written by students which show the required notations and footnotes** that should accompany this assignment. You can regard these examples as models to emulate and adapt in a way that will give you guidance in writing your own assignments.

However, before doing so, we first offer a superb example of a few paragraphs by a student which is a wonderful introduction of the value of writing as self-expression using the Mother Tongue or naturally spoken language.

This excellent example of student writing vividly describes the value and virtue of mutual dialogue and conversation in the common Mother Tongue (or one's native cultural language).

Such mutual dialogue and exchange is the seed and fountainhead of personal formation and integration, of social fellowship, and – in time – of that intellectual development and imaginative craft that can blossom into professional and enduring writing.

As such, the selection is a superb initial example of **Writing as Self-Expression.**

On Bed Talks

by Cecilia, Jinan University, Guangzhou

When talking about our dormitory life, and probably all students' dormitory life, we should never leave out one thing: bed talks. Nothing will stop us from deliberately starting a heated (or lively) discussion right after lights are out. It was our favorite and only way to end each day, and we were as punctual for it as our parents are for work.

Psychiatrists say that to lie comfortably in bed is the only way to make someone open his mind. Therefore, during bed talks, we were able to touch the most intrinsic part of others. What were the topics? Almost everything – making nicknames for ourselves, school life, classmates, tutors, boys (of course), and even politics, policies, communication theories, and more.

I assume that this is how those bed talks changed us. I was amazed at realizing the great difference among people in terms of their ways of thinking, and the diversity of personalities. This may change our attitudes towards others, because it is also a process of sharing.

Assignment 1
Model Compositions by Students

One Paragraph #1 **Bungee Jumping**
Aram Messina

One of the things I have always wanted to do in my life before I die is to go bungee jumping.**1** The thought of free falling down from a thousand feet up gives you this thrilling, exhilarating, and invigorating feeling that sends shivers down your spine.**2** Once I do go bungee jumping, I know that feeling will hit unexpectedly and unknowingly and surprisingly.**3** Hopefully, I can go bungee jumping in the near future.

Sentence Forms:

1) 3V infinitive
2) 2S Standard Series; 3V Present Participle
3) 3V Gerund (2); 2S Lyrical Series

One Paragraph #2 **Benefits of Exercise**
Allen Terrance

Exercise is therapeutic – therapeutic for the mind, therapeutic for the body, and therapeutic for overall health.**1** When you exercise, a study shows that your brain releases endorphins. Endorphins create a feeling of well being, thus relieving stress.**2** It has been proven that relieving stress takes pressure off the body and the mind.**3** Just as exercise strengthens the body, so also it clears the mind from stress, giving way to a sense of well being.**4** Swimming, boxing, and running are all exercises that make you look and feel great as well as relieve stress.**5** Not only will you look your best with daily exercise, you will feel your best.**6** With the new energy you experience from exercise, you will feel empowered – with renewed mental and physical health.**7** So, exercise today and every day, experiencing the benefits that follow.**8**

Sentence Forms:

One Paragraph #3 Coping with Humidity
Jill Friend

The weather is humid outside. It makes me feel miserable, hot, and crabby.**1** I have to make sure to drink a lot of water.**2** If I don't, then I will start to feel weak as well as sluggish.**3** In weather like this, it is important to stay alert, stay hydrated, stay in the shade, and stay alive.**4** If I don't plan on becoming a hot weather casualty, I need to attend to my health and above all stay hydrated.**5**

Sentence Forms:

One Paragraph #4   Spring   Aaron Marshall

The season of love, warmth, and beauty, spring is one of the best seasons.**1** Not too hot, not too cold, not too bright, not too dark, it marks the balance of the extreme seasons, summer and winter.**2** No heavy coats, no bathing suits, only light clothing is needed.**3** Picnicking in the park, people find many different ways to enjoy the weather and beauty of a spring afternoon.**4** Many sports are played outdoors such as baseball and soccer and golf.**5** The more free time that we spend outdoors, the more we can enjoy the season of spring.**6**

Sentence Forms:

1) 2S Standard Series
2) 5R word
3) 4C supplement
4) 3V Present Participle; 3V Infinitive; 2S The Pair
5) 2S Lyrical Series
6) 4C more less

One Paragraph #5   Summer

Thomas Dockery

Summer is the season one loves most. I wish the weather would stay hot all year around, but that would be too good to be true.**1** There are many great sports played outdoors in the summer season: basketball, baseball, soccer, and football to name a few.**2** I love running outside in the warm, inviting, beautiful weather.**3** And don't forget swimming!**4** I always jump in some sparkling water at a park or beach.**5** The outdoor picnics and cookouts are also fabulous.**6** I eat all the barbecued hotdogs, the corn, the hamburgers, and the grilled chicken and ribs.**7** Summer wouldn't be the season one desires without the warm weather, without swimming at the beach, without the outdoor sports, without the picnics and the cookouts.**8** Summer is the best season of all.

Sentence Forms:

1) 3V Infinitive
2) 2S Standard Series
3) 3V Gerund; 2S Triple Force
4) 3V Gerund
5) 3V Present Participle

193

One Paragraph # 6 Fall Rita Chung, Ronald Wright

It is the season when the rain pours, the warmth of the summer fades, baseball ends, and football begins.**1** Crisp, fallen leaves and cool, fresh breezes bring this season forgotten by those who delight only in spring and summer.**2** It is the season of Fall – by far my favorite season. With Fall come the holidays of Halloween and Thanksgiving, two holidays notable for their fun, relaxed times, and variety of tasty foods.**3** Fall has also the ideal temperature for outdoor fun with a next door neighbor, bike riding with a close friend, and soothing walks around the park with a loved one.**4** Fall strikes the perfect balance in temperature with mild mornings and invigorating nights.**5** The trees turn into a brilliant variety of colors, and crumbling leaves underfoot yield their familiar sound.**6** Fall lasts only a short time, but it is intense and invigorating, vivid and unforgettable.**7**

Sentence Forms:

1) 2S Standard Series
2) 2S Compact Duo; 3V Past Participle
3) 2S The Pair; 5R Key Word; 2S Standard Series
4) 2S Standard Series; 3V Present Participle; 3V Past Participle
5) 2S The Pair
6) 3V Present Participle
7) 2S Rhythmical Pairs

photos from trim/yC7d and yC7A

Language is like a snow plough at the front of a great locomotive, a *logo*motive, clearing the tracks of fuzzy thought and approximation, exposing the usable rails of understanding and mutuality.

Sentence Combining As an Aid to Writing and Especially a Great Aid to Teaching Students Re-writing

Students can then go on to practice sentence combining. After they have learned the ten basic forms, the **practice of sentence combining is especially effective in teaching the importance of re-writing the original drafts. They learn that re-writing involves selection of not just the first and only thing they think of writing, but that they must choose the best among many options**.

Students can be provided with kernels of sentences written by someone else, and then must combine these using various stylistic options. Students are less embarrassed when they have to manipulate and rewrite other people's initial thoughts and words, rather than their own. They are forced to think about how to combine kernel sentences and re-write their compositions effectively.

Inevitably, there is a huge variety of narrative possibilities, and a wide variety of other sentence combining techniques and materials. By sharing their work with the class and publicly seeing the possible changes that can be made once something is on the paper, students will learn to write with economy, vision, and clarity.

Students do not have to spend undue time creating initial drafts, but can spend time on rewriting itself and working at a higher level of complexity, sentence structure, and style.

Two books by William Strong (1973, 1981) provide plenty of examples and exercises. Students will learn to write sentences with greater variety. Within the class, sentence kernels will be transformed into a wide array of interesting sentences – all done by the students.

Critics may argue that the content in sentence-combining textbooks is contrived or unimaginative, the drab and dull product of an author who may be much older than the students. But practice brings perfection, and no all coaches use the same method. The victory will certainly go to the practitioner who has practiced sufficiently, reviewed various game plans, and who will therefore excel in performance when called upon to do so.

Clustering

Clustering is an outlining technique that uses a graphic method of arranging ideas, often called a *mind map, topic tree, bubble diagram,* or *idea map.* It is a diagram in which the writer writes down a main idea in a bubble or oval in the center of the page, and then adds newer spokes to older spokes with related ideas big and small. This is best done on an erasable surface. The writer then organizes and clusters them using bubbles (ovals) and larger spokes, giving them a sequence. Having spent a few minutes planning, the student will be able to proceed with confidence in making a logically organized and well-framed initial draft.. Here is a sample start for a topic tree for the topic of the power of the symbol of the hand.

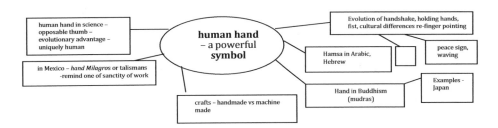

The student then begins to write, constructing simple kernel sentences. After that, the student is challenged to combine the kernel sentences into longer and more varied sentences. Finally, the student should link the sentences into paragraphs and the paragraphs into an essay or composition that is within the required word limit (if there is one).

6 (CC) Coordinating Conjunction Forms

This conjunction joins **two equal and independent clauses. Either clause could be a sentence by itself.** A **comma** is placed before the coordinating conjunction.

6.1	**and**	• Jane will do the report, **and** Sally will present it. • I'll find the firewood, **and** you get the matches.
6.2	**but**	• She was in a hurry, **but** the bus didn't come. • Kurt was ready to go to the airport, **but** Coco couldn't find her ticket.
6.3	**or**	• Job conditions must get better, **or** I'll quit. • We have to buy a new car, **or** we will be walking.
6.4	**nor**	•I was not hungry, **nor** was I thirsty. (Note: S-HV switch) • The dog would not sit, **nor** would he roll over.
6.5	**for**	second part explains reason for first part • I went for a walk in the evening, **for** I had been inside all day. • We stayed in a hostel, **for** we were low on funds.
6.6	**so**	first event leads to occurrence of second event • My class is starting just now, **so** I have to run. • My neighbor dropped by, **so** we decided to order Chinese food.
6.7	**yet**	like *but*, but not as strong • The leader had died two weeks ago, **yet** the public still piled flowers on her grave. • I had finished my English homework, **yet** I still had lots more to do before going to bed.

Configuration of 7 Coordinating Conjunctions in 3 Rows

(for ease of memory)

And		But	association/opposition
Or		Nor	choice
For	So	Yet	cause/consequence/ elegant opposition

The 7 Coordinating Conjunction are ordered logically in 3 groups:

I. **Association and Opposition**

(a) **And –The Association** Coordinating Conjunction;

(b) **But** – The **Opposition** Coordinating Conjunction

II. **Choice**

(c) **Or** –The **Positive Choice** Coordinating Conjunction;

(d) **Nor** – The **Negative Choice** Coordinating Conjunction

III. **Cause, Consequence, Elegant Opposition**

(a) *For* –The **Cause** Coordinating Conjunction;

(b) *So* – The **Result or Consequence** Coordinating Conjunction

(c) *Yet* – The **Elegant Opposition** Coordinating Conjunction

6 CC Coordinating Conjunction Forms

A coordinating conjunction joins two equal and independent clauses. Either clause could be a sentence by itself. Always, a comma is placed before the coordinating conjunction.

6.1 CC and

- She was late for class, **and** her research paper was due.
- Josh will clean his room, **and** Jeremy will take out the trash.
- Forgive us our trespasses, **and** deliver us from email. ● Tom washed the car, **and** Brenda cleaned out the garage. ● She sorted the mail, **and** I sorted the trash. ● I'll find the rake, **and** you get the mower. ⌘

6.2 CC but

■ John went to school, **but** he did not feel well. ■ Nobody lives in the Empire State Building, **but** it has many floors of offices and shops. ■ Her mother was a Phys. Ed. teacher, **but** she wanted to be an astronaut. ■ In North America there is the shopping mall, **but** in South Korea there is the shopping building. ⌘

6.3 CC or

- I'll contact you by email, **or** you can call me in a few days.
- We will have to raise the workers' wages, **or** they will quit.
- You can catch a flight at 9:00pm, **or** there is a train leaving this afternoon at 2:35pm. ● We'll visit the Parthenon and Acropolis, **or** we'll travel to a nearby Greek island by boat. ⌘

6.4 CC nor

Note: The second independent clause has an inverted subject/auxiliary verb word order.

■She won't listen to the advice of her parents, **nor** will she seek the guidance of any of her friends. ■None of the students aced the exam, **nor** did any of them do well in the community service category. ■The business was not doing well, **nor** were its owners keeping healthy lifestyles. ■I don't approve of that expenditure, **nor** will I assign any funds for such related matters. ■He will not be allowed to go out to play, **nor** will he be allowed to watch television. ⌘

6.5 CC for

Note: The second part explains the reason for or justifies the first part.

●I came inside, **for** it had started to snow. ●I went for a walk in the evening, **for** I had been inside all day. ●She wanted to go, **for** skating was one of the joys of her life. ●James read the book, **for** he was interested in computers. ●He was thinking of changing his minor, **for** Psychology doesn't quite interest him enough. ●The people returned to the store, **for** the service was outstanding. ●The meeting went late, **for** many people stayed back and asked the speaker questions. ⌘

6.6 CC so

Note: In our use here, *so* is a logical connector, equivalent to *and therefore*. The first event leads to the occurrence of the second event.

■My class starts in a few minutes, **so** I have to run. ■My neighbor dropped by, **so** we decided to order *rotis*. ■My class finished early, **so** I went for a walk to see the cherry blossoms. ■It was a beautiful morning, **so** he decided to walk to work. ■The bus hadn't arrived, **so** I took a taxi. ■When she saw the ice cream vendor Mary realized she was short of money, **so** she ran all the way back home to get more. ■I have a lot to do right now, **so** I won't be able to meet you today. ⌘

6.7 CC yet

Note: The second part is a strange or surprising event that almost contradicts the first part

●The player is short, **yet** he still gets by the tall players and scores baskets. ●Sidney Poitier came from a poor background in the Bahamas, **yet** he went on to prove himself an excellent actor in Hollywood cinema. ●He wanted to move to Mongolia, **yet** he hesitated because he knew the salary would be quite lower.　　●I hate being busy, **yet** I hate being bored even more. ●He went to his school guidance counselor for assistance, **yet** the counselor offered little help. ●Many people chose to handwrite their essay, **yet** the easiest way is to type it on a computer. ⌘

Short Code Chart for Coordinating Conjunction Forms

6 CC Coordinating Conjunctions			
NUMBER	SENTENCE FORM LETTER CODE	DESCRIPTION OR FORMULA	SUBFORM NOTATION (NAME OR SHORT CODE)
6.1	CC	and	6CC and
6.2		but	6CC but
6.3		or	6CC or
6.4		nor	6CC nor
6.5		for	6CC for
6.6		so	6CC so
6.7		yet	6CC yet

7 (AC) Adverbial Clause Forms

Cause	7.1	● **Because the snow had melted**, the river ran high.
	7.2	● **Since we were away on vacation**, the plant died of thirst.
Condition	7.3	● **If anyone calls for me**, please take a message.
	7.4	● **Whether we win or lose**, we know we tried our best.
	7.5	● **Unless you save for your retirement now**, you could end up living on a prayer and a shoestring.
	7.6	● **Until you master these forms**, you may get lost reading English sentences.
	7.7	● **Once he saw the pattern**, he could compose many variations using it.
Concession	7.8	more frequent and casual ● **Though she isn't tall**, she can still play basketball well. ● **Though the police surrounded the bank**, the thieves still got away.
	7.9	more formal ● **Although she was lacking experience**, her enthusiasm and cheerfulness got her the job.
	7.10	more emphatic ● **Even though it's 2:30am**, I am not really tired.
Time	7.11	● I'll call you from the airport **when I reach Cebu**.
	7.12	● **As the parents slept**, the teen chatted online.
	7.13	● **Before you apply for a passport**, you need photos. ● I always write in my diary **before I sleep**.
	7.14	● **After they broke up**, they still were good friends.
	7.15	● **While the babies slept**, the mothers chatted.
	7.16	● **Since moving to Toronto**, she has opened a hair salon that specializes in dreadlock, French, cornrow, and interlock braid styles.

Adverbial Conjunctions Configured as the 3Cs and a T for Ease of Memory

The 15 Adverbial Conjunctions are conveniently arranged in 4 groups which we can remember as **CCCT** or **3Cs and a T**.

CAUSE	CONDITIONAL or HYPOTHETICAL	CONCESSION (or Qualification)	TIME
because since	if once whether unless until	though although even though	when as while ---------------- before after ---------------- since

7 AC Adverbial Clause Forms

Subordinate adverbial clauses start with easily identifiable subordinate adverbial conjunctions. They are called **subordinate** because they are *dependent* clauses, not *independent*. They are *dependent* because they cannot stand on their own and make sense alone. We change the name to **adverbial** because they explain *why, when,* or *how* the action of the main verb was or is or will be done.

These adverbial conjunctions fall into four categories: **Cause, Condition, Concession**, and **Time** (C-C-C-T). **Students should memorize these conjunctions as signifying markers or red flags: they are not the main part of the sentence, but introduce a clause with a subject and verb, and this clause explains the event of the main verb in the main clause**.

A **comma** is used <u>after the adverbial clause</u> when it begins the sentence. *Usually*, the adverbial clause at the end of a sentence *is <u>not</u>* preceded by a comma.

CAUSE

The adverbial clause gives a reason for the event or action or occurrence in the main clause.

7.1 AC Ca because

- **Because she had an appointment**, she left work right at 5:00.
- **Because I had a flat tire on the way**, I arrived late for the job interview. •**Because the snow has melted**, the rivers run high.
- **Because the cheese has melted**, I have to wait a bit for the burger to cool off. •**Because he was broke**, he could not sign up for the class. •**Because there were many tribal languages**, Native Americans developed a sign language in order to communicate

together. ●**Because they wanted to save money**, the family decided to plant their own vegetables and bake their own bread. ●She ran **because the bus was starting to pull away from the curb**. ●I love snakes **because they are smooth, sleek, and powerful**. ●He started to run **because bees were chasing him**. ⌘

7.2 AC Ca since, now that

■**Since I have little money**, I'll have to eat instant noodles for dinner. ■**Since it is late**, I'd better go home. ■**Since it snowed**, all traffic slowed down to a crawl. ■**Since you insist**, I had better write a sentence with *since* in it. ■**Since I have moved to New Delhi**, I've had several intense, enlightening experiences. ■**Since we did not want to live in an apartment**, we decided to rent a house. ■**Since the plant died while we were away**, my mother decided to buy a new one. ■My legs really hurt **since I climbed Mount Sorak last weekend**. ■I'm really tired **since I stayed up until 2:30 last night**. ■**Now that he has become a parent**, he has gotten much closer and friendlier to his own parents and parents-in-law. ■**Now that the monsoons are over**, I can work on replacing the palmyra leaves of my roof. ■**Now that you have learned a few more of these forms**, you should have no problem in composing interesting sentences of your own. ⌘

CONDITION

A condition is described in the adverbial clause, and the main part of the sentence gives the consequence if the condition is true or is met. However, information in an *as if* clause is assumed to be true when in fact it is not.

7.3 AC Co if, as if

■**If anyone calls for me**, please take a message. ■**If you're healthy**, you're wealthy. ■**If the waves don't get smaller**, we'll have to cancel the surfing contest. ■**If you buy it on the installment plan**, you'll end up paying a bit more. ■Don't give the child any dessert **if she refuses to eat dinner**. ■She looked at me **as if she knew me**. ■You treat me **as if I am a juvenile**. ■The woman drove wildly, **as if she was in a hurry**. ■You look at me **as if you think I know nothing at all about teaching children**. ⌘

7.4 AC Co whether

This conjunction offers a kind of yes-no or diametrically opposite situation in the adverbial clause, but then presents a third situation that must be done or met regardless of the first two.

■**Whether all workers are there or not**, the meeting will begin at 4:30. ■**Whether you win or lose**, it's more important how you play the game. ■**Whether you like it or not**, you will still have to correct your mistakes in your sentence forms homework. ■It's not important **whether you were born in the countryside or the city**. ■**Whether it snows or not**, we will still try to enjoy our year-end holidays. ■**Whether the economy is good or bad**, I will still try to give the best service I can to each and every customer. ■**Whether** the food tastes good or strange, it is still good manners to compliment the chef at a formal summit dinner. ■We will continue construction of the complex **whether the weather is warm or freezing**. ⌘

7.5 AC Co unless

■**Unless I really pour it on now**, I won't be able to win this race. ■**Unless the weather clears up**, the game will be cancelled. ■**Unless you join the club**, you won't receive any of the benefits. ■**Unless we get more sales**, we may slide into bankruptcy. ■I won't be able to go **unless I can get some more money together**. ■**Unless more students show up**, we'll have to postpone today's lecture. ■**Unless there is greater equality**, there will never be any peace. ■**Unless you think now about your old age and retirement**, you could end up in the poor house. ■**Unless it rains**, we will lose this summer's wheat crop. ⌘

7.6 AC Co until

●**Until both groups agree to put down their guns**, there can be no hope of peace. ●**Until you master these forms**, you may get lost reading English sentences. ●**Until I get in contact with the bank**, I will not be able to take out any money. ●I can't wait **until I see you**. ●I'll wait at the track **until you come**. ●He will continue at the same job **until he retires**. ●Hold her head back **until her nosebleed stops**. ●I can't get my allowance **until my parents come home**. ●They stayed in the shelter **until the hurricane was over**.

7.7 AC Co once

■**Once you've seen how the system works**, you can never forget it. ■**Once Melinda ate**, she felt better. ■**Once she got off work**, she called her boyfriend. ■**Once you've finished sweeping the dance floor**, mop and wax it. ■**Once you drink the herbal medicine**, you'll feel better. ■**Once the lake freezes over**, trucks will drive over the ice as a shortcut route to the towns in northern Manitoba. ■**Once she arrives**, we can start the meeting. ■**Once the stain has dried on the wooden sofa**, you can apply the first topcoat of lacquer on it.

> Peer criticism is the most *real* writing students will ever do as students.
>
> Kenneth Bruffee *A Short Course in Writing 1980*

QUALIFICATION/CONCESSION

The adverbial clause describes a concession, qualification or circumstance that gives rise to an unexpected or surprise result in the main clause.

7.8 AC Q though (more frequent and casual)

●**Though she was not tall**, she could still play basketball well. ●**Though my legs felt like rubber**, I knew I had to continue my mountain trek. ●**Though you might not believe it**, women have a larger connection between the two sides of their brain than men have. ●**Though I had been there before**, I found my second visit to China much more interesting than the first. ●**Though some people think that a university degree is necessary to become financially stable**, there are still many people who have proven that the converse is true. ●**Though he plays cards well**, he can't play dominoes. ●She completed her homework assignment **though she was extremely tired.**

7.9 AC Q although (more formal)

■**Although they lost the game**, they were not too disappointed. ■**Although Ron and Chrissy broke up as a campus couple**, they still remain friends and meet every once in a while. ■**Although his work was not finished**, he went home early. ■**Although the experience was not good**, the job did not pay enough. ■**Although the man works as a carpenter**, he is also an electrician. ■Everybody sat on the edge of the stage **although we could have sat at the tables.**

7.10 AC Q even though (more emphatic)

●Even though it's raining, I'll go jogging. ●Even though it looks easy, snowboarding takes a while to master. ●Even though the skater tilted off balance after one jump, she still won top marks at the figure skating competition. ●Even though he couldn't swim, he still managed to get to shore after the raft tipped over. ●Even though she grew up in a wealthy neighborhood, she still did not care much about getting a good-paying job. ●They kept the cow even though they had no meat to eat. ●I went to work even though I had a splitting headache.

<u>Variation</u>: *even though* with a comma in front

●Jim went to the club, **even though he had parental duties at home.** ●They say there will be a clear sky to see the full moon tonight, **even though it's pouring rain right now.**

Time
The action in the adverbial clause precedes, is simultaneous with, or follows the action of the main clause.

7.11 AC T when

●When I leave class today, I have to get a shot. ●When she goes home, she will stop by the daycare center to pick up her kids. ●When you join our academy, you will be expected to do some homework almost every day. ●"When companies operate in synch, everybody wins." (Michael Hammer *The Agenda*) ●Who was at the wheel when the crash took place? ●We will start the party when Dana arrives. ●Call me when you're finished. ●The de-briefing of the astronauts will take place on Tuesday when their spaceship returns to Earth. ⌘

7.12 AC T as

■**As I was leaving**, I remembered to bring the letter. ■**As it was getting late**, I decided to head home and zonk out. ■**As she stood in front of the cheering crowd of fans**, she realized that her dream had come true. ■**As the family slept**, the burglar picked the lock and stealthily entered the house. ■**As you slowly inhale and exhale**, be sure to focus also on your spine. ■The results of the survey are disappointing **as you predicted they would be.**

Variation: *like* instead of *as*

■**Like you said**, some sentences are hard to understand. ■I don't know if I will ever feel **like I did then.** ■Life is just **like Grandma said it would be.**

7.13 AC T before

●**Before you lock the door**, don't forget to turn on the security alarm. ●**Before you jump to any conclusions**, I'd like to give you the full scoop on what happened - and that may take a while. ●**Before you do your piano practice**, could you please feed the fish? ●**Before the guest arrived**, we thoroughly cleaned the house. ●**Before we went to class**, we had to memorize the Two Hands chart. ●**Before you marry**, you should take a course together to make sure you understand the many aspects of your commitment. ●You should make a bag lunch **before you go.** ●Wash your hands **before you eat.** ●You have to learn to walk **before you can run.** ●Remove your shoes **before you enter the living room.**

7.14 AC T after

■**After she went home,** she cooked some spicy tuna and fermented cabbage soup. ■**After we broke up,** I had a near-death experience. ■**After families celebrate Christmas and New Year,** the parents are usually in debt. ■**After the decision had been made,** Jim wished he had voiced his opinion. ■**After we saw** *Lord of the Rings,* we went for a pizza. ■**After it got mild,** the snowman melted. ■**After you take a bath,** make sure to moisturize your skin to prevent dryness. ■You can play computer games **after you finish your lunch.** ■Refreshments will be served **after the ceremony is over.** ■Construction will begin on the Tata Nano Housing Project **after the Mumbai city central committee approves the urban design and financial plans.**

7.15 AC T while

●**While you are waiting for the bus,** you can also review some vocabulary. ●**While the sun shone,** the birds sang and chirped. ●You shouldn't talk on your cell phone **while** you are driving. ●**While their parents were gone,** Jill and Jen had a party. ●Students are not allowed to talk **while the teacher is lecturing.** ●The chicken was being baked in the oven **while the rice was boiling in the pressure cooker.** ●**While the baby was asleep,** the mother studied over the internet. ●Make hay **while the sun shines.**

Note: *while* can also be used to show not a concurrent time event, but a contrast: "Amateurs built the Ark, *while* professionals built the Titanic." [Anodea Judith in *Waking the Global Heart*] In a like manner, **whereas** can be used similarly.

7.16 AC T since, ever since, now that

■Since I moved to Guam, my life has been exciting and interesting. ■Since she has begun her studies abroad, she has become responsible and mature. ■I've been working part-time or full-time since I was 14 years old. ■I feel better since I quit smoking. ■They had to use public transportation since their car broke down. ■They've been at war ever since the Xanadulians invaded in 2183. ■My Mom has had short hair ever since I can remember. ■She's been feeling uneasy ever since the family dog died. ■Now that you mentioned it, I think that security control is of vital importance. ■Now that spring is here, we can all go for beautiful walks.

Short Code Chart for 7 AC
Adverbial Conjunction Forms

NUMBER	SENTENCE FORM LETTER CODE	DESCRIPTION OR FORMULA	SUBFORM NOTATION (NAME OR SHORT CODE)
		Cause	
7.1		because	7AC Though
7.2		since	7AC Since
		Condition	
7.3		if	7AC If
7.4		whether	7AC Whether
7.5		unless	7AC Unless
7.6		until	7AC Until
7.7		once	7AC Once
	A	**Qualification or Concession**	
7.8		though	7AC Though
7.9	**C**	although	7AC Although
7.10		even though	7AC Even though
		Time	
7.11		when	7AC When
7.12		as	7AC As
7.13		before	7AC Before
7.14		after	7AC After
7.15		while	7AC While
7.16		since	7AC since

8 (RN) Reference and Noun Clause Forms

		Reference Clause	Noun Clause
8.1	who	Sam, **who is our coach,** runs every morning.	I don't know **who used the** bicycle last.
8.2	where	Toronto is the city **where I was born.**	I know exactly **where I will** go on my trip.
8.3	when	This is a time **when** everyone should be glad.	She doesn't know **when she will be finished.**
8.4	why	~	I wonder **why she hasn't** called yet.
8.5	what, whatever	That feeling, **what the** French call *ennui*, sets in sometimes, and life seems boring.	Did you hear **what I said?** **Whatever you do** is fine. by me.
8.6	how	~	It depends on **how you do in the** qualifying matches.
8.7	that	The house **that Jack built** is beside his beanstalk.	I understand **that you spent three years on a tropical island.**
8.8	which	The hat **which you bought** is very becoming.	You'll have to decide **which is best.**
8.9	whose	I rented a car **whose radio was broken.**	I'll try to find out **whose book it is.**
8.10	whom	The person **whom you met yesterday** is from Alpha Centauri.	I don't know **whom you're talking about.**
Reference and Noun Clause Forms — the odd one			
8.11	**Missing [that]**	The comic books [that] I bought are funny.	I think [that] it's time to go.

217

The Usual Configuration of 10 with 3 Sets of 3 and One Alone by Itself
(for ease of memory)

Who	Where	When	person-place-time
Why	What	How	order of priority of asking (high to low)
That	Which	Whose	order of frequency (high to low)
	Whom		

There is an interesting observation here: From the above 10 words, 9 of them (all except *That*) constitute **the most Fundamental Questions asked in the English language**.

All good writers – especially reporters and journalists – must continually ask and answer questions that contain these words.

Likewise, every person should ponder such questions as they relate to him or herself.

8 RN Reference and Noun Clause Forms

A **reference clause** starts with a *wh-* word[1] or *that,* and the clause *refers back* to the preceding noun or pronoun. The clause adds to the noun like an adjective does; thus, <u>all reference clauses are adjective clauses</u>. It is our renaming of the traditional *relative clause* (which is too confusing).

A **noun clause** starts with a *wh-* word, *how* or *that,* and the clause functions as the subject or an object in the sentence.

Both clauses can't stand by themselves and are subservient to the main clause of the sentence in which they occur.

8.1 RN who, whoever

REFERENCE CLAUSE

● She **who studies hard** will get some respect in the working world. ● Bill Gates, **who is the owner of Microsoft**, has entered the video game industry. ● Tom, **who is a co-worker of mine**, will be teaching the calligraphy class. ● The president, **who met with CIA and FBI officials yesterday**, has scheduled a press conference for 2:00pm.

NOUN CLAUSE

● She wanted to know **who stole her money**. ● We still don't know **who sent the flowers**. ● The new evidence did not help pinpoint conclusively **who murdered Atria Fusa**. ● **Whoever did the gag** meant no harm.

---

[1] *who ,whoever, where, when, whenever, why, which, whose, whom*

REFERENCE CLAUSE

■The house **where he lived** is for sale. ■South Korea is the country **where the 1988 Summer Olympics were held.** ■I plan to vacation in Bali, **where the weather is always warm.** ■I will go to Christchurch, **where my parents live.** ■"I want to live in a world **where I belong.**" [UK pop group Travis in *Turn*] ■We will go **where we are wanted.** ■I looked **where you said**, but couldn't find it.

NOUN CLAUSE

■Australia is **where you can find the kookaburra bird.** ■I know exactly **where I want to live** – Santiago. ■On the rack is **where you should place your hat.** ■Let's decide **where we should put the sofa.**

8.3 RN when

REFERENCE CLAUSE

<u>Note</u>: This signifying marker may cause some confusion, since it is also an adverbial conjunction of time used in the subordinate adverbial clauses in Form 7AC. To spend large amounts of time debating whether a clause that starts with *when* is a reference or adverbial clause would seem to us to be waste of time. It is more important that you learn to recognize and compose such sentences.

●Spring is the season **when we all rejoice with nature.** ●It is a time **when all people like to walk outdoors.** ●This is the time **when you can speak your mind freely.**

NOUN CLAUSE

●**When I sleep** is when I'm happiest. ●I don't know **when I** will be going there. ●How will I know **when you arrive?** ●We need to decide **when we'll meet next.** ●**When I was in my twenties** was the most exciting time of my life.

8.4 RN why

NOUN CLAUSE

■I don't know **why I didn't do my homework.** ■Hinduism's versatility is **why I find it interesting.** ■I don't know **why I can't stop thinking about her.** ■Her sparkling eyes are **why I find her so attractive.** ■I wonder **why he left in a hurry.** ■He wants to know **why you are late.** ■**Why I didn't think of that sooner** really eludes me. ■Although someone tried to explain it to me, I still don't get **why water expands when it turns to ice.** ■The ultimate philosophical question is **why is there something and not nothing?**

8.5 RN what, whatever

REFERENCE CLAUSE

●Fatigue in concrete buildings – **what engineers call** *creep* - limits their life spans. ●A strong feeling of boredom, **what French people call** *ennui*, slowly crept into their relationship. ●That feeling – **what sociologists call** *sibling rivalry* – is a factor that is present in families with more than one child.

NOUN CLAUSE

●**What I like most** is the small town atmosphere. ●No one understood **what the new policy stated.** ●Did you hear **what I said?** ●She always knows **what he is thinking.** ●I don't know **what I was thinking when I joined the military.** ●He accomplished **what every human dreams of doing** - walking on the moon. ●I will make do with **what I have.** ●I'm okay with whatever you decide to do. ●I will do **whatever it takes to complete this project.**

8.6 RN how

NOUN CLAUSE

■Do you know **how to make** *kimchi?* ■Tracy was contemplating **how to get rich.** ■**How they survived two weeks adrift at sea** is a real miracle. ■She doesn't know **how she got there.** ■Show me **how to cook** *tortillas.* ■She wondered **how she would ever get all the work done in time.** ■Do you think I will ever learn **how to speak Mandarin?** ■They teach you **how to set up a solar charging unit.**

8.7 RN that

REFERENCE CLAUSE

●The houses **that the three pigs built** would not pass modern construction standards. ●The report **that you sent me last week** was impressive. ●The possibility **that there was something wrong with the rocket engine** started to bother the astronauts. ●A hammer is a tool **that you usually use when making a house out of wooden planks and beams.**

NOUN CLAUSE

●I can't assume **that you understand all of this.** ●I realize **that you will be busy next week.** ●It was obvious **that he was the better player.** ●The big news is **that the company president has resigned.**

8.8 RN which

REFERENCE CLAUSE

■The hat **which I bought** is very warm. ■The argument **which you put forth** is a good one. ■The song **which you wrote** sounds beautiful. ■That **which is done** is not always that **which is intended**. ■The store **which is on the corner** gives the best deals on books.

> REFERENCE CLAUSE WHICH REFERS TO THE BASE SENTENCE
> Here, *which* refers back to the whole base sentence which precedes it; it does not refer to the word immediately before it.
> ■They argued continuously **which later resulted in a fight.**
> ■I fell down the stairs **which caused me to break my leg.**
> ■My husband always came with me to every one of my prenatal checkups, **which meant that he also got to hear the baby's heartbeat at ten weeks.**

NOUN CLAUSE

■You'll have to decide **which is best.** ■It's not important **which one you do first.** ■I can't figure out **which piece is connected to the wingnut.** ■Have you decided **which college you want to attend?**

8.9 RN whose

REFERENCE CLAUSE

●The man, **whose lawyers were very good**, was acquitted. ●Teddy, **whose house is made from home-made bricks and a palm leaf roof**, recently bought a Rajdoot motorcycle. ●I met my neighbor **whose dog had just died.** ●I rented a car **whose heater was broken.** ●Bill Clinton will always be remembered as the president **whose marital infidelity almost caused his**

223

impeachment.

NOUN CLAUSE

●I don't know **whose boy that is.** ●They couldn't figure out **whose DNA it was.** ●There was nothing left at the scene of the attack that could further lead investigators to determine **whose prayer shawl it was.**

8.10 RN whom

REFERENCE CLAUSE

■The lady **whom you met yesterday** is related to Ann Landers.
■The officer **whom I talked with last week** is not here today.
■The student **whom I gave the prize to** later went on to become a lawyer.

NOUN CLAUSE

■I don't know **whom you're referring to.** ■The architect for **whom I worked last year** has moved her offices to Mumbai.
■The woman on **whom the greatest responsibility rests** is now the president of the country.

8.11 RN missing *that*

In the following sentences, the *that* is shown for the first few examples, but left out for the final few examples. To show that you understand this form, find the place in the latter where *[that]* should go, and write it in.

REFERENCE CLAUSE

●Some of the people [that] you meet in life make it all worthwhile. ●The next slide [that] I want to show you illustrates the IIO philosophy for language learning. ●The comic books I bought are funny. ●The suitcase [that] Dad gave me is old but useful. ●The CD I bought is exceptionally good. ●"It destroys all evidence it was ever there." [Crichton *Jurassic Park*]

NOUN CLAUSE

●I think [that] she'll be happy if you get her some flowers. ●I know [that] you did your best. ●The computer [that] I bought is really great. ●I think it's time to go. ●I think we need more practice. ●We know you tried your best.

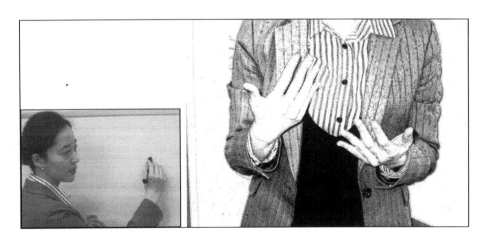

Short Code Chart for Reference & Noun Forms

8 RN Reference and Noun Conjunctions			
NUMBER	SENTENCE FORM LETTER CODE	DESCRIPTION OR FORMULA	SUBFORM NOTATION (NAME OR SHORT CODE)
8.1	R N	who	8RN who
8.2		where	8RN where
8.3		when	8RN when
8.4		why	8RN why
8.5		what	8RN what
8.6		how	8RN how
8.7		that	8RN that
8.8		which	8RN which
8.9		whose	8RN whose
8.10		whom	8RN whom
8.11		missing *that*	8RN missing *that*

ASSIGNMENT #2 2 TO 3 PARAGRAPHS WITH FORMS 1
TO 5 BUT NOW ALSO INCLUSIVE OF FORMS 6 TO 8

In the previous assignment, you were asked to incorporate several different examples of the First 5 Simple Sentence Forms into your paragraphs. In this second assignment, you will should again try to include 2 or 3 examples of the First Five Simple Sentence Forms; however, in addition, you should also now incorporate 2 to 4 examples of the Compound and Complex Sentence Forms 6, 7, and 8 into a theme with a length of two or three paragraphs. Once again, you should supply **a focused title**, and *you should **notate and footnote** the Sentence Forms that you choose to employ.*

Below are some examples of how earlier students completed this assignment to serve as models for you to follow.

In the model paragraphs below, we have notated and footnoted most, but not all of the Sentence Forms, used. The aim is simply to highlight a representative sample of the Sentence Forms employed, not to necessarily designate every single form used. Occasionally, we also notate and footnote, by way of foreshadowing, some of the upcoming Form 9 Sentence Forms. By foreshadowing and notating certain select instances of the upcoming, all important Form 9, we hope to gradually introduce students to the pivotal and central importance of Form 9 for the full mastery of effective prose.

The third assignment will deal exclusively with learning and incorporating various examples of Sentence Form 9.

Student Compositions Forms 6, 7, 8

Lending a Helping Hand by Hee Gon Yang

I think that I have accomplished plenty of things in my short life.**1** Of all the accomplishments, the one that I recall most vividly is volunteering to refurbish the worn-down library of an elementary school in a small village in Romania.**2** Volunteering just meant a little time out of my day, yet it meant the world to the children who attended that school.**3** The building required new walls, a new roof, and repainting.**4** The work was strenuous, but it was very rewarding and satisfying.**5**

The image that will permanently be burned in my memory of that day will be the gratitude and joy, playfulness and friendship on the faces of the children.**6** Though most of the children barely spoke English, we could sense a special bond building between us.**7** We definitely had an eventful day. Although volunteering took most of our free time that day, I believe it was time very well spent.**8** Because on that day, we fostered friendship that will last a lifetime.**9**

Sentence Forms

1) 8RN That
2) 8RN That; 3V Gerund; 3V Infinitive
3) 3V Gerund; 6CC Yet; 8RN Who
4) 2S Standard Series
5) 6CC But; 2S The Pair
6) 8RN That; 2S Rhythmical Pairs
7) 7AC Though; 3V Present Participle
8) 3V Gerund; 7AC Although; 8RN Missing that
9) 8RN That

Mom's Applesauce by Caroline Daniels

When it comes to food, I have never been very picky.**1** For me as a child, however, the taste of store bought applesauce wasn't appealing to me. The consistency of the sauce slid across my tongue like slime. Even though I knew the slimy sauce was made from apples, I couldn't understand why it didn't taste like apples.**2** It almost reminded me of rotten pears.**3** My mother, after an exhausting battle, finally stopped serving it to me.**4** She had another plan. She was going to prove to me that I would like applesauce.**5**

    I came home from school one day and walked into the kitchen. My mother was cutting the most gorgeous Granny Smith apples. I just assumed she was cutting slices for us to eat, but when I picked up a slice, she slapped my hand gently and told me they weren't ready yet.**6** I didn't understand why they wouldn't be ready.**7** They were already cut into slices. I wondered what else she was planning on doing with them.**8** I proceeded to go into my room and put my school bag down. I knew I wouldn't be able to help my mother without washing my hands, so I went straight to the restroom and scrubbed them clean.**9** My next step was to find out what she had planned for those absolutely beautiful apples.**10**

    I walked back into the kitchen, and I noticed that my mother had cut the apples into much smaller pieces than before.**11** She motioned for me to come closer and handed me a knife.**12** I smiled. I always liked helping in the kitchen.**13** I began to cut the apples into small pieces. When all the apples were cut, I helped her put the pieces into a pot on the stove.**14** I kept asking her what we were making, but she refused to tell me.**15** "You'll see, you'll see," she kept saying. She poured water, sugar, and cinnamon into the pot and began stirring.**16** After about 20 minutes, the smell of the sauce caressed my senses and made my stomach rumble with anticipation. It was almost ready and I was excited.

    Finally, the applesauce was done. By then, I knew it was applesauce, but I didn't care.**17** My mom made it, so I figured it had to taste good.**18** She served me only one spoonful, and I gave her a look that could kill. "Well, you don't like applesauce," my mother sarcastically stated. I just politely asked for more and she served me a bowl's worth. The apple chunks were sweet and soft.**19** I chewed the delectable sauce slowly to enjoy every bite. I absolutely loved it. It was sweet and sugary; it did not feel slimy.**20** It wasn't boring or unpleasing.**21** It was perfect. My mother laughed as I sighed with pleasure after every bite.**22** My mother had proved me wrong: I loved applesauce.**23**

Sentence Forms:

1) 7AC When
2) 7AC Even Though; 8RN Why
3) 3V Past Participle
4) 3V Present Participle; 3V Gerund
5) 8RN That
6) 8RN Missing *that* (2); 6CC But; 7AC When
7) 8RN Why
8) 8RN What
9) 8RN Missing *that*; 3V Infinitive; 3V Gerund; 6CC So;
10) 3V Infinitive; 8RN What
11) 8RN That;6CC And
12) 3V Infinitive
13) 3V Gerund
14) 7AC When
15) 8RN What; 6CC But
16) 2S Standard Series; 3V Gerund
17) 6CC But
18) 6CC So; 8RN Missing *that*
19) 6CC And
20) 2S The Pair
21) 2S Choices
22) 7AC As
23) 9PP Explanation Colon

Combat Medic by Jill Friend

Combat medics have one of the most exciting and interesting, mentally and physically challenging jobs in today's army.**1** We are the ones that see all of the guts and gore.**2** We are expected to help the bleeding soldiers, with amputated limbs and spurting blood.**3** Neither books nor pictures can prepare you for what types of injuries you encounter.**4** You have to keep your head and work quickly to get casualties to safety.**5**

Not only do we save lives on the battlefield, but also in the TMCs [Troop Medical Clinics], clinics, and hospitals.**6** We take care of all soldiers as well as their families.**7** Since we work long hours and holidays, we have little time off.**8** Until you stand in our shoes, you don't know all the things that we go through and all the graphic and painful things we have to see.**9** I love my job, and I love what I do: Medical Aid and Support!**10**

Sentence Forms

1) 2S Rhythmical Pairs
2) 8RN That; 2S The Pair
3) 3V Infinitive; 3VPresent Participle; 3V Past Participle; 3V Present Participle
4) 4C Neither Nor; 8RN What
5) 3V Infinitive (2)
6) 4C Not Only, But; 2S Standard Series
7) 4C As Well As
8) 7AC Since; 2S The Pair
9) 7AC Until; 8RN That; 2S The Pair
10) 8RN What; 9PP Explanation Colon

Words of Wisdom by Kareem Byam

Words of wisdom have an important and powerful influence on the human body.**1** My grandmother always provided words of wisdom to me. She always said "Wisdom will make you very strong and knowledgeable in life". The first time I rode a bike, I couldn't stay on it for a long time, and I kept falling and falling – until one day when my grandmother saw me trying and trying to stay on the bike.**2** She then told me, "Kareem, you have to be like a lion chasing after a zebra".**3** I thought about her words of wisdom for many days. But finally one day, it hit me – like a baseball thrown to you at 100mph.**4** I understood what my grandmother was telling me that time: have bravery, courage, and determination, and toughness, too.**5** I learned how to ride and stay on a bike for a long period of time, day or night.**6**

My grandmother's words of wisdom were spiritually moving and physically touching.**7** I still can't express how I feel about her words of wisdom.**8** They fostered my evolution – like a new creation being touched by God.**9** No other woman's words could ever replace my grandmother's words of wisdom.

However, it was my mother, and not my grandmother, who told me, when my uncle had passed away a few days earlier, "Your favorite uncle is looking down at you every day, and he wants the best for you".**10** When my mother told me that, I got a Spiderman sense, as if he was right there in the room with me.**11** That touched me, and from then on, I have always been strong in heeding words of wisdom. My mom's and grandmother's words and wisdom will always flow through my veins and blood, and be passed to my son.**12**

Sentence Forms

1) 2S The Pair
2) 6CC And; 9PP Dash E Adverb Phrase; 7AC When; 3V Present Participle (2)
3) 3V Present Participle
4) 3V Past Participle
5) 8RN What; 9PP Explanation Colon; 2S Standard Series
6) 8RN How
7) 2S The Pair; 3V Verbal Present Participle (2)
8) 8RN How
9) 3V Present Participle
10) 6CC And
11) 7AC When; 7AC As If (supplemental)
12) 2S The Pair (3)

Long Awaited Trip   by Addonis Hawkins

"Good morning," I said to my wife as I rolled out of bed.**1** She replied the same to me as she peeped through the covers.**2** This is the morning we waited so long for: we were going on our honeymoon cruise to the Bahamas!**3** I grabbed my list to ensure that I didn't forget anything: luggage packed, tickets in hand, kids at grandparents, check, check and check!**4** Now we were off to the docks to board the ship and hit the casino. As the ship pulled away from the dock, my wife and I waited at the stern waving good-bye as if we would never return.**5** As I stood in amazement at the glory of this huge city on water, I noticed the shoreline getting further and further away.**6**

Not only did the shoreline disappear, but the ship began to sway back and forth and up and down.**7** I began feeling dizzy which I thought was caused by the four Martini's that I drank earlier, but then I realized that it was my first drink.**8** I couldn't believe what was happening to me.**9** I was getting seasick, and we had just got underway, yet still my wife was unaffected from what was happening around us.**10** Since this was our honeymoon, I didn't want to ruin it for my wife, so I hurried to the ship doctor to retrieve some motion sickness pills.**11** About an hour after I took the pills, I started feeling a whole lot better.**12** When I finally found my wife, she said to me, "I didn't even know that you were gone!" – as she pulled the handle on the slot machine, shouting "BIG MONEY!"**13**

Sentence Forms:

1) 7AC As
2) 7AC As
3) 8RN Missing that; 9PP Explanation Colon
4) 3V Infinitive; 8RN That; 9PP List Colon; 3V Past Participle
5) 7AC As; 3V Present Participle; 7AC As (supplemental)
6) 7AC As
7) 4C Not Only, But
8) 8RN Which; 8RN That (2); 6CC But
9) 8RN What
10) 6CC And; 6CC Yet; 8RN What
11) 7AC Since; 6CC So; 3V Infinitive (2)

12) 7AC After
13) 7AC When; 8RN That; 7AC That; 3V Present Participle

The Bald-Headed Truth by Charlie Sanders Jr.

A lot of people ask bald-headed people why they shave their head, as if they have to have a reason why they do it.**1** There are a lot of reasons why people shave their heads. Here are just a few of the reasons: some do it because they are starting to go bald; some do it for fashion; some do it for medical reasons; and some do it because it's quick and easy.**2** There are additional reasons why people shave their heads, but these are just some of the main reasons.**3**

Personally, I just like to shave my head. I remember the first time I did so.**4** I was cutting my head with my clippers, and my son, who was five at the time, hit me between the legs.**5** Needless to say, I then had a large section on my head without hair. Since I had messed up my hair, I just cut it all off.**6** That was the start of my shaving my head.**7** I guess I just got used to having my head bald, as well as paying less to having it cut professionally.**8** To be truthful, the only time I miss my hair is during the winter months.

Sentence Forms
1) 8RN Why (2); 7AC As If (supplemental)
2) 9PP Explanation Colon; 9PP Trio Semicolon
3) 6CC But; 8RN Why
4) 8RN Missing that
5) 6CC And; 8RN Who
6) 7AC Since
7) 3V Gerund
8) 8RN Missing that; 3V Gerund (2); 4C As Well As

234

Running on Faith by Alphonse Arlene

One summer night at sunset, while I was visiting in a quaint little town in Georgia, I took a long leisurely walk down a back road to enjoy one of my favorite views of the countryside.**1** While walking, I heard the sound of thunder rolling, and it seemed as if it was headed in my direction.**2**

It was so majestic and magical, magnificent and grand.**3** I turned to see ten wild horses running freely.**4** The night revealed these most beautiful creatures in their natural habitat, moving together as if they were going somewhere, anywhere, nowhere.**5** They appeared to be running on faith, naturally following God's lead, just knowing that they were heading in the right direction.**6** At that moment, I also understood and knew what it feels like to be heading in the right direction.**7**

Sentence Forms

1) 7AC While; 3V Infinitive
2) 3V Gerund; 3V Present Participle; 6CC And
3) 2S Rhythmical Pairs
4) 3V Infinitive; 3V Present Participle
5) 3V Present Participle; 7AC As If (supplemental); 2S Triple Force
6) 3V Present Participle (2); 8RN That
7) 2S The Pair; 8RN What

Benevolent Mountains by Littlejohn

Mountains are something mysterious. I used to wonder about their source of strength, their height, and their unshakable essence.**1** They are not easily understood.

Well, I've given much thought and attention to the quality and characteristics of mountains, and I have walked them many times.**2** Hence, I have come to respect and feel a connection to mountains in a personal way.

Mountains are strong and serene, making their presence known out of utter silence.**3** I find that kind of cool and breath-taking. Not many things I know possess those qualities. Mountains don't bend for nature or man. Whether or not animals inhabit them, and man exploits them, they still remain standing.**4** They stand on their own, and are independent.

Mountains provide shelter from the elements to all creatures that run to them; therefore, I believe that they are defenders of the helpless.**5**

Mountains are unshakable. Whether or not a disaster comes so that mountains are stripped and bare, still they stand there, as stubborn as a mule, as if to say, "You have to do better than that."**6**

I respect mountains for all these qualities that seem so benevolent.**7** Mountains don't change their design with time. They are rough and jagged, full of justice and provision for weary creatures.**8** For all these reasons, mountains constitute an imposing, enduring, and under-appreciated feature of nature.**9**

Sentence Forms

1) 2S Standard Series
2) 2S The Pair (2); 6CC And
3) 2S The Pair; 3V Present Participle
4) 7AC Whether
5) 9PP Expansive Semicolon
6) 6CC So; 2S The Pair; 7AC As If (supplemental)
7) 8RN That
8) 2S The Pair (2)
9) 2S Standard Series

Motto Emphasizing Balance
and Moderation in Writing

Not too little, not too much — just in the middle.

Not too many words, not too few — just in the middle.
Not too little formal language, not too much formal language — just in the middle.
Not too little casual language, not too much casual language — just in the middle.
Not too few commas, not too many commas — just in the middle.
Not too few semi-colons, not too many semi-colons — just in the middle.
Not too few dashes, especially not too many dashes — just in the middle.
Not too few short sentences, not too many short sentences— just in the middle.
Not too few long sentences, not too many long sentences — just in the middle.
Not to few Latin or Greek words, not too many Latin or Greek words — just in the middle.
Not paragraphs that are too short, not paragraphs that are too long — just in the middle.

A skillful writer has an extensive repertoire of options at his or her command — a large vocabulary of words and a large vocabulary of syntactic structures — and enough sensitivity to the rhetorical situations to make wise choices.

Nora Bacon

The Well-Crafted Sentence: a writer's guide to style (2009)

9 (PP) Power Punctuation Forms I

10 9 8 7 6

Three COLONS		*(a STOP sign)*
9.c 1	**NUMERIC PRECURSOR Colon** marks off a set of items or instances that refer to a preceding numbered quantity	• **Three** things keep me here: **good food, good people, clean air.** • **One** thing matters on this team: **how fairly you play.** • I had **two** things to do after class: **post a letter and workout at the gym.**
9.c 2	**LIST Colon** specifies items or instances of a general word that precedes the colon	• Our design has <u>advantages</u>: **portability, simplicity, and low cost.** • The following <u>athletes</u> will compete: **Abe, Vanna, Brown.** • The recipe has just a few <u>ingredients</u>: **eggs, milk, sugar, flour.**
9.c 3	**EXPLANATION Colon** explanation of a significant word or whole clause preceding the colon	• Today is **unforgettable:** *I got my driver's license.* • The bread was **flat:** *the yeast was too old.* • I love my **job:** *it is always interesting and challenging.*
Two Supremely Important SEMI-COLONS *(a STOP Sign)*		
9.sc 1	**ASSOCIATION Semi-Colon**	• It was early evening; the reds of the sunset gave way to the hood of night.. • The wind is picking up; a storm is brewing.
9.sc 2	**OPPOSITION Semi-Colon**	• Some people dream of being something; others stay awake and are. Robert Kennedy • Min Joo is vegetarian; Bill eats all kinds of food.

238

9 (PP) Semi-Colon Forms II

Five Useful SEMI-COLONS

9.sc 3	**CONSEQUENCE** Semi-Colon	● It stopped raining; I went outside. ● The weather is too dry: my cello cracked. ● The cat was too loud; I put it out.
9.sc 4	**EXPANSIVE** Semi-Colon	● The traffic was heavy; *however*, we weren't late. ● The class is small; *nonetheless*, the group interacts well. ● The results are negative; *consequently*, you have no polyps.

Common Conjunctive Adverbs

A **conjunctive adverb** is a word or phrase that qualifies or extends the clause preceding it and transitions to the clause following it. These adverbs generally convey an attitude or feeling of the writer or speaker. Like train track switch signals, they show where one's train of thought is going.

Consequence	consequently	therefore	as a result
	then	hence	
Adding Information	furthermore	moreover	in addition
Emphasis	in fact	indeed	then
Overcoming Obstacle; Indicating Exception or Unusual Alternative	nevertheless	however	rather
	nonetheless		
Specifying or Exemplifying	namely	specifically	in particular

9.sc 5	**TRIO** Semi-Colon	●Nam plays guitar; Eddy plays bass; Snow sings. ● The food was delicious; the music was great; the talk was inspiring.
9.sc 6	**STYLISH** Semi-Colon	● One day there's rain; the next, fog. [note omitted verb] ● I ordered salad; Lisa, shrimp.
9.sc 7	**COMPLICATED** Semi-Colon	● The phone rang, and he was quick to answer it; he was waiting for her call.

9(PP) Semi-Colon Forms III

Two Difficult SEMI-COLONS
Separating Items in a Series

	### FIRST Separating Semi-Colon clearly divides **items in a series** in which **one or more items has a comma in it**
9.sc8	● This Korean New Year I gave gifts to each member in my family: to my brother, an organizer; to my mother, a book she really wanted to read; to my father, a handkerchief. ● Everyone brought something to help make the party a success: Jim, his mp3 boom box; Jan, cabbage rolls; Han, fruit punch; Colly, potato salad; Jansirani, *idlis*; Zooey, her strobe light; and Jeff, board games. ● "Second, we have all the problems of a major zoo – care of the animals; health and welfare; feeding and cleanliness; protection from insects, pests, allergies, and illnesses; maintenance of barriers; and all the rest." M. Crichton *Jurassic Park* ● Our collection... includes directions in assorted shapes and sizes; handwritten or typed narratives; free-form, all-too-creative maps with little stick figures, cars and houses; on colored paper and white; some photocopied, others dictated casually over the phone..." Anne Bernays *Take a Left Turn Onto Nowhere Street* from Skwire *Writing with a Thesis* 10the ed.
	### SECOND Separating Semi-Colon clearly divides **items in a series** in which **the items may lack commas, but in which one or more of the items are long**
9.sc9	● The team's success comes from training that pushes one's limits: a coach who inspires confidence and knows all the strategies; team members who pour on the heat every minutes of every game and workout. ● This exercise encapsulates my philosophy of education, which is based on the word *respect*: respect between student and teacher; respect for our cultural heritage; and respect for our natural neighbors. Robert Bateman *Thinking Like a Mountain*

9(PP) Power Punctuation – Dash Forms I

The DASH – The Highlighter, The Commentator, The Amplifier As a speed controller, the dash is like a **Yellow Light**.

		A dash followed by a summary word can be used to **wrap up an introductory series.**
DASH BEGINNING LIST WRAP-UP	9.d1	• Jordan, Pippen, and Rodman — **all were part** of the Bull's last three championships. • San Diego, San Francisco, Los Angeles — **these** are cities in California that have friends who are dear to me.

		A **pair of dashes** is used to **highlight** material inserted in the middle of the sentence. The inserted material amplifies, comments on, or clarifies *a word or idea in* the main part of the sentence .
DASH MIDDLE	9.d2	Word	• The singer waited her turn — **nervously** — in the wings. [highlights]
	9.d3	Prepositional phrase	• The hockey player — **of Russian origin** — dazzled the crowd. [amplifies]
	9.d4	Verbal phrase	• Her goal - **to master databases** — was reached in less than 14 months. [clarifies] • The music star — **forgotten by almost everyone** - released a new hit that shot straight to #1 on Billboard. [amplifies & clarifies]
	9.d5	Noun phrase	• The injured youth — **hours from death** — was taken by police to the hospital. [highlights] • The price — **100,000 won** — reflects the rarity of the bowl. [clarifies]
	9.d6	Adjective phrase	• The soup — **thick and chunky** — tasted delicious. [amplifies] • Her skirt — **short and tight** — brought many comments at the party. [amplifies & comment on]
	9.d7	Adverb phrase	• Tom — **rarely late** — had not arrive yet at the office. [highlights]
	9.d8	Appositive, Series of Appositives	• A big surprise — **a banner** — greeted him as he stepped down from the train. [clarifies] • Of all the four seasons — **Spring, Summer, Fall, Winter** — I like Spring the best. [amplifies]

9(PP) Power Punctuation
– Dash Forms II

			A **dash** can be used **at the end** to highlight or emphasize a concluding **word** or **phrase**.	
DASH END	9.d9	Word	●Psychologists say that one time of your life influences you later more than any other — **childhood.** ● One side dish was now noticeably missing from my meals — **kimchi.**	
	9.d10	Prepositional phrase	● I finally found my keys — **under the car seat.** ● Isabel is engaged — **to the man** *she saw in her vision.*	
	9.d11	Verbal phrase	● The gazelle paced back and forth — **cornered** *now by the newly-erected wire fences.*	
	9.d12	Noun phrase	● The robotic rover clocked more than 1000 kilometers roaming on the Martian surface — **a new distance record** *for a remote-controlled vehicle on the planet.*	
	9.d13	Adverb phrase	● I will have some copies made soon — **hopefully** *by early next week.* ● She doubts if she will stay long at her new job — **precisely** *because of having to work split shifts.*	
DASH LIST	9.d14		● The product was tested under a **variety** of condition — **illumination, irradiation, immersion.** [amplifies]	
			On occasion, the dash can be used to indicate a **Sudden Break** or **Shift in Direction** or **Departure** from the starting idea.	
DASH SUDDEN SHIFT	9.d15		● The movie was memorable — **but for all the wrong reasons.** ● They were in love — **and geographically only 3233 kilometers apart!**	

9 PP Power Punctuation Forms

There are three power punctuation marks used in English: the **colon**, the **semi-colon**, and the **dash**. They are each used for different purposes. We list them all here a second time without examples for ease of quick review.

9 PP	Power Punctuation Forms		
COLON: Dramatic Pointer			*(a STOP-sign)*
:	9.c1	Numeric Precursor COLON	
	9.c2	List COLON	
	9.c3	Explanation COLON	
SEMI-COLON: The Balancer			*(a STOP-sign)*
2 Supremely Important SEMI-COLONS			
	9.sc1	Association SEMI-COLON	
	9.sc2	Opposition SEMI-COLON	
5 Useful SEMI-COLONS			
;	9.sc3	Expansive SEMI-COLON	
	9.sc4	Consequence SEMI-COLON	
	9.sc5	Trio SEMI-COLON	
	9.sc6	Stylish SEMI-COLON	
	9.sc7	Complicated SEMI-COLON	
2 Difficult SEMI-COLONS Separating Items in a Series			
	9.sc8	First Separating SEMI-COLON – series items with commas	

| 9.sc9 | Second Separating SEMI-COLON – long series items without commas | |

DASH: The Highlighter, The Commentator, The Amplifier *(a YELLOW light)*

Beginning List Wrap-Up – dash followed by a summary word

| Dash Beginning | 9.d1 | DASH Beginning List Wrap-Up | |

Amplify, Clarify, Comment on, or Add an Afterthought

	9.d2	DASH Middle Word	
— Dash Middle	9.d3	DASH Middle Prepositional Phrase	
	9.d4	DASH Middle Verbal Phrase	
	9.d5	DASH Middle Noun Phrase	
	9.d6	DASH Middle Adjective Phrase	
	9.d7	DASH Middle Adverb Phrase	
	9.d8	DASH Middle Appositive, or Series of Appositives	
Dash End	9.d9	DASH End Word	
	9.d10	DASH End Prepositional Phrase	
	9.d11	DASH End Verbal Phrase	
	9.d12	DASH End Noun Phrase	
	9.d13	DASH End Adverb Phrase	

| Dash end list | 9.d14 | DASH End Informal List | |

| Dash shift or change in direction | 9.d15 | DASH END Shift or departure in the Content, Thought, or Direction of the Sentence | |

244

Power Punctuation - The Colon

The first power punctuation mark is the *colon*. It indicates an abrupt stop in the flow of the sentence.

9.c1 PP Numeric Precursor COLON

Note: The colon – which we call one of the **STOP** signs punctuation marks – draws attention to the list that follows it. This means that it requires a **full stop or pause** when reading. ***Comparatively, the colon is more formal than the dash when used to start a list.***

● We draw your attention to **three** advantages: portability, simplicity, and low cost. ● The Galapagos Islands are the home of **two** very interesting lizards: the marine iguana and the land iguana. ● The small town now had to deal with **three** problems: flood damage to roads and bridges, contaminated drinking water, and temporary housing. ● **One** thing I saw plainly: I was now able to leap up the stairs two at a time and not feel tired. ● My wife had **two** things to accomplish: one was shopping, and the other was mailing a letter. ● "**One** thing's for sure: If we keep doing what we're doing, we're going to keep getting what we're getting." [Stephen Covey in *First Things First Every Day*]

245

9.c2 PP List COLON

- This is what we need for our camping trip: **a tent, the sleeping bags, the cooler full of food, canned soft drinks, mosquito repellant, and the fishing gear.** • "We must counter the horrors of a world that doesn't care: **a system that spews darkness, media that spew violence, governments that spew apathy, and industries that spew poison.**" (Marianne Williamson *A Woman's Worth*) • I greatly enjoy the following activities: **sleeping, watching movies, listening to music, and bouldering.**
- You should always go to morning formations with these three things: **shaved face, pressed uniform, and shined boots.**
- In some places, the following foods are considered delicacies: **snake (any part), pig (intestines), monkey (brains), chicken (gizzard or feet), fish (head).** • The newspaper has many sections: **world news, editorial, lifestyle, sports, the classifieds, and the arts.** • The baby's toys were scattered on the floor: **a robot, a spaceship, a LEGO tower, and a yellow ball.**

9.c3 PP Colon: Explanation

Note: There are three examples of this colon. The first two are easy to use, because it simply requires one to explain a preceding word which we have put in bold-face below. They are similar to the Form 9.c1 where we explain the Numeric Precursor. The third example is more difficult but important to learn to use effectively. If you practice the first two kinds of colons, you will naturally get a sense for the third kind. Basically, when you see a colon, you stop and say *Why? How? What? Where? When?* Answer the question in the given context, after the colon, and you probably got it right.

explanation of adjective or participle before a noun

● It was **early** morning: only the crickets, the cicadas, and a few birds were awake.   ● Spring on the east coast is for me a **miserable** season: the pollen count is far too high.   ● It was a **foggy** day: the mountains, the houses, the fields were all shrouded in mist.   ● It was a **smoggy** day: the city was wrapped in a dense cloud of dirty air and polluted fog.   ● September 11, 2001 was a **devastating** day of terror in American history: thousands of lives were lost, and symbolic landmarks desecrated.

explanation of distant descriptor

● The laundry was still **wet**: it had rained all day.   ●The cake is **flat**: I forgot to add baking powder.   ●The movie was **boring**: all they did was hit and shoot each other.

explanation of whole statement

● **Everybody knew why he was smiling**: he had won the national lottery.   ● **I like to wear sandals**: they keep my feet nice and cool.   ● **The Empire State Building is a popular spot for proposals and weddings**: there is a wedding ceremony there each year on St. Valentine's Day.   ● "Hospitals breathed by night: there were generators and footsteps, life and crises instead of the sterile death of empty rooms in an empty home." (Frances Fyfield *Deep Sleep*)

Power Punctuation - The Semi-colon

The second power punctuation mark is the **semi-colon**. Like the colon, it indicates a full stop in the flow of the sentence. It is an equalizer or a balancer. It divides equal independent clauses or equal long items in a series, and then places the equal independent clauses or equal long items in a series in a **balanced relationship of close association or opposition**.

9.sc1 PP Association SEMI-COLON

Note: The first form using the semi-colon joins two independent clauses in close association:

association: the two clauses are closely connected or associated in meaning or in content to one another

- I just bought a car today; it has a standard gearshift.
- Writing is a skill; it has to be learned.   • I like to wear the color orange; it's very bright and beautiful.   • The wind is really getting stronger now; a hurricane must be approaching.
- Aroma filled the air; dinner must be ready soon.   • The computer processor is slow; I guess it's time to upgrade.   • My ballpoint pen was a gift; it was given to me when I retired.
- Just be yourself; no one can tell you that you are doing it wrong.   • A person isn't born with wisdom; he acquires it.
- The birds are singing; spring is here at last.   • The lightning streaked across the sky; thunder quickly followed.

9.sc2 PP Opposition SEMI-COLON

Note: This form joins two independent clauses to show contrast.

contrast: *the two clauses are directly opposed or contrasted in their meaning*

●Min Joo is a vegetarian; Bill eats all kinds of food.   ●"We're not in control; principles are." [S.Covey *First Things*]   ●In Canada, a newlywed couple may look forward to owning a detached home or a townhouse; in South Korea, many newlyweds look forward to having a condo in a high-rise building.   ●In daytime, the Beijing Financial Street beats with the pulse of a vibrant financial economy; at night, it dances with the breath of fashionable life.   ●"When structures and systems are aligned, they facilitate empowerment; when they aren't, they work against it." [Covey *ibid*]   ●Some walked right by; others stopped and looked on.   ● "The ultimate purpose of ancient knowledge was the contemplation of reality, either sensible presence or ideal form; technological knowledge aspires to substitute a universe of machinery for the real reality." (Octavio Paz *The Bow and the Lyre* quoted in Blaser *The Fire*)   ● In many Western duets, singers perform at the same time; in the typical Indian duet called "*Kahbi, Kahbie*," the singers almost always alternate singing.

9 (PP) Semi-Colon Forms II

Five Useful SEMI-COLONS

9.sc 3	**CONSEQUENCE** Semi-Colon	• It stopped raining; I went outside. • The weather is too dry: my cello cracked. • The cat was too loud; I put it out.
9.sc 4	**EXPANSIVE** Semi-Colon	• The traffic was heavy; *however*, we weren't late. • The class is small; *nonetheless*, the group interacts well. • The results are negative; *consequently*, you have no polyps.

Common Conjunctive Adverbs

A **conjunctive adverb** is a word or phrase that qualifies or extends the clause preceding it and transitions to the clause following it. These adverbs generally convey an attitude or feeling of the writer or speaker. Like train track switch signals, they show where one's train of thought is going.

Consequence	consequently	therefore	as a result
	then	hence	
Adding Information	furthermore	moreover	in addition
Emphasis	in fact	indeed	then
Overcoming Obstacle; Indicating Exception or Unusual Alternative	nevertheless	however	rather
	nonetheless		
Specifying or Exemplifying	namely	specifically	in particular

9.sc 5	**TRIO** Semi-Colon	• Nam plays guitar; Eddy plays bass; Snow sings. • The food was delicious; the music was great; the talk was inspiring.
9.sc 6	**STYLISH** Semi-Colon	• One day there's rain; the next, fog. [note omitted verb] • I ordered salad; Lisa, shrimp.
9.sc 7	**COMPLICATED** Semi-Colon	• The phone rang, and he was quick to answer it; he was waiting for her call.

9(PP) Semi-Colon Forms III

Two Difficult SEMI-COLONS
Separating Items in a Series

	FIRST Separating Semi-Colon clearly divides **items in a series** in which **one or more items has a comma in it**
9.sc8	● The morning meal usually consists of several common breakfast foods: bacon and eggs; toast, butter, and jam; pancakes and syrup; and a variety of fruits. ● This Korean New Year I gave gifts to each member in my family: to my brother, an organizer; to my mother, a book she really wanted to read; to my father, a handkerchief. ● Everyone brought something to help make the party a success: Jim, his mp3 boom box; Jan, cabbage rolls; Han, fruit punch; Colly, potato salad; Jansirani, *idlis*; Zooey, her strobe light; and Jeff, board games. ● "Second, we have all the problems of a major zoo – care of the animals; health and welfare; feeding and cleanliness; protection from insects, pests, allergies, and illnesses; maintenance of barriers; and all the rest." M. Crichton *Jurassic Park*
	SECOND Separating Semi-Colon clearly divides **items in a series** in which **the items may lack commas, but in which one or more of the items are long** †
9.sc9	● The team's success comes from training that pushes one's limits: a coach who inspires confidence and knows all the strategies; team members who pour on the heat every minutes of every game and workout. ● This exercise encapsulates my philosophy of education, which is based on the word *respect*: respect between student and teacher; respect for our cultural heritage; and respect for our natural neighbors. Robert Bateman *Thinking Like a Mountain*

9.sc3 PP Consequence SEMI-COLON

Note: Here the event in the second independent clause is an obvious consequence or follow-up to what happened in the first clause.

consequence: the event(s) in the second clause is (are) an understandably immediate consequence of the events in the first one

- Ravindra sprained his ankle; he'll miss the next game. ● The moon came out from behind the cloud; the gathering started to chant again. ● There was an accident on the highway; we got there late. ● The shirt was very pretty; I decided to buy it for Mother's Day. ● Meowing loudly, the cat kept scratching at the pantry door; I put him outside for the rest of the night.

9.sc4 PP Expansive SEMI-COLON

Note: This semi-colon form places a **signal marker** - a **conjunctive adverb** - after the semi-colon. There are 18 common conjunctive adverbs. They were first listed for you in the Connectors section of grammar. They facilitate flow and transition in thought. These adverbs can be put into 5 groups according to the kind of change they indicate in the thought flow.

consequence: _consequently, therefore, then, hence, as a result_

Note: In the previous form, Form 9.sc3, there is no bridge word that helps the reader understand that what follows is a direct consequence of the event or action in the first clause. The connection by consequence is implied rather than stated. Here, however, we assist the reader with the use of the above five conjunctive adverbs. They help lay out the logic better.

- I can still see some streaks under the fresh black paint;

consequently, we will have to give the car another coat of paint. ●Sam never took time to study; **consequently,** he failed the course.   ●The Communications Exposition will take place in four weeks; **therefore,** preparations for it are being made now. ●Chinese New Year is in three weeks; **therefore,** I must finish my shopping soon. ●The turkey will be frozen; **therefore,** we must thaw it out tonight.   ●Get settled first; **then,** we will assess your schedule. ●His grandmother died; **as a result,** he didn't attend Wednesday's class. ●The flowers are hand-pruned, hand-watered, hand-picked, and hand-delivered; **hence,** the price is a bit more than the floral chain shops.

adding information: _furthermore, moreover, in addition_

●Gino loves gospel music; **furthermore,** he sings with a choir in Daegu.   ●They have not seen that film; **moreover,** they have not gone to the cinema for almost a year.   ●She's a vegetarian; **in addition,** she is a running enthusiast and an advocate of all aspects of fitness and hygiene.

emphasis: _in fact, indeed, then_

●Sruti is hilarious; **in fact,** he could be professional comedian. ●An arthroscope helps a doctor examine the inside of an injured knee; **in fact,** the use of this instrument can prevent unnecessary surgery.   ●He was surprised to get the call to fill in for Jon Anderson as the lead singer for _Yes;_ **indeed,** it looks like Benoît David will be joining the progressive rock group for good.

overcoming obstacles: *however, nevertheless, nonetheless*

●The traffic was very heavy; **however**, we did make it to the party on time.   ●The car was low on fuel; **however**, I made it to work.   ●My mom was really tired from work; **nevertheless**, she helped me with my homework.   ●The team suffered a great defeat; **nevertheless**, they showed great sportsmanship.   ●The troops were called in to sandbag against the rising river were tired; **nonetheless**, they toiled late into the evening stacking the bags to make a dike to prevent the farmhouse from being flooded.

exception or unusual alternative: *however, rather, nonetheless*

●The seniors group is quite small; **however**, we are a close-knit group. ●I could use this free time to study; **however**, my favorite show *Farscape* is on.   ●The little girl loved to play in the grass; **however**, she had severe allergies, and was forced to play inside.   ●Susan argued with her husband; **however**, she still loved him.   ●The old bike was ten years old; **nevertheless**, it worked well and hardly ever broke down.   ●After his release from prison he no longer wasted time playing cards; **rather**, he devoted all his spare time and energy into mastering the fundamentals of computer networking.

specifying or exemplifying: _namely, specifically, in particular_

●A foreigner should always try to learn the customs of the host nation; **in particular**, the visitor should become familiar with the greeting and eating protocol, acceptable discussion topics, and family and interpersonal customs.   ●After joining the club, you will have more choices; **specifically**, you will have a say in determining the format, the frequency, and the content of our free monthly news digest.

> So what was it that erased the sentence, wiped what had been the _"forefront in composition research today ...at the cutting edge of research design"_ in 1980 off the radar screen of composition studies?
>
> Robert J. Connors
> _The Erasure of the Sentence_
> from _Selected Essays of Robert J. Connors_ (2000)

Eight Ways to Express Association and Opposition

Eight Ways or Options to Express Association or Combination in Prose

1. by the singular conjunction "and";
2. by the singular correlative "also"
3. by the correlative expression "not only , but also";
4. by the correlative expressions "as well as":
5. by the correlative expression "in addition to";
6. by the Sixth Sentence Form 6.1 : "CC and";
7. by the Ninth Sentence Form 9.1: "The Associative Semicolon";
8. by the Ninth Sentence Form 9.4: "The Clause Adverb Semicolon (moreover, furthermore, etc.)"

Eight Ways or Options to express in Opposition in Prose

1. by the singular conjunction "but" ;
2. by the singular conjunction "yet";
3. by the correlative expression "this, not that";
4. by the Sixth Sentence Form 6.2: "CC but";
5. by the Sixth Sentence Form 6.7: "CC yet";
6. by the Seventh Sentence Form 7.19: "AC while";
7. by the Ninth Sentence Form 9.2: "The Oppositional Semicolon";
8. by the Ninth Sentence Form 9.4 : The Clause Adverb Semicolon (however)";

9.sc5 PP Trio SEMI-COLON

Note: This form is an extension of Form 9.sc1 Association SEMI-COLON. Three or more short clauses are put together in a sentence, separated by semi-colons.

Examples:

● The song was touching; it brought back memories; I had to cry.   ● Debbie is good at spiking; Sung Min is good at setting; Gyeong Ae is good at serving the ball over the net.   ● Paula is unique; Kissa is exciting; Vanta is dull.   ● Keiko wants to go to California; Bahiyyih wants to go to Geneva; I just want to go to Rota.   ● MiSook sculpts; MiHee paints with acrylics; Dawn sketches with pencil.   ● Bees eat nectar; birds eat seeds; fish eat plankton and worms.   ● Molly grew up to be a singer; Desmond plays bass in a band; Derrick manages a blues group.
● "Some speculated that he [David Livingston] really was dead; others that he was in hiding; still others that he had discovered the fabled ancient cities of Christian Ethiopia and their mythical king, Prester John." (Arthur Herman *How the Scots Invented the Modern World*) ● In Canada, you get gasoline at a *gas station*; in Britain, they call it a *petrol station*; in Korea, they call it an *oil bank*.
● Jenny rides a recumbent bike; Sarah powers a racing bike; Ian commutes on an electric scooter.   ● "All was dark; all was doubt; all was confusion." [Virginia Woolf *Orlando*]   ● "What they know very well, however, is that their lives are stretched to the breaking point; their children suffer from asthma, obesity, and a continuous bombardment of sex and violence on TV and of ads promoting junk food; and they are unable both to keep bread on the table and to supervise their children." [D. Korten *The Great Turning*]

257

9.sc6 PP Stylish SEMI-COLON

Note: The main verb of the second independent clause is omitted. A comma is placed after the subject in the second independent clause. It is parallelism with a minimalist twist.

- I like potatoes; MaryAnn, beans. ● Robert ordered melted tuna for lunch; Lee, shrimp and salad. ■ My dog is a sweetheart; my cat, a pest. ● One of Joanne's gifts was a watch; the other, a ring. ● The Chinese government is communist; the Canadian government, democratic. ● One day there's rain; the next, fog. ● My shirt is too small; my shoes, too big. ● Many of the families were wealthy; the others, poor. ● Johnny plays slide guitar; Frank, blues harmonica. ● Betty makes clothes; Barb, pottery. ● Some plants like a lot of sunshine; others, shade.

9.sc7 PP Complicated SEMI-COLON

Note: In this form, three clauses are joined. Two of them contain a coordinate conjunction preceded by a comma to form the longer part of the sentence. The third clause is separated from the other two by a semi-colon.

complicated semi-colon — first half has coordinating conjunction in it

- You can sing, and I can dance; Tom plays flamenco guitar.
- Sam pushed the car, and Sally steered it; they were out of gas and in the middle of nowhere. ● We boarded the plane at 6 pm, but our flight was delayed; we didn't take off for another hour.

complicated semi-colon — second half has coordinating conjunction in it

●Tomorrow is Saturday night; I would like to go out with my friends, but I should stay home with my family. ● He was gorgeous; he had a beautiful car, but his personality was the pits. ●I baked a cake; I followed all the directions, yet it tasted awful. ●"Some of these [icebergs] were as broad as a bowling green and as high as a house; others no bigger than a man's hat, but most fantastically twisted." [Virginia Woolf *Orlando*]

●"The name of the coachman was John Manley; he had a wife and one little child, and they lived in the coachman's cottage, very near the stables." [Anna Sewell *Black Beauty*]

●"There was a fine drizzle outside; the hair of the priest rose in a frizz, but he did not seem to mind." **(Frances Fyfield *Shadow Play*)**

optional omitted comma (if the pair of clauses having the coordinating conjunction are short)

●The wind blew[,] and the rain poured; an ominous funnel-shaped cloud loomed at the horizon. ●Students laughed[,] and parents smiled; the principal was an excellent speaker with a good sense of humor.

TWO DIFFICULT SEMI-COLONS SEPARATING ITEMS IN A SERIES

First Separating Semi-colon

9.sc8 PP Series items having commas SEMI-COLON

Note: This is the **first instance in which the semi-colon is not used to separate independent clauses**. Its main use in this form is to separate **items in a series in which one or more items has at least one comma in it**.

●This Christmas I bought gifts for the men and women in my family: for the men, I bought ties and socks; for the women, I bought scarves and purses. ●We installed a new, synchromesh, autonomous clutch; repaired the dent on the left side; and painted the whole car a bright, glossy red. ● We have everything we need for the party: plates, napkins, cutlery; different colored streamers, confetti, and balloons; savory and sweet finger foods; party hats and favors. ● I have lived in several US cities: Bethany, Missouri; Houston, Texas; Los Angeles, California; ●"This is why we tend to focus on such things as processes for community dialogue; quality of life indicators such as the ones introduced in Chapter 2; multiple viewpoint drama such as Anna Deavere Smith's work in Chapter 8; systems thinking; and the creative use of media as an ongoing, perceptive 'mirror' for the community." Tom Atlee *The Tao of Democracy*   ●My job at the zoo involves all aspects of animal care: health, treatment, and welfare; feeding, exercise, and cleanliness; protection from insects, pests, allergies, other predators, and illnesses; maintenance of enclosures and their barriers; and all the international paperwork related to the capture and transfer of old, newly born, and released animals.

●I like all things automotive: cars, red and fast; motorcycles, sleek and powerful; autoshops, clean and modern. ●Every member of my family has their favorite type of movie: my wife, comedies; my son, animation; my daughter, horror flicks; me, action movies.

> To achieve an effective style, a writer needs enough knowledge of sentence structure to be aware of the range of options for expressing an idea, enough understanding of the rhetorical context to predict a sentence's impact on readers, and enough commitment to the idea itself to keep testing options until the sentence rings true.
>
> Nora Bacon
> *The Well-Crafted Sentence: a writer's guide to style*
> (2009)

Second Separating Semi-colon

9.sc9 PP Series long items usually having no commas SEMI-COLON

<u>Note</u>: This is the *second instance in which the semi-colon is not used to separate independent clauses*. Its main use in this form is to *separate items in a series in which the items contain no commas, but are long*.

● "Most campuses have more serious and ancient problems: faculties still top-heavy with white males of the monocultural persuasion; fraternities that harass minorities and women; date rape; alcohol abuse; and tuition that excludes all but the upper fringe of the middle class." (Barbara Ehrenreich *The Snarling Citizen* 1995)

●Peace involves the greater involvement of women in all levels of decision-making; a massive campaign to eradicate illiteracy and to improve education for all; a systematic and methodical sharing and distribution of all the planet's fossil and renewable resources; the adoption of a universal script and language that will become the global secondary language spoken and understood by all.   ● I have to launder my stuff and pack; clean up the place so it looks presentable when we come back; notify our neighbors to keep watch and to collect the mail and newspaper; and set the automatic lighting to go on at sunset.

● The platoon's success in the practice battles came from hard work; a leader who implemented a great strategy; soldiers that were devoted to their platoon.   ● The play's instant success came from the incredible talent of the actors; the dedication and inspiration of the directors; and the ability of the playwright to instantly transport the audience to another world.

9(PP) Power Punctuation – Dash Forms I

The DASH - The Highlighter, The Commentator, The Amplifier As a speed controller, the **dash** is like a **Yellow Light**.

A **dash** followed by a summary word can be used to **wrap up an introductory series**.		
DASH BEGINNING LIST WRAP-UP	9.d1	●Jordan, Pippen, and Rodman — **all were part** of the Bull's last three championships. ● San Diego, San Francisco, Los Angeles — **these** are cities in California that have friends who are dear to me.

A **pair of dashes** is used to **highlight** material inserted in the middle of the sentence. The inserted material amplifies, comments on, or clarifies *a word or idea in* the main part of the sentence .

DASH MIDDLE	9.d2	Word	● The singer waited her turn — **nervously** — in the wings. [highlights]
	9.d3	Prepositional phrase	● The hockey player — **of Russian origin** — dazzled the crowd. [amplifies]
	9.d4	Verbal phrase	● Her goal - **to master databases** — was reached in less than 14 months. [clarifies] ● The music star — **forgotten by almost everyone** - released a new hit that shot straight to #1 on Billboard. [amplifies & clarifies]
	9.d5	Noun phrase	● The injured youth — **hours from death** — was taken by police to the hospital. [highlights] ● The price — **100,000 won** — reflects the rarity of the bowl. [clarifies]
	9.d6	Adjective phrase	● The soup — **thick and chunky** — tasted delicious. [amplifies] ● Her skirt — **short and tight** — brought many comments at the party. [amplifies & comment on]
	9.d7	Adverb phrase	● Tom — **rarely late** — had not arrived yet at the office. [highlights]
	9.d8	Appositive, Series of Appositives	● A big surprise — **a banner** — greeted him as he stepped down from the train. [clarifies] ● Of all the four seasons — **Spring, Summer, Fall, Winter** — I like Spring the best. [amplifies]

263

9(PP) Power Punctuation
– Dash Forms II

A **dash** can be used **at the end** to highlight or emphasize a concluding **word** or **phrase**.			
DASH END	9.d9	Word	• Psychologists say that one time of your life influences you later more than any other — **childhood.** • One side dish was now noticeably missing from my meals — **kimchi.**
	9.d10	Prepositional phrase	• I finally found my keys — **under the car seat.** • Isabel is engaged — **to the man** *she saw in her vision.*
	9.d11	Verbal phrase	• The gazelle paced back and forth — **cornered** *now by the newly-erected wire fences.*
	9.d12	Noun phrase	• The robotic rover clocked more than 1000 kilometers roaming on the Martian surface — **a new distance record** *for a remote-controlled vehicle on the planet.*
	9.d13	Adverb phrase	• I will have some copies made soon — **hopefully** *by early next week.* • She doubts if she will stay long at her new job — **precisely** *because of having to work split shifts.*
DASH LIST	9.d14		• The product was tested under a **variety** of condition — **illumination, irradiation, immersion.** [amplifies]
On occasion, the dash can be used to indicate a **Sudden Break** or **Shift** in **Direction** or **Departure** from the starting idea.			
DASH SUDDEN SHIFT	9.d15		• The movie was memorable — **but for all the wrong reasons.** • They were in love — **and geographically only 3233 kilometers apart!**

Power Punctuation – The Dash

The dash is used to highlight one or several of the following: (1) an elaboration and amplification; (2) an afterthought; (3) a short explanation; (4) a commentary; (5) a break in time; (6) a break in the continuity of expression; (7) a summary sentence that follows a list; (8) a sudden break, departure, or shift in the direction of the sentence.

Dashes are longer than a hyphen. Also, according to typographic tradition, there are **2 types of dashes** that are used – the shorter *en dash* (–) and the longer *em dash* (—). Although style preferences vary, the more popular style (perhaps) is the one we have used here – an **en dash** with a single space on both sides. See http://en.wikipedia.org/wiki/Dash for further information on the uses of each.

9.d1 PP Dash Beginning list wrap-up

Note: In this form, a dash is used after a short or medium-sized list or series. What follows the dash is *one or more summarizing words which sum up the list* and usually function as the subject of the sentence. Examples of summary words are *all, these, many, each, some, such.*

●Ginous, Larry, Aldo – **all three** were on last year's slow pitch team. ●Dispatches, load plans, and licenses – **all** are needed to drive a humvee. ●Research papers, vocabulary, sentence structure – **these** are the things I despise most in Composition class. ●Parent-teacher conferences, my children's performances, charity fundraisers – **these** are things that I always try to attend at my children's school. ●Yogurt, *kimchi*, *injera, idli* – all **these** foods are made using fermentation. ●Claudius, Polonius, Gertrude, Ophelia – **all** are characters in Shakespeare's tragedy *Hamlet*. ●Jordan, Pippen, and Rodman – **all** were part of the Bull's last three championships. ●Respectability, neatness, accuracy – **all** are required to be a good secretary.

Comment on PP Dash Middle Sentence Forms

Note: Each of these numbered forms for the Middle of the sentence using the Dash has many sub-forms. Indeed, so many are the sub-forms that they can overwhelm the students. **Therefore, it is only necessary that the student write several examples of *any of the sub-forms*.** We simply provide a wealth of examples to be comprehensive. Slowly, skill and understanding of the use of the Dash will improve.

9.d2 PP Dash Middle Word

●The football club needed one thing above all else – **teamwork** – to win the final championship. ●One ingredient – **friendship** – was missing in their relationship.   ●"Wisdom is a marriage – a **synergy** – of heart and mind." [S. Covey *First Things First Every Day*]   ● A big blessing – **rain** – finally came to the village.   ●One word – **carelessness** – accounts for the tragic accident.   ●Their viewpoint – **ultra-orthodox** – met with frequent resistance. ●The dog – **a collie** – pleased the buyer at the pet store. ●The new style of the furniture – **contemporary** – suited the décor of the hotel. ● One factor – **money** – seems to always enter the equation, but never leaves it. ●His thoughts – **scattered** –

resulted in his making many wrong decisions when he was young.
●The rat – **terrified** – fled from the cat. ●The victims of the robbery called – **frantically** – for help. ●The student – **submissively** – pleaded for an extension of the deadline. ●"While you can be efficient with things, you can't be efficient –

effectively – with people." [S.Covey *First Things First*]

In this sub-form, we may occasionally have a word set off between dashes that we can see is in direct apposition or side-by-side replacement position, since that word (which we call an **appositive**) could very well be substituted for the noun to which it refers without little or no loss in meaning.

So we would include this sentence here:
   ●Our basketball coach – **Tina** – is great.

We could add more to the appositive to get an **appositive phrase**
   ●Our basketball coach – **Tina** *from Tijuana* – is great.

This would belong further down the list.

But what if we put together more than one appositive, making a **series of appositives**? Is it an Appositive phrase, or a multi-word unit, and do we include it as an extension of the Dash M Word sub-form?

Because the series of words is more "loosely" arranged without the binding that a phrase has, we chose the latter.

So, here are some examples of Appositive (Multi-)Word in Mid-Sentence.

multi-word appositive unit = series of appositives

●Three ingredients – **bacon, lettuce, and tomato** – are the main ingredients in the toasted BLT sandwich. ● He then decided he needed to go to Italy . . . in order to build up a visual data bank of classical designs and motifs – cornices, friezes, figures, bas-reliefs, vases, altars, columns, windows, and doorways – which he could use for his own designs. (A.Herman *How the Scots Invented the Modern World*) ●My favorite food – **pizza, lasagna, and spaghetti** – are all Italian foods. ●"And our world starts to seem polluted in fundamental ways – **air, and water, and land** – because of ungovernable science." [Michael Crichton *Jurassic Park*]

We likewise can consider several "unbound" adjectives strung together in a multi-word unit as being an extension of the Word sub-form, rather than in the Adjective Phrase sub-form.

multi-word adjective unit = adjective + [conjunction or comma] + adjective

Note: This sub-form is quite effective and easy to use. It is a The Pair Series made using two adjectives.

Examples: ● CJ's truck – *rusty and old* – had been in the auto shop for weeks. ● Kim's dress – *short and tight* – made everyone stare at her. ● His behavior – *rude and uncalled for* – was embarrassing to everyone. ● The teacher's lecture – *long and boring* – made everybody sleepy. ● The new car – *lightweight and battery-powered* – was the envy of all car enthusiasts at the auto show. ● The lost hikers – *weary and starving and distraught* – straggled out miraculously from the forest after nine days. ● "Jonesy looked up and saw a dozen glaring lights – *some* red, some blue-white – dancing around up there." (Stephen King *Dreamcatcher*) ● "Within months, plans to incarcerate us – *alien and citizen, rich and poor, sick and well* – were implemented." (Wakako Yamaguchi *Otoko* in *The Riverside Reader* ed by J.Trimmer)

9.d3 PP Dash Middle Prepositional Phrase

●Her wandering was – **at best** – episodic yet it enables her to learn many things about the world.   ●"The early Sixties' vision of peace, nonviolent reform – **of ending poverty** and racism – evaporated." [B. Shulman *The Seventies*]   ●"Iris patterns fulfill these requirements, as do – **to varying degrees** – fingerprints, face shapes, hand geometries, voices, and signatures." [Corrina Wu *Science News*]   ●"So I applaud – **with one hand, anyway** – the multiculturalist goal of preparing us all for a wider world."

(Barbara Ehrenreich *The Snarling Citizen*)   ●The face of fortune smiled on her – **during her youthful years** – as she began a life of unimaginable wealth, luxury, and freedom.   ●"But the market – **in particular**, *starting new businesses* – became the favored means for personal liberation and cultural revolution." [B. Shulman *The Seventies*]   ●The youth – **on a raft** *made of bamboo and balsa wood* – sailed up the west coast of Chile.   ●"For all across the region – **in Japan** *and South Korea as much as in China and North Korea* – one finds the same remarkable gift for regimentation and self-surrender, for hard work and discipline." [P.Iyer *Falling Off the World*]

9.d4 PP Dash Middle Verbal Phrase

verbal (infinitive) + its object

●Her ambition – **to complete her bachelor degree** – came true after seven years of hard work.   ●Her idea – **to rid the neighborhood** *of drug-dealing, drug-taking, and prostitution* –

required some convincing, but she and her noble assistants finally purged the hood of such hindrances to community well-being. ●Her action group with its one goal – **to help the needy** *and homeless in the city core* – eventually evolved into NPO agency that organized rural/urban youth exchange visits, homeless soccer competitions, a cadet corps, and drop-in learning centers for adults and students in need.

verbal (present participle) + its object

●Most of the townsfolk – **including those** *who have just recently moved to the neighborhood* – feel the same way about keeping the young mayor. ●A package – **containing candy**, *flowers, and a teddy bear* – arrived at my doorstep on Valentine's Day.

verbal (past participle) + prepositional phrase

●The country's first multi-party democratic election – **supervised by UN observers** – ran smoothly with a large turnout. ●The orphaned youth – **raised by his aunt and uncle** – managed to get a good education and became an active advocate for poor children both at home and around the world. ●The poacher – **waiting in camouflage gear** *with a high-powered repeater rifle* – targeted the endangered panda. ●The students – **stunned by the madman's rampage** *and murder of seven of their teachers and classmates* – could not understand the motives that might have led to such a horrendous act.

9.d5 PP Dash Middle Noun Phrase

A **noun phrase** is defined as *a noun* (called **header** or first word) *plus its attendant and attached elements*. A **header** is the central word around which a phrase or multi-word unit revolves; often, it is often the first word in the phrase.

For example, it can be a noun that is followed by: a *prepositional or verbal phrase*; a *lone participle*; a *reference clause*; or *more nouns (in series)*.

Students need only give *a couple of examples* of any of these, but should *not have to practice all the sub-forms in this form*. We simply provide a wealth of examples for their review and understanding, and to be comprehensive.

noun phrase = noun + prepositional phrase

● It is life's noise – the **noise of the news** – that sings 'It's a Small World After All' again and again to lull you and cover the silence while your love boat slips off into the dark." (A. Dillard *For the Time Being*) ● At the meeting, there were women – **women of all hues** – and their excited chatter proved how quickly women can establish rapport with their own gender. ● The perspective of the week prompts us to plan for renewal – **a time for recreation and reflection** – weekly and daily. (S. Covey *First Things First Every Day*) ● She had endured enough now – **nights of loneliness**, arguments of rage, episodes of deceit – and she knew it was curtains for their relationship.

noun phrase = noun + verbal phrase

●The new school had many restrictions – **rules to cover** all types of activities – that were hard for many students to accept. ●The huge Eden Project biome domes near Cornwall have plant species – exotic **ferns** and palms and fruit trees **obtained** from countries such as Malaysia, Cameroon, and the Seychelles – that have never before rooted in English soil. ●Someone has taped his blue umbilical cord – the **inch** or so **left** of it – upward on his belly." (Annie Dillard *For the Time Being*)

noun phrase = noun + lone participle (absolute construction)

●The Malaysian triathlon team – the **clock ticking** – scaled the steep Moroccan cliff, and passed the New Zealand team to take over the lead in the 1998 480 km Eco-Challenge expedition race. ●The amateur singer advanced to the stage – **heart pounding** – and then took the mike and started to sing.

9.d6 PP Dash Middle Adjective Phrase

The **adjective phrase** will be defined as *an adjective* followed by:

☐ *a prepositional phrase;*
☐ *[conjunction or comma] + adjective;*
☐ *[+adjective]+ noun (noun preceded by many adjectives);*
☐ any of the above plus any extending attachments

adjective phrase = adjective + prepositional phrase

●The tie you wore last night — the flashy neon colored one — looked really great. ●The girl — *happy at the prospect of graduation* — began to consider various universities and their special programs. ●The father — *elated by the safe birth of his first daughter* — could not stop bragging about it to his co-workers. ● Robert — *furious at not making the final cut* — decided to confront the coach for an explanation.

adjective phrase = adjective(s) in front of a noun

● "The late Sixties had favored the peace sign – *index and middle fingers in a V* – which proclaimed a world of possibilities, the emphatic conviction that young Americans could build a new and better world." Bruce Shulman *The Seventies*

adjective phrase = adjective + [,] + adjective
● "Mr. Gray drove the Subaru nearly three miles up East Street — *muddy, rutted, and now covered with three inches of fresh snow* — before crashing into a fault caused by a plugged culvert." Stephen King *Dreamcatcher*

273

9.d7 PP Dash Middle Adverb Phrase

An adverb string will be defined as a ***single-word adverb*** followed by:
- □ *one or more nouns with or without attachments;*
- □ *one or more adjectives;*
- □ *a prepositional phrase;*
- □ *a verbal phrase*

In other words, it is a combination of words and/or phrases that fit together and follow a single-word adverb.

adverb phrase = adverb + noun with its associated attachments

In the following example, we have an adverb header followed by a noun and its front or back descriptors. These back attachments of the noun usually refer to a prepositional phrase. The prepositional phrase is often not autonomous, but is integrally involved with the earlier words and is read as a unit with the earlier words.

● Mosquitoes – ***frequently*** *unwelcome visitors in the summer* – bother me less than they do most people.   ● Dinner – ***once***[2] *a common thing in our house* – has become a special event.   ● Sgt. Mark A. Linnell – ***previously*** *a police officer in the Royal Canadian Mounted Police* – has volunteered more than 8000 hours setting up Cadet programs for Métis youth in Alberta.

adverb phrase = adverb + adjective(s)

● The dragon boat paddling crew – ***always*** *keen and feisty* – plied the waters with their wide paddles in the powerful strokes; they brought the WanChu dragon boat first across the finish line.   ● Tom – ***rarely*** *late* – didn't show up for work the next day.   ● The hotel – ***although*** *old and obviously showing a past not present grandeur* – still offered

---

[2] *once* is an adverb here that means *at some time in the past, but not now.*

excellent service at an affordable price.   ●The man's salary –
although *rather large* – was not enough for him to reduce his debts.

adverb phrase = adverb + prepositional phrase or extended phrase

● "In 139 of these visits – ***ostensibly*** *for a flare-up of chronic hip pain* – the correct treatment would have been acetaminophen but no anti-inflammatory drugs." (N.S. in Science News vol. 152 1997.10.4)   ●The young salesman – ***rarely*** *at home because of his job* – racked up huge monthly phone bills calling his wife and daughter every evening.

adverb phrase = adverb + participle with its associated attachments

● Thawed-out rat skin cells – ***earlier*** *frozen* for 25 years – exhibit daily rhythms of gene activity that suggest that cells maintain their own biological clocks.   ●The election – ***strictly*** *supervised* by UN observers – ran smoothly without any problems.   ● The couple – ***forever*** *gazing* into each other's eyes – enjoyed their honeymoon at Montezuma Bay.

9.d9   PP Dash End word or multi-word unit

Footnote Code: 9PP DASH E Word or Multi-Word
Note: In fact, what follows the dash can be one or more words that explain, amplify, or add a telling comment, an observation, or an afterthought about the first part of the sentence. *Stock phrases or collocations will be kept intact and considered as a one-word unit*.

Examples:

● I have only one favorite color – *blue*.   ●The librarian stressed one thing with the students – *quietness*.   ● After the battle the soldiers wanted one thing – *rest*. ● China's ancient capital is gearing up for the year's most important traditional celebration – the *Spring Festival*.

multi-word units at the end of the sentence

● "Ecologists use a computer model to explore how the different types of patches shift around in space and in time – *and why*." (Mari N. Jensen *Ecologists Go To Town* Science News Vol 153 1998.4.4)
● She was tall – *even statuesque*. ● Valentin Abe's aquaculture action plan meant only one thing for the villages — **poverty reduction**. ● Their decision was a recipe for one thing – *mutual happiness*.

9.d10 PP Dash End prepositional phrase

Note: We can place a prepositional phrase at the end of a sentence after a dash plus any elements extending or following from it.

Examples:

● The former high school grads decided to meet after the alumni reunion at their favorite meeting spot – **at Marla's Diner.**
● I finally found my keys in the one place I hadn't checked – **under the car seat.**   ● The nightclub was strict in its refusal to admit young people based on two criteria – **under age,** *and inappropriately attired.*   ● The picture would look good anywhere – **on that wall** *over there, on the big wall in the kitchen, or above the media console in the living room.*   ● Each person in the group felt better able to cope with Life's stresses and challenges – **after undergoing a period** *of spiritual purfication.*   ● "It's a very flimsy craft – **like a tissue-paper spacecraft.**" (Jim McDivitt quoted in *Moon Shot* by Alan Shepard and Deke Slayton)
● "You'll sauté my delicious dollops of doctored data into a confection that everyone will swallow – **per my instructions,** *of course.*" (Bruce Bower in *The Deep Blue Sleep* in *Science News Vol .152* 1997.12)
● "Their family is performing a *yajna,* Vedic fire ceremony – **at 4a.m.** *in the morning!*" (Linda Forman in *Hinduism Today* Feb. 1998)

● "The power to create quality of life is within us – **in our ability** *to develop and use our own inner compass so that we can act with integrity in the moment of choice.*" (Stephen Covey *First Things First Every Day*)

9.d11 PP Dash End verbal phrase

This includes the **initial verbal phrase** complete with any **objects** if they are required, plus any other **extended attachments** to the verbal or its objects.

infinitive

● "Only the president, Carter insisted, could be counted on to make a policy for the nation as a whole – **to consider freezing tenants** *in Boston as well as oil barons in Austin.*" (Bruce Shulman *The Seventies*)   ● "For my part, whatever anguish of spirit it may cost, I am willing to know the whole truth – **to know the worst** *and provide for it.*" (Patrick Henry in M.Scott Peck *Abounding Grace*)   ● "Yet I still have faith in this country's unique destiny – **to create generation** *after generation of hyphenates like me, to channel this new blood, this resilience and energy into an ever more vibrant future for all Americans.*" (Eric Liu in *A Chinaman's Dream* in *The Riverside Reader*)

gerund

● The entire season is a rehearsal for one goal – **reaching the playoffs.**   ●His hobbies were all active ones – **climbing mountains**, *playing squash, photographing wildlife.*

present participle

● "Nearby, other people were doing as I was – *squinting* east into the wind." (Annie Dillard *For the Time Being*)   ● "The hope and energy of the 1960s – *fueled not only by a growing economy but by all the passions of a great national quest* – is long gone." (Rosemary Bray in *So How Did I Get Here?* in *The Riverside Reader*)   ● "For some unknown length of time (probably no more than five minutes, although it felt like longer) they watched those brilliant lights run across the sky – *circling, skidding, hanging lefts and rights, appearing to leapfrog each other.* (S.King *Dreamcatcher*)   ● "The man loves trains

— riding them, photographing them, even listening to them."
(Rebecca Barry *Chicken Soup for the Teenage Soul*) ● "However, since World War II, agriculture has been undergoing a transformation — *moving from a family enterprise to big business."* (Janet Raloff *Dying Breeds* in Science News 1997.10.4 vol. 152 p. 217)

9.d12 PP Dash End noun phrase

noun phrase = noun + prepositional phrase

● Today was a good day — *a **day** of rest, a day of relaxation.*
● The child became a major concern — *a two-legged **dynamo** with endless energy and curiosity requiring constant supervision.* ● "Sly and the Family's music evinced an incredible freedom — **freedom** *of form, with band members trading lead vocals and instrumental solos."* (Bruce Shulman *The Seventies*) ● "The two astronauts swooped toward the lunar landscape in their landing craft — *the **first** of their kind to descend on the moon."* (Alan Shepard and Deke Slayton *Moon Shot*) ● "Instead of having a separate message photon as well as an entangled pair, De Martini and his coworkers used two aspects of each particle of the entangled pair — *the **polarization** and direction of motion."* (Ivars Peterson in *Instant Transport* in Science News Vol 153 1998.1.17)

noun phrase = noun + reference clause

● "So we have come to cash this check — *a **check** that will give us upon demand the riches of freedom and the security of justice."* (Martin Luther King, Jr. in *I Have A Dream*) ● "To hear conscience clearly often requires us to be 'still' or 'reflective' or 'meditative' — *a **condition** [that] we rarely choose or find."* (S.Covey in *First Things First Every Day*) ● Thornton's doubt was strong in his face, but his fighting spirit was aroused – *the fighting* **spirit** *that soars above the odds, fails to recognize the impossible, and is deaf to all save the clamor for battle.* (Jack London) ● "As recently as 1894, bubonic plague killed 13 million people in Asia – *the same* ***plague*** *that killed twenty-five million Europeans five and a half centuries earlier."* (Dillard *For the Time Being*) ●"The Department of Defense launched the MSX satellite in part to study what natural patterns exist in the atmosphere – *a* **prerequisite** *for being able to distinguish the signature of a warm trail left by a ballistic missile."* (R. Monsastersk in *Storms paint bull's-eyes in stratosphere* in *Science News Vol 153* 1998.4.4) ● "He didn't want to trouble my mother – *a* **course** *that backfired, because the imagined is always worse than the reality."* (Rose del Castillo Guilbault in *Americanization is Tough on "Macho"* in *The Riverside Reader*) ● Most people were against the proposed clear-cut logging except a few – *the* **loggers** *who worked for Fergus Paper Mill.* ● "Feminists campaigned for subsidized child care for working mothers and stricter sanctions against deadbeat dads – ***those*** who did not meet their financial obligations to their children." (Shulman *The Seventies*)

noun phrase = nouns in a correlative at end

● "My discovery of America was also a discovery of feminism – **not only** *Ms. magazine and The Feminine Mystique* **but also** *the open and straightforward manner of young American women I met."* (Cathy Young in *Keeping Women Weak* in The Riverside Reader) ● "We choose – **either** *to live our lives* **or** *to let others live them for us."* (Covey *First*)

noun phrase = noun + adverb + (adjective)

● The Mobile WiFi technology is made for villagers worldwide – **people moderately** *poor but who enjoy some of the new communications technology.* ● "British paper currency, which his team examined this summer, has more rounded fibers and far smaller holes — **none apparently** *large enough for the cocaine crystals to enter.* (from Why greenbacks make good 'drug money' *Science News* 1997.10.4 vol. 152 p 213)

noun phrase = noun + verbal phrase

● The hurricane swept across the prairie — a vacuum **cleaner** *ripping up trees and houses and buses high into the sky, and then letting them all smash mercilessly to the ground.*   ● "When glaciers melt, they leave in outwash plains boulders, rocks, gravels, sand, and clays — the **sand** *ground to floury powder.*" (Annie Dillard *For the Time Being*)   ● "Rather, they realized that the first step in building SDI would be the development of ground-based missile defenses — **weapons** *designed to protect U.S. missiles from attack.*" (Shulman *The Seventies*)   ● "In the United States, it took shape as the nuclear freeze — a massive social **movement** *encompassing a wide spectrum of social activists across America.*" (Shulman *ibid*)

9.d13   PP Dash End adverb phrase

Note: The **header** is usually a **single-word adverb**.

● She doubts if she will stay long at her new job — **precisely** *because of having to work split shifts.*   ● She finally got her degree — **nearly** *seven years after she started to take evening classes at U.S.Q. in Australia.*   ● "They made grants that reinforced their notions of what was best and most deserving — **overwhelmingly** *New York-based abstract art.*" (Shulman *The Seventies*)

• Maybe it wouldn't be such a bad idea to talk to Sylvia's parents – **better still**, *her sister*.

9.d14 PP Dash End less formal list

Footnote Code: 9PP Dash E List
Note: A dash can follow a list (as seen in Form 9.d1), or the dash can introduce a list, as we have here. As such, it highlights or draws attention to the list, though in a *more casual and flowing manner than the more formal colon.*
Examples:

• "Segregation disappeared in arenas of casual contact between Americans – **restaurants, airports and train stations, hotel lobbies**. (Bruce Shulman)   • "The reason that Li finally gave for his appreciation of crab was that it was perfect in the three requisites of food – **color, fragrance, and flavor.**" (Lin Yutang *The Importance of Living*)   • "They constructed alternative institutions – **food co-ops, underground newspapers, free medical clinics.**" (B. Shulman)   • There are many biometric approaches – **fingerprinting, face recognition, hand geometry, voice printing, and signature verification.**   • "Bjornstam could do anything with his hands – **solder a pan, weld an automobile spring, soothe a frightened filly, tinker a clock, carve a Gloucester schooner which magically went into a bottle.**" (Sinclair Lewis *Main Street*)   • "Dumpster things are often sad – **abandoned teddy bears, shredded wedding albums, despaired-of sales kits.**" (Lars Eighner *My Daily Dives in the Dumpster* in *The Riverside*

Reader) ● "Imagine a B & B[3] run by the Phantom of the Opera –
huge chandeliers, voluminous drapes, richly patterned
carpets, 14-foot high ceilings, dramatic shadows." (Kerry McPhedran
Feb/Mar. 2000 issue *Elm Street*)

9.d15 PP Dash End Departure DASH

Footnote Code: 9PP Dash E Departure
Note: A dash can be used to indicate a sudden break or shift in
direction of thought or departure from the starting idea.
Examples: ●She was charming and agreeable – *but only when
she wanted to be.* ● He was an eloquent speaker – **when he
wasn't drunk.** ● It's a nice house – **only it's on the wrong
side of the river.**

---

[3] bed and breakfast – a type of hotel accommodation where people rent rooms in
a large family house and get a breakfast included

For this third assignment, you will concentrate on incorporating the all-important Form 9 Sentence Forms, using the punctuation marks of the **colon**, **semicolon**, and the **dash** in your sentences. What distinguishes excellent from only average writers is often the precise and effective use of the colon, semicolon, and dash, so the practice of writing and incorporating the various sub-forms of Form 9 into essays is critical to success in writing.

You should write on a theme of two or three paragraphs with a **focused title**, and as before, should incorporate 3 or more different examples of Forms 2 to 8 in their paragraphs; however, you should now also incorporate 2 or 3 examples of Form 9 in your paragraphs, employing the colon, semicolon, and dash. As always, *you should **notate and footnote** all the various Sentence Forms that you choose to highlight.*

Below are examples by earlier students to serve as models for this assignment.

Compositions using Form 9

FROM UKELELE TO GUITAR BY MATTHEW ORMITA

There is only one thing that I want to do with my life.**1** I want to play music.**2** My musical career began in Hawaii three years ago, and since then, it is all that I think about.**3**

In Hawaii, there are two instruments of choice: the guitar and the ukulele.**4** Many of my family members can play the ukulele. They motivated me to learn also.**5** I have always loved attention, and in Hawaiian music, the ukulele player is the star; the guitar player, the supporter.**6** Troy Fernandez and Ernie Cruz Jr., Jake Shimabukuro and Jon Yamasato, Israel Kamakawiwo'ole and Louis Kauakahi are all perfect examples of star ukulele players and their supporting guitarists.**7** Because the ukulele gets all the attention, that is what I wanted to play.**8** So in 1997, I began taking ukulele lessons. Just as I expected, when my skills began to develop, so too did the attention on me.**9** I enjoyed playing the ukulele; however, all the music to which I listened did not use ukuleles.**10** Within a year's time, I had grown tired of playing the ukulele; I now started to play the guitar.**11**

The guitar, like the ukulele, took a while to feel comfortable playing.**12** Anger, frustration, despair – these were all emotions I felt throughout the learning process for both instruments.**13** The guitar, however, was not as difficult since I had been playing the uke for a year straight.**14** I have continued playing and learning the guitar for over two years now, and I am sure that the hunger and desire will never stop.**15** I will never be able to master an instrument, but I will be able to play it well enough to satisfy my soul.**16**

Sentence Forms:

1) 1F There is; 8RN That; 3V Infinitive
2) 3V Infinitive
3) 6CC And; 8RN That
4) 9PP Numeric Precursor Colon
5) 3V Infinitive
6) 9PP Stylish Semicolon; 6CC And
7) 2S Rhythmical Pairs (extended)

8) 7AC Because; 8RN What
9) 4C Just As; 7AC When
10) 3V Gerund; 9PP Expansive SemiColon
11) 9PP Association SemiColon
12) 3V Infinitive; 3V Gerund
13) 9PP Dash B Wrap-up; 8RN Missing that; 3V
    Present Participle
14) 7AC Since
15) 3V Gerund (2); 6CC And; 8RN That; 2S The
    Pair
16) 3V Infinitive (3); 6CC But

SEARCHING FOR A TOPIC BY RICHARD PEACE

Today's writing assignment is to write two paragraphs; however, I do not have anything on my mind to write about.**1** I gave some thought to writing about penguins, or ostriches, or other birds that can't fly.**2** Writing about these birds would be silly, for I know little about them.**3** I have knowledge of the outdoors, so I should save that topic for a more important assignment.**4** The random thoughts bouncing in my head all lead to one conclusion: I must start writing soon, or I will never finish.**5**

After my break, I continue my search for just one thing – a topic.**6** My situation is turning desperate; head scratching, brainstorming, random doodling – nothing seems to help.**7** I am going to need a good excuse: I was sick; I had to work; the dog ate it.**8**

Sentence Forms:

1) 9PP Expansive Semicolon; 3V Present
   Participle; 3V Infinitive (2)
2) 2S Choices; 3VGerund; 8RN That
3) 3V Gerund; 6CC For
4) 6CC So
5) 3V Present Participle; 9PP Explanation Colon;
   3V Gerund; 6CC Or
6) 9PP Dash E Word
7) 9PP Association Semicolon; 9PP Dash B Wrap-
   up (variation); 3V Gerund (3); 3V Infinitive
8) 3V Infinitive; 9PP Explanation Colon; 9PP Trio
   Semicolon

LOSING WEIGHT BY BRANDIE STEVENS

Many people these days say they need to lose weight.**1** They try to lose it in many different ways: dieting, not eating at all, exercising.**2** I have found that cutting back on certain types of food (pizza and potato chips) and exercising more helps me lose weight.**3**

The first thing I did when I got pregnant was eat anything; I did not care what it was, or if it was healthy.**4** Now that I look back, I realize that I should not have done that - eating and eating and eating – because I gained 50 pounds by the time I had my son.**5** I started out at 170 pounds and went up to 220 pounds.

I tried many different programs to lose weight. Workout videos, metabolism increasing pills, Atkin's diet – all are things that I tried and failed as methods for losing weight.**6** After losing only eight pounds, I decided to try something new, something miraculous, something doable.**7** I needed something that would work for me.**8**

I started eating less food that had sugar and carbohydrates.**9** I did not eliminate them completely because then I would have broken down and pigged out on all of the food I missed.**10** I ate more chicken, steak, fruit, vegetables.**11** But I steered clear of fried, greasy foods, like fried chicken, pizza, and french-fries.**12** I also stopped watching TV while I ate.**13** I still had a brownie or a popsicle every once in a while, though.

The other exercise I did to start losing more weight was walking and running and step aerobics/*tae bo*.**14** I first started jogging and walking until I could handle running a full four miles.**15** And I also started aerobics/*Tae Bo* class two to three nights a week. The way I kept motivated was to have someone – my 1st Sargent – working with me.**16**

Slowly but surely, I started running faster and farther, and started losing body weight and body fat. By the end of 6 months – from January to June – I had lost 30 pounds, going from 214 pounds to 184 pounds, and also losing 5% of my body fat in the process.**17** The best way for me to lose weight was to eat more conscientiously and to exercise more.**18**

And I am still trying!

Sentence Forms:

1) 8RN Missing that; 3V Infinitive
2) 3V Infinitive; 9PP List Colon; 2S Triple Force; 3V Gerund (3)
3) 8RN That; 3V Gerund (2); 2S The Pair; 9PP M (appositives); 3V Infinitive Missing *to*
4) 8RN Missing *that*; 7AC When; 9PP Association Semicolon; 8RN What; 2S Choice; 7AC If (or 8RN If/Whether supplemental)
5) 7AC Now That supplemental; 8RN That; 9PP Dash M Appositives; 2S Lyrical Series; 5R Key Word; 7AC Because; 8RN Missing *That*
6) 2S The Pair; 2S Triple Force; 9PP Dash B Wrap-up; 8RN That; 2S The Pair; 3V Gerund;
7) 3V Gerund; 3V Infinitive; 5R Word; 2S Triple Force
8) 8RN That
9) 3V Gerund; 8RN That; 2S The Pair
10) 7AC Because; 2S The Pair; 8RN Missing *that*
11) 2S Triple Force (extended)
12) 2S Compact Duo; 2S Standard Series
13) 3V Gerund; 7AC While
14) 8RN Missing that; 3V Gerund (3); 2S Lyrical Series
15) 2S The Pair; 3V Gerund (3); 7AC Until
16) 8RN Missing that; 3V Infinitive; 9PP Dash M Appositive; 3V Present Participle
17) 4C From To (2); 9PP Dash M Prepositional Phrase; 3V Present Participle (2)
18) 3V Infinitive (3)

WHAT I DO BY BETTY WARREN

I cannot count the times that I have been asked the same question "What do you do?"**1** Hmm, let me think about that for a moment. Even though I know exactly what they are referring to, I still feel compelled to answer with a question of my own: "What do I do, when?"**2** Since they have obviously never seen me in an office, never seen me behind a desk, and never seen me anywhere, that would imply that I am unemployed.**3** Why then, do they ask what I do?**4**

I am not trying to be rude: I am simply being defensive.**5** Because I am a housewife, I do not want people to assume that I do nothing.**6** I do a number of things: I care for my family; pay the bills; do the taxes; coordinate moves; plan vacations; and generally keep our lives in order.**7** The list is endless, for I am a housewife.**8**

And that is what I do.**9**

Sentence Forms

1) 8RN That
2) 7AC Even Though; 8RN What; 3V Infinitive
3) 7AC Since; 5R Key Word; 2S Standard Series; 8RN That
4) 8RN What
5) 3V Infinitive; 9PP Explanation Colon
6) 7AC Because; 3V Infinitive; 8RN That
7) 9PP Long Items in a List
8) 6CC For
9) 8RN What

FOOTBALL 101 BY CARLOS JONES

America is in need of its own Shakespearean type amphitheater to play out the modern day dramas of life; consequently, football was created.**1** Since I am from the city of Houston, football dictates that I should be a Houston Texan fan; however, I am actually a Dallas Cowboys fan.**2** There are so many virtues which football brings to our world: teamwork, competition, a healthy life, dedication.**3** Ming, Roman, British – all three were great empires that were arguably built around the central virtue that football is built around.**4** Those empires, like every football fan, knew that only one factor – loyalty – can bring about the fruits of victory.**5**

Such are my reflections when I am silent, serene, and secluded with my thoughts.**6** Football surely has to be God's gift to mankind! Where else can you see a spectacle so simple in its rhythm, so complex in its intricacies, so brutal in its passion?**7** The stories of everyday life are played out in each new game: See the team go from rags to riches; Delight in the pain and punishment of the sport; Bear witness to the world of football in all of its glory.**8** There are no cowards here, only warriors.**9**

And on the eighth day, God created FOOTBALL . . .
and He said, IT IS GOOD!

Sentence Forms:

1) 9PP Expansive Semicolon; 3V Infinitive
2) 7AC Since; 8RN That; 9PP Expansive Semicolon
3) 1F There Are; 8RN Which; 9PP Colon List
4) 2S Triple Force; 9PP Dash B Wrap-up; 8RN That (2)
5) 9PP Dash M Word
6) 7AC When; 2S Standard Series
7) 2S Triple Force; 5R Word
8) 9PP Explanation Colon
9) 4C No, Only (supplemental)

PHYSICAL TRAINING BY JIMMY CURRIE

Physical training is a good thing for you; it builds the body's endurance.**1** I work out hard daily to stay physically fit.**2** I have three favorite activities: pushups, sit ups, and running; all three are part of the army physical fitness test.**3** Sometimes it makes your body really sore; however, the exercise is good for the body.**4** My muscles scream, ache, tremble while I lift the heavy weights, but I feel better afterwards.**5**

Racquetball, football, basketball – all are sports that give a person a good cardiovascular workout.**6** Before working out, I like to stretch my muscles, do warm up exercises, and mentally prepare myself.**7** The stretch and warm-up is good for sports or weight training as well as for aerobics workouts.**8** If one works really hard, if one sticks to a workout program, if one doesn't quit, he will be on his way to becoming physically fit.**9** Once you are physically fit, you are primed to succeed and win in all aspects of your life.**10**

Sentence Forms

1) 9PP Association Semicolon
2) 3V Infinitive
3) 9PP Numeric Colon; 2S Standard Series; 9PP Association Semicolon
4) 9PP Expansive Semicolon;
5) 2S Triple Force; 7AC While; 6CC But

6) 2S Triple Force; 9PP Dash B WrapUp
7) 3V Gerund; 3V Infinitive; 2S Standard Series
8) 2S The Pair; 2S Choice; 4C As Well As
9) 5R Adverbial Conjunction *If*; 3V Gerund
10) 7AC Once; 2S The Pair

BEING ALONE BY GEORGE C. PINEDA

Today was unforgettable: I chatted with my kids.**1** It's been a long time since I talked to them, and I really miss them very much.**2** I had several things to do after I chatted with them: I sent a package by mail and started taking pictures for them to see what I do here in Korea.**3**

Some people cannot cope with being alone and far away from their family; I, on other hand, try to occupy myself with work and liberty.**4** That way I won't get depressed when I miss my children.**5** I try to be strong for them, so that I can live through being stationed here for another two years without them with me.**6** So, I try to keep very busy; with my hectic schedule and overloaded work, I never even thought of myself being alone until now.**7**

Sentence Forms:

1) 9PP Explanation Colon
2) 7AC Since; 6CC And
3) 9PP List Colon; 2S The Pair; 3V Gerund; 3V Infinitive; 8RN What
4) 9PP Opposition Semicolon; 2S The Pair (2); 3V Infinitive
5) 7AC When; 3V Gerund
6) 3V Infinitive; 6CC So That supplemental; 3V Gerund; 3V Past Participle
7) 9PP Association Semicolon; 3V Past Participle; 3V Gerund

TIPS ON WORKING RETAIL BY CAROLINE DANIELS

Working retail can be described as challenging and mildly interesting.**1** It is not exactly a bad experience, but it's not exactly a good one either.**2** There are two qualities you must possess to make it through the day: patience and understanding.**3** Some people who work retail leave work drained and angry; others can leave the building and still be calm and collected.**4** The difference is how much you let the customers upset you.**5** Long days of dealing with disgruntled customers can be stressful; however, if you know to contend with their problems, you can lower your stress level significantly.**6**

Anytime you're serving others, there will always be people who are not exactly the kindest or most appreciative.**7** Days like this are almost inevitable: it's karma.**8** If customers complain about something, the first rule is to try to understand their point of view.**9** The policy of most companies is that the customer is always right.**10** Usually this isn't true, but you have to pretend it is if you wish to keep your job.**11** So smile; you know they're wrong.**12** Smiling then looks good on the outside and feels good on the inside.**13** No matter what happens, just remember three things: smile, be patient, and understand their point of view.**14** With these three rules, you should be able to get through your day with no problems.**15**

Sentence Forms:

1) 3V Gerund; 2S The Pair
2) 6CC But
3) 8RN Missing That; 3V Infinitive; 9PP Numeric Colon; 2S The Pair
4) 9PP Opposition Semicolon; 2S The Pair (2)
5) 8RN How
6) 3V Gerund; 9PP Expansive Semicolon; 7AC If; 3V Infinitive
7) 8RN Missing That; 8RN Who; 2S The Pair
8) 9PP Explanation Colon
9) 7AC If; 3V Infinitives (2)
10) 8RN That
11) 6CC But; 8RN Missing *that*; 7AC If; 3V Infinitive
12) 9PP Association Semicolon

13) 3V Gerund; 5R Key Word
14) 9PP Numeric Colon; 2S Standard Series
15) 3V Infinitive

MY SECOND DRIVING SKILL BY TRUCQUYNH HUA

Learning is a process.**1** Learning is an occupation you never retire from.**2** You learn something new every day, at any age throughout your life.**3** For example, I learned how to ride a bicycle when I was at the age of seven. Then, when I was seventeen, my father taught me how to drive an automatic transmission car; however, I didn't learn how to drive a manual transmission car until two years ago.**4** In my opinion, driving a manual transmission car – better known as driving a stick shift – requires lots of time, lots of patience, and lots of practice.**5** Learning the skill to operate a manual vehicle is not easy, yet it can be done.**6** While I was stationed in Sigonella, Italy, I decided to learn how to operate a manual car.**7** My friend Mitchell taught me how. It was a unique and wicked experience.**8** I was a little bit nervous during my first driving lesson, but Mitchell said I would be fine.**9** We got into the car, and I started it. He told me to adjust the seat and mirrors so that it would be comfortable for me.**10** Then he said, "Put on your seat-belt and let's go!" Mitchell gave me simple instructions on what to do: he pointed out what each of the foot pedals were; he explained in words how to start a manual transmission, and at what speeds to move into the next shift and how to downshift; he also reminded me to always use the emergency brake when I parked.**11**

The instructions seemed pretty easy, and I was ready to go.**12** I began practicing the maneuvers in my head: left foot on clutch, right on brake, put it into first gear, gently press the gas and lift off the clutch.**13** I thought I could do it, but I was wrong.**14** It stalled. I started it again, yet it stalled again.**15** The third time, I failed; then, the fourth time, too.**16** I was very upset, and I wanted to give up; but Mitchell looked at me and said, "You are doing just fine. Just keep practicing, and soon enough you will get it."**17** I could not believe how hard it was.**18** It looked so easy and fun when he drove.**19** I took a deep breath and sighed and decided to give it another try.**20** Concentrating on releasing the clutch and pressing the gas pedal down at the same time, I finally shifted into first gear.**21** I drove for approximately 100 meters, and before I shifted into second gear, the car stalled again; however, I was happy because I felt like I accomplished the first step of my goal – to drive the manual car.**22** I kept practicing (releasing the clutch and pressing the gas pedal) and concentrating (feet, hand, and eyes in coordination) for several hours.**23** Finally, I was able to drive out of the parking lot and onto the road without a stall.**24**

Learning to drive stick shift was not easy for me, but I did it because I didn't give up.**25** I devoted my heart, my time, and my patience to it.**26** Once I learned the driving skill, it will never be forgotten; it will stay with me for the rest of my life.**27**

Sentence Forms:

1) 3V Gerund
2) 3V Gerund; 8RN Missing *that*
3) 10TP E Prepositional Phrase
4) 7AC When; 3V Infinitive (2); 9PP Expansion Semicolon
5) 3V Gerund; 9PP Dash M Verbal Phrase; 5R Word; 2S Standard Series
6) 3V Gerund; 3V Infinitive; 6CC Yet
7) 7AC While; 3V Infinitive (2)
8) 2S The Pair
9) 6CC But; 8RN Missing *that*
10) 2S The Pair; 7AC So that supplemental
11) 9PP Explanation Colon; 9PP Difficult Semicolon / List Items With Commas; 8RN What; 3V Infinitive (4); 7AC When
12) 7AC And; 3V Infinitive
13) 3V Gerund; 9PP List Colon
14) 6AC But; 8RN Missing *that*
15) 6AC Yet
16) 9PP Stylish Semicolon
17) 6CC But; 9PP Complicated Semicolon; 3V Gerund; 6CC And
18) 8RN How
19) 2S The Pair; 7AC When
20) 2S Lyrical Series
21) 3V Present Participle (2); 3V Gerund

22) 6CC And; 7AC Before; 9PP Expansion
Semicolon; 7AC Because; 9PP Dash E Verbal
Phrase
23) 9PP M Verbal Phrases; 3V Gerund (4); 9PP E
Words
24) 3V Infinitive
25) 3V Gerund; 3V Infinitive; 6CC But; 7AC Because
26) 2S Standard Series; 5R Word
27) 7AC Once; 9PP Association Semicolon

10 TP Three Places Forms

This 10th Form involves an understanding of **more complicated sentences**. It involves making simple or more complex additions to a sentence in one of **Three** possible **Places**. Depending on the location of the addition, these types of sentences can be grouped and labeled as:

(1) TP - B (beginning of sentence)
(2) TP - M (middle of sentence)
(3) TP - E (end of sentence)

ADDITIONS AT THE BEGINNING, MIDDLE, AND END OF A SENTENCE SET OFF WITH COMMAS OR PARENTHESES

A **sentence addition** refers to something that is placed at the *beginning, middle, or end of a sentence*, and is usually separated from the rest of the sentence by a punctuation mark. The punctuation mark for the beginning and end of sentence additions is a *comma*. The punctuation mark before and after the mid-sentence addition or interruption can be a *dash* (discussed in Form 9), *comma*, or *parenthesis*. The interruption itself can be a series of appositives, an explanation, a comment, or an afterthought. The interrupting portion can be removed, and the remaining sentence makes complete sense and is grammatically correct. The information contained in the interruption is useful, therefore, but is not essential for the meaning of the sentence.

Basically, there are **_25 possible kinds of additions_** that can be added to the three places (locations) mentioned above.

The *beginning of the sentence* and the *end of the sentence* refer to elements placed at either or both of those two locations.

By the *middle of the sentence* is meant such possible locations as
1) anywhere between a subject and main verb;
2) anywhere between a main verb and its object;
3) before a coordinating conjunction in a sentence with compound main verbs; or
4) after another introductory interrupting element.

A chart for determining which punctuation marks are most appropriate for enclosing the interrupting mid-sentence element follows later.

10 (TP) Three Places
Sentence Forms – Introduction

Additions to a sentence build it up, giving it a unique topography, adding density and greater texture. Francis Christensen explains: *If a writer adds to few of his nouns or verbs or main clauses and adds little, the texture may be said to be thin. The style will be plain or bare. The writing of most of our students is thin – even threadbare. But if he adds frequently or much or both, then the texture may be said to be dense or rich. One of the marks of an effective style, especially in narrative, is variety in the texture, the texture varying with the change in pace, the variation in texture producing the change in pace.*

He later adds: *The real problem in writing is to reconcile these two seeming opposites – to pack much into little, but to pack it so that it can be readily unpacked.*

We divide the Forms (1) according to whether additions are placed at the beginning, middle, or end of the sentence; and (2) within each of these 3 groups, **we further divide the Forms – into Primary, Secondary, or Tertiary – according to their stylistic value, their frequency of use, and ease of learning**.

Initially, instructors may choose to have students learn and practice only the Primary Sentence Forms (since they are the really essential ones) in each of the 3 groups, and later have them return to practice the Secondary and Tertiary Sentence Forms.

Primary 10 (TP) Three Places Sentence Forms – Beginning

10.1	Word or multiple words	● Loudly, Beth spoke over the megaphone. ● Desperately, the mouse tried to outrun the cat. ● Weary and worn-out, the traveller looked for a cheap hotel.
10.2	Prepositional phrase	●On my way home, I got hit by a drunk driver. ●Across the open fields, you could see the next village. ● After lunch, many Chinese people take a nap.
10.3	Verbal phrase	● Waiting for the bus, I listened to a podcast. ● Running behind the pack, the small wolf struggled to keep up. ● Seated on the bench, the old man read a book.

Secondary 10 (TP) Three Places
Sentence Forms – Beginning

10.4	Noun phrase	●**Hat in hand**, the beggar went from door to door. ●**Mind in a daze**, the student struggled to remember. ●**Pen in hand**, the student sat ready to begin the examination. ● **Bottle in hand**, the alcoholic voiced his discontent loudly to fellow winos in the downtown park.
10.5	Absolute construction (noun + verbal participle)	●**Heart pounding** *in anticipation*, he knocked on her front door. ●**Legs pumping** *furiously*, the cyclist stormed to the finish line. ● **Purse missing**, she started to panic. ●**Hair flying** *in the breeze*, Nick rode his motorcycle across the outback towards Killarney. ● **Homework done**, Jenny flopped onto her bed.

Tertiary 10 (TP) Three Places Sentence Forms – Beginning

Three Places – beginning of sentence - tertiary

10.6	**Adjective phrase** adjective is header	•Familiar *with all the topics*, the student found the exam a push-over. • **Upset** *after the loss*, the youth decided to seek help.
10.7	**Adverb phrase** or string of related words reading as a unit	• **Sometimes** *after rain*, I go out for a walk. • **Early** *next week*, I will finish this manuscript. • **Largely** *through science*, billions of us live on one small world, densely packed and intercommunicating. M.Chrichton *Jurassic Park* • **Up ahead**, there was a flashing red light. • **More often than not**, Carol was an open book where her thoughts and feelings were concerned. Fern Michaels *The Guest List*

Beginning Sentence Primary Form 10.1:
Word at beginning of Sentence before subject and main verb

Code: 10TP B Word

Note: The word is set off by a comma. The word is usually an adverb, but it sometimes is an adjective.

Intent: The pausing gives attention to the isolated word.

Examples:

10TP B Word

adverb

● **Frantically**, Elaine searched for her I.D. card. ● **Reluctantly**, Bert obeyed his wife and went in for therapy. ● **Calmly**, the doctor explained the fatal disease to the patient. ● **Angrily**, the father beat his fist upon the wall. ● **Happily**, the little girl went outside to play. ● **Remarkably**, I won a lottery. (Ha Eun-hoon, Korea)

● **Suddenly**, the building was broken down. Eddie, Gumi, Korea, 2HA class 2001.11

● **Recently**, many people have lost their jobs. Eddie, Gumi, Korea, 2HA class 2001.11 ● **Blindly**, the criminal fired his gun. Seol-Mee-ryeon of Gumi, Korea, 2HA class 2001.11   ● **Carefully**, you take care of your baby. Song Jun Woo of Korea, 2HA class 2001.11 ● "**Previously**, humanity had to rely on solar flow and on wind, water, and animal power for its sources of energy,..." Jeremy Rifkin *The Biotech Century*   ● "**Year-round**, the wail and hum of traffic comes with the urban territory." Kerry McPhedran in *The Rescuers* in Feb/Mar. 2000 issue *Elm Street*

adjective or participle

- **Exhausted**, the soldier continued to fight.   - **"Aching**, I gave up on sleep and ventured out with my tin cup in search of coffee." R.Solnit *Sierra* 1991 Sept/Oct.   - **Frustrated**, she continued to stare at the blank sheet of paper, unable to compose a single sentence.   - **'United**, there is little we cannot do in a host of cooperative ventures." John F. Kennedy in his *Inaugural Address*

- **"Dazed**, I pulled up to my feet." Richard Wright *The Ethics of Living Jim Crow: An Autobiographical Sketch*

Beginning Sentence Primary Form 10.2:
Prepositional phrase at beginning of Sentence before subject and main verb (usually an adverb phrase)
Code: 10TP B Prepositional Phrase

Note: This form also includes sentence that have extended phrases at the beginning of the sentence.

Examples:

10TP B Prepositional Phrase

- **Against the odds**, I learned to write. - **In the house**, we played games. - **Above the trees**, there flew a flock of birds. - **In the distance**, we could see gazelles, zebras. - **With style and grace**, the models strolled down the runway. - **Of all the students**, Mi Gyeong is the tallest. - **On the first day of school**, I had to fill out many forms. - **On Friday**, the convention will officially open. - **During the closing decades** *of* the *nineteenth century*, a number of people tried to photograph motion. - **In Korean culture**, the family is the most important aspect of life.   ● **Along every road in the valley**, festive lanterns could be seen.   ● **Without the support of my husband**, my success would not have been possible.   ● **On a beautiful day like today**, I enjoy an outdoor barbeque.   ● **In response to your recent inquiry**, we hereby enclose several maps and pamphlets of Kilwa Kisiwani, and hope that you will one day be able to visit this scenic and historic spot off the coast of Tanzania.   ● **After the rain**, I went outside.   ● **Before dawn**, the fishermen set out.

● **Between the two of us**, I have to admit that I find you irresistible.   ● **"Among living animals**, erect posture occurred only in warm-blooded mammals and birds." (Crichton *Jurassic Park*)

● **"Without this**, they will forever play catch-up, both in school and in the job market." (Carol Jago in *English Only – For the Kid's Sake*)

extended phrases

● **"At the feet of the adults**, baby velociraptors skittered and chirped." (M. Crichton *Jurassic Park*)

● **With an explanation** *in English*, the performances are from the Beijing Peking Opera Theatre.

● **"By the light** *of a melon slice of moon*, Yiban told us the news." (Amy Tan *The Hundred Secret Senses*)

● "In sunny Singapore where the heat never lets up, it's no surprise that fruit juice bars and takeaway counters have sprouted up along Orchard Road and the business district like oases in a desert." (from *Straits Times* *-web page removed* - accessed 2002.03.05)

● "Among some species *of stalk-eyed flies*, the guy with the longer eye stems gets the girl." (from *Female flies pick mates with sexy eyes* in *Science News* 1998.01.17)

● According to bylaw 230(a) *in the jurisdiction of Hastings County*, we hereby give you notice that the icicles hanging dangerously from your eaves must be removed before they break off and hurt someone.   ● Beside this man *in blue flannel shirt, baggy khaki trousers, uneven suspenders, and vile felt hat*, she was small and exquisite. (Sinclair Lewis *Main Street*)

prepositional phrase with verbal object

● After cleaning my teeth, I combed my hair and put on my makeup.   ● After seeing the doctor, the patient had her prescription filled at the pharmacy.   ● After brushing my teeth, I flossed and rinsed with mouthwash.   ● After passing the security check, the traveler went to the immigration desk to get clearance to exit the country.

● On learning that Sung Min had got a higher mark than me on the last test, I resolved to study non-stop in preparation for the next test.   ● In order to understand the case, the lawyer hired a detective to get more information. ● **In order to do these sentences right**, I need to use the correct subordinate adverbial conjunction. ● **Before dating Julie**, Tom had never had a girlfriend for more than three months. ● **While riding on the commuter train**, you can also read a book or newspaper. ● (extended) **Wanting to eat better**, *have more energy, and of course lose weight*, the contestants each made some adjustments in their already demanding lives.

Beginning Sentence Primary Form 10.3:
Verbal Phrase at the Beginning of a Sentence

Code: 10TP B Verbal Phrase Present/Past Participle or Infinitive

Notes: Verbals (present or past participles) and their attendant words or phrases start off this type of addition.

Examples:

10TP B Verbal Phrase Present / Past Participle or Infinitve

● **Outlining her stand on taxes**, the politician received a standing ovation. ● **Leaning on the fence**, the cowboy surveyed the herd of cattle. ● **Looking into each other's eyes**, the young couple saw the most beautiful sight that was better than any website or historical site that a packaged tour could offer to any place in the world. ● **Leaving a tip** *on the table*, I put my coat on, paid the bill, and slipped out into the inky night. ● **Reaching the summit** *of Mt. Gumoh*, the hikers had a magnificent view of the city of Gumi. ● **Waiting for** the bus, I studied Hausa [language of Nigeria]. ● **Having been neglected as a child**, the young man did not know how to be compassionate.   ● **Writing all night**, the student finished the essay.   ● **Thrashing back and forth in the swimming pool**, the boy shouted for help. ● **Meowing loudly**, the cat kept scratching at the pantry door. ● **Jolted by the shock of the electric fence,** the elephant turned jerkily away from the village compound. ● **Born of a movie projectionist father and an amateur actress mother**, Qin learned to dance at the Local Children's Palace not long after she was able to walk. ● **Founded in 1909**, the Beijing Library has remained open 365 days a year since 1998.   ● **To dry the** clothes, she hung them on the balcony in the sun. ● **To repel the mosquitoes,** she soaked her mosquito netting in the special pesticide.

Beginning Sentence Secondary Form 10.4:
Noun Phrase at the Beginning of a Sentence
Code: 10TP B Noun Phrase
Examples:

10TP B Noun Phrase

● **Umbrella in hand,** I headed out into the misty morning rain.

● **Hat in hand,** the beggar went from door to door. ● **Diploma in hand,** the graduate stepped down from the stage and smiled for the photographers. ● **Arm in arm,** the newlyweds walked triumphantly down the busy Vancouver street. ● **Money in short supply,** the family had to economize on everything. ● **Hand in hand,** the couple walked dreamily through the park.

● **Wildflowers everywhere,** the children reveled and played on the Alpine mountain slope. ● **Arms akimbo,** my mother waited at the top of the stairs with a very serious expression on her face. ● Brightly colored tissue **caps on each head,** the children celebrated their friend's birthday in a fun and festive style.

Beginning Sentence Secondary Form 10.5:
Absolute Construction at the Beginning of a Sentence
Code: 10TP B Absolute Construction

Note: This Form, shown without explanation earlier, places additional information into the sentence though the information lacks a clear grammatical connection to the sentence. It stands grammatically alone, loosened or separated (Latin *absolūtum*), by itself, so it is called an *absolute construction*.

Examples:

10TP B Absolute Construction (noun + participle)

- **Prices skyrocketing**, the public held back on its spending.

- **Cap switched** *backwards*, the youth spent some time skateboarding in the mall parking lot. • **Poncho slung** *over his shoulders*, Pedro climbed over the Mexican hills in the cool morning mist. • *His* **blanket torn**, Linus cried on Charlie Brown's shoulder. • **Pistols drawn**, the cops were going to shoot the suspect. • **Teeth clenched**, she held on as the roller coaster ride began. • *His* **legs aching**, the soldier finished the fifteen kilometer cross-country march. • "*Its electric* **motor whirring**, the cart raced forward down the dark underground tunnel." (M. Crichton *Jurassic Park*) • **Feet shod** *in a new pair of high-tech runners*, I ran outside to catch the school bus. • **Face beaming and arms waving**, the child ran to greet her father, clutching her new report card in her hand. • **Plasma ad screens parroting their products** *all along the metro platform*, the commuters waited.

Beginning Sentence Tertiary Form 10.6:
Adjective String at the Beginning of a Sentence
Code: 10TP B Adjective Phrase
Examples:

10TP B Adjective Phrase

● *Late for class*, the student went to the principal's office to get a note. ● *Limp and paralyzed in one leg at the age of two*, Wilma Rudolph conquered polio and the taunts and jibes of her high school classmates, and went on to become the first women ever to win three gold medals in one Olympiad. ● *"Pale, shivering, with rigid features and compressed lips,* she looked an entirely altered being from the soft and timid creature she had been hitherto." (H. Beecher Stowe *Uncle Tom's Cabin*)

Beginning Sentence Tertiary Form 10.7:
Adverb Phrase at the Beginning of a Sentence
Code: 10TP B Adverb Phrase
Examples:

10TP B Adverb Phrase

● *Early yesterday morning*, the scout group packed up and slipped away in their canoes to a new frontier. ● *Sometime next week*, I have to finish typing my report and hand it in. ● *Perhaps, as a result of all her training*, Li is now a strong-minded and independent woman. ● *"Largely through science,* billions of us live on one small world, densely packed and

309

intercommunicating." (Crichton *Jurassic Park*) ● *"Up ahead,* the rectangular maintenance shed emerged from the fog." (Crichton *Jurassic Park*) ● *"More often than not,* Carol was an open book where her thoughts and feelings were concerned." (Fern Michaels *The Guest List*) ● *"Properly executed,* any of these methods can work." (Carol Jago *English Only – For the Kid's Sake* in *The Contemporary Reader* 6/e) ● *Overly excited on her birthday,* the child ran constantly to look out the front bay window to see who was arriving next for her party.

variation

● *"Moments later,* Donovan came in from the garage." (Fern Michaels *The Guest List*) ● *Last **Friday** while leaving,* I noticed a yellow envelope on the defendant's desk.

"If you know sentences, you know everything. Good sentences promise nothing less than lessons and practice in the organization of the world." p.7

'It is true that you can't get from form to content, **but it is also true that without form, content cannot emerge.** . . . Despite the familiar proverb, **it's not the thought that counts. Form, form, form, and only form is the road to what the classical theorists call "invention,"** the art of coming up with something to say. It follows that **familiarizing yourself with form independent of any content you might want to elaborate later is the way to learn how to write a sentence."** p.27

"A discipline in form is a discipline in thought." p.48

Stanley Fish
How to Write a Sentence: and how to read one (2011)

10(TP) Mid-Sentence Interruptions
Set Off with Paired Punctuation Marks

A chart for determining which punctuation marks are most appropriate for enclosing an interruption in the middle of sentences is given below:

\multicolumn{4}{Three Punctuation Marks to Set Off Interruptions}			
Covered In ...	Punctuation Mark	Property or Nickname	Intended Literary Effect
Form 9	**dash** (non-list)	*the emphasized, outstanding or highlighted comment*	used to highlight, emphasize, or make conspicuous the addition
Form 10	**comma**	*the simply expressed, usual or normal comment*	used for regular, ordinary, or mild emphasis
Form 10	**parenthesis**	the w*hispered, very slightly emphasized comment*	whispers or very slightly emphasizes the addition, almost as an afterthought or an aside

Mid-Sentence Interruptions in Form 10 Set Off with Paired Commas and Parentheses

In the previous section of the forms of Dashes in the Middle of the sentence (Form 9.d), we looked at the use of the dash to punctuate mid-sentence interruptions. In this form, we look at the use of the second and third punctuation marks (commas and parentheses) used as pairs to separate the interruption from the main part of the sentence.

A **pair of commas** or a **pair of parentheses** is used to set off a word, phrase, or clause placed in the middle of a sentence. This addition could be called an *interruption*. This means that the flow of the kernel or core part of the sentence has been deliberately interrupted somewhere about midway with the intention of adding some information that supplements in a major or minor way the information in the core part of the sentence.

In both cases, one should make sure that the inserted interruption **adds to the main idea**. Occasionally, the interruption is a kind *of candid remark from the writer,* generously offering us a tidbit of helpful or even surprising optional background information.

311

Primary 10 (TP) Three Places
Sentence Forms – Middle

10.8	Word	• I regret to say, **however**, that I will be going away soon. • It is, **undoubtedly**, the best example yet.
10.9	Noun phrase	• They lay in the shade, **their coats** *as pillows*, and talked of when they were young and carefree. • She walked on, **the heavy pot** *of water on her head*, for still another hour before she reached home.
10.10	Appositive Phrase	• Zuda (**a herb** *from the Amazon jungle*) can cure cancer. • Eva, **an undergrad** *at Jinan*, is in fine arts. • Tom and Jerry (**enemies** *since their creation*) are still cartoon favorites.
10.11	Adjective phrase	• The parents, **certain that their son was lost**, looked for the nearest police station. • Sobs, **heavy and loud**, shook the chair. [Harriet Beecher Stowe in *Uncle Tom's Cabin*]

Secondary 10 (TP) Three Places
Sentence Forms – Middle

10.12	Prepositional phrase	• Juanita, **in her first film**, is simply astonishing. • The new student, **from South America**, was warmly welcomed by the class.
10.13	Verbal Phrase	• The girl scouts, **preparing for their trip**, talked excitedly. • A mother, **loving and caring** *for her children*, cannot be replaced.
10.14	Absolute construction	• They travelled at night, **the moonlight shining down**, on foot, by horse, by train. • She danced, **her mind fixed** *on every aspect of her routine*, and went on to win.

Tertiary 10 (TP) Three Places
Sentence Forms – Middle

10.15	Adverb phrase	• Delaney's Delight (**always a good bet**) won the race with ease. • The police car, **like a cheetah** *running after its prey*, chased the speeding truck.
10.16	Insertion	• "All car owners," **he said**, "should have their car checked." [identifying speaker signal, dialogue in quotation marks] • She's better off now (**isn't she?**) than she was before. [anecdotal remark] • Ronald Reagan was an effective communicator (**some would say just a good storyteller**) when he served as president. [anecdotal remark]

Punctuation Marks for Middle of Sentence

Recall our chart of the punctuation marks that are used to demarcate additions:

Three Punctuation Marks to Set Off Additions		
Punctuation Mark	**Property or Nickname**	**Intended Literary Effect**
dash (non-list)	the *comment with flair*	used to highlight, <u>boldly emphasize, or make conspicuous</u> the addition
comma	the *comment that clarifies*	used for regular, ordinary, or <u>mild emphasis</u>
parenthesis	the *comment that whispers*	whispers or <u>very slightly emphasizes</u> the addition, almost as an afterthought or an aside

One may ask how to know which punctuation should be used to set off or enclose an addition. A student must choose whether to use **dashes** or **commas** or **parentheses** for each mid-sentence addition. In each case, the student should **read the sentence aloud**, and try to note **the degree of emphasis that is placed on the addition. As you go down the above chart, the degree of emphasis on the addition decreases; the presence of the addition is more subdued.**

Some of the **punctuation marks**, along with the sentence length and the amount of branching, collectively act in a way as an **emotional barometer**. Through them, the intensity and tone of the writer's spoken voice and mood comes through together with the message of the words. For example, **abrupt, short sentences** ending in periods may indicate tension or anxiety or panic, or in the case of a beginning learner of English – shyness; an **exclamation mark** shows excitement or surprise; question marks reflect the

315

speaker's curiosity; a **dash or pair of dashes** could show pride or congeniality on the part of the writer for including something just thought of that suddenly seems special and relevant; a **semi-colon** can show a logical or rational approach to the topic at hand; a **long, branching or complex sentence** can indicate that one is almost wallowing in delight in talking about the subject matter at hand, and has no problem in stitching together the component pieces that are intelligible and interesting into lengthy sentences.

Middle Sentence Primary Form 10.8:
Interrupting Word at Middle of Sentence
Code: 10TP M Word
Note: A word set off by a pair of commas.
Examples:

10TP M Word

• The lioness, **surreptiously**, paused by the thicket and watched the gazelle in the distance. • I understood, **clearly**, what you meant. • Yee Yeong, **carefully**, jumped over the vase. • "He could hear them, **faintly**, on the other side of the door." (Crichton)
• I regret to say, **unfortunately**, that your job performance is far below par. • Between them sat three half-buried bluish spheres — the eggs , **presumably** , of some desert monstrosity. (David W. Goldman *Reunion*) • Tawantinsuyu, **evidently**, consisted of an empire center at Cuzco with the four *suyus* (regions) placed to the north, south, east, and west.

Middle Sentence Form Primary 10.9:
Noun Phrase at Middle of Sentence
Footnote Code: TP M Noun Phrase
Examples:

10TP M Noun Phrase

● Jim and Jane lay in the shade, *their **coats** under their heads*, talking very little. ● Jane walked slowly, *a grocery **bag** under each arm*, thankful that there was enough food for the next week. ● Bill, *his **wallet** now gone*, stood at the corner wondering what to do next.

Middle Sentence Primary Form 10.10:
Appositive Phrase at Middle of Sentence
Code: 10TP M Appositive Phrase
Note: In most cases, the header or controlling word is usually the first word in the phrase, but for the appositive, there are often one or more adjectives in front of it.
Examples:

10TP M Appositive Phrase

● The Cowboys, *America's favorite football **team***, are riddled with criminal problems. ● Tracy, *both a masculine and feminine **name***, was the name they chose for their son. ● We, *the **staff** of Earlybird English magazine*, are starting a new column next month especially for you. ● They took a pedicab, *a **tricycle** with a wide enclosed back seat and a driver who has to peddle very hard*, back to the hotel.

parentheses

● Sarah (*once a brilliant **writer***) is now a housewife.

● Tom and Jerry (***enemies** since their creation*) are still cartoon favorites. ● My class project (*A **Model** of the Solar System*) won the Science and Math competition. ● A

317

herbal drink (*a **mixture** of honey, boiled onion roots, and ginger*) helped clear up his cold and sore throat quickly. • The Worldmapper website produces density-equalizing maps (**equal area cartograms**) that re-size each territory according to the data values for the variable (**literacy**, **longevity**, etc) being mapped.

***

Middle Sentence Primary Form 10.11:
Adjective Phrase at middle of Sentence
Code: 10TP M Adjective Phrase
Examples:

10TP M Adjective Phrase

• The traveler, **certain that she was lost**, looked for the nearest police station.   • The young man, **happy at the thought of seeing her again**, counted away the days and hours remaining until they would meet.   • The Christmas tree, **tall and glowing with strings of lights**, gave the living room a wonderful pine scent.   • "The animal's huge leathery wings, **translucent in the sunlight**, flapped broadly on both sides of her." (M. Crichton *Jurassic Park*)   • The marathoner, **fit and long-winded from hours of pounding the pavement**, moved into the lead in the last kilometer, and never looked back.   • Tom, **resolute and firm**, told the workers that they would have to improve production or else face layoffs.

***

Middle Sentence Secondary Form 10.12:
Prepositional phrase at middle of Sentence
(usually an adverb phrase or extended phrase)
Code: TP 10M Prepositional Phrase
Examples:

10TP M Prepositional Phrase

- They heard the news, **over the loudspeaker**, at noon the next day.
- Her eyes, **like two luminous stars**, can pull you with the gravity of black holes.
- I went to my hometown last weekend, **by bus**, and had a great time with all my middle school buddies.
- I wrote my answers recklessly, **in a hurry and without thinking**, and immediately regretted that I hadn't studied more.
- Tyrone, **because of his past criminal record**, was prevented from entering the civil service.
- The horses, *in the solitude of their stalls in the barn*, pricked up their ears when they heard the sound of footsteps.
- The porcelain doll, **of unknown origin**, fascinated archeologists far and wide.
- When I was a freshman, **in 1994**, I drank and played pool a lot. (Ha Eun Hoon, Korea)
- Martha, **because of her weight**, was unable to join the military.
- "They are, **according to the tags clipped to their pockets**, obstetricians, gynecologists, pediatricians, pediatric nurse practitioners, and pediatric RNs." (Dillard *For the Time Being*)
- "And sure enough, our mouths, **like those fireflies**, bobbed and weaved toward each other." (Amy Tan *The Hundred Secret Senses*)
- The baby, **after gurgling and cooing like a little doll**, slept peacefully through the night.

Use of Parentheses Parentheses are used as asides or additional explanations to enclose information or thoughts that (1) clarify for those who may need a bit more **clarification** to understand the first part of the sentence or the context of the sentence as a whole; or (2) a sudden thought that can be added for **humor** or for a more **personal** or **sobering** effect; (3) an **extra detail** which is woven in for interest's sake but could have been left out.

- Many of the 49 percent (**of women earning $100,000 or more who are childless**) don't want children now and probably not in the future. ● The time of youth (**roughly from age 15 to 25**) is a time of great energy, vision, idealism, and drive.
- Enthusiasts (**of all shapes and sizes**) crowded together at the starting line of the Boston Marathon. ● The children (**like a herd of turtles**) walked together towards the playground.
- The music (**like a choir of singing angels**) brings tears to my eyes. ● Then suddenly (**I never would have guessed it**), my high school classmate, Mirindi, announced that she was pregnant.

Middle Sentence Secondary Form 10.13:
Verbal phrase at middle of Sentence
Code: 10TP M Verbal Phrase
Examples:

10TP M Verbal Phrase

- The team coach, **wearing a new black sweat suit**, called the players into the change room for an important discussion.
- There he sat, **rocking back and forth** in the hammock, in the cool shade of the porch at the front of the big old house built by his grandfather.
- The wind, **giving us now a favor**, changed direction, and we were able to sail home.
- The H_2 comes from a chemical reaction, **called dissociation**, that splits the hydrogen from water.
- A mother, **loving and caring** toward her children, cannot be replaced.
- A picture, **taken professionally**, can be beautiful.
- The boy scouts, **preparing themselves** for their camping trip, could not wait until the following day.
- Magnolias and cherry blossoms, **blooming beautifully** at the start of spring, lined the campus roads.
- A single open staircase, **lit by clerestory windows above**, joins the two floors mid-building." (Kerry McPhedran in Feb/Mar. 2000 issue *Elm Street*)
- "International Women's Day, **first held in 1911**, is celebrated on March 8." (Judy Rebick *Radical Chic* Feb/Mar. 2000 issue *Elm Street*)

<u>**parentheses**</u>

- The thief (**thinking he could scale the barrier)** ran to the brick wall at the end of the alleyway.
- The mouse (**shaking like a leaf**) cowered in the corner.
- NewTurf's excellent investment profits (**made mostly from real estate**) have doubled in the last five years.

Middle Sentence Secondary Form 10.14:
Absolute Construction at Middle of Sentence
Code: 10TP M Absolute Construction
Note: Absolute construction consists of noun followed by a participle and its attendant words.
Examples:

10TP M Absolute Construction

- The trekkers, **backpacks bulging** *with tents and supplies,* pressed on to the second base camp. ● Tony and Suzy, **arms** *clasped like ivy around each other,* danced and slinked slowly and dreamily around the dimly lit cafetorium dance floor. ● "Abby stood, **her foot rooted** to the concrete, until the yellow cab was swallowed up in traffic." (Fern Michaels *The Guest List*) ● "After they left the hotel, **fingers interlocked,** they entered dirt roads to walk slowly past yellow bungalows and shafts of deep green Nipa palm." (Peter Bollington *Salvos*)

Middle Sentence Tertiary Form 10.15:
Adverb String at middle of Sentence
Code: 10TP M Adverb Phrase
Examples:

10TP M Adverb Phrase

● "The Inka homeland, **uniquely high**, was also uniquely steep, with slopes of more than sixty-five degrees from the horizontal."

(Charles C. Mann *1491: New Revelations of the Americas Before Columbus*)   ● The newborn giraffe, **awkwardly adjusting to the world outside the womb**, stood momentarily on all fours, but then fell down when he tried to walk.   ● The shuttle, **like a needle pointing to the stars**, blasted off at daybreak.   ● "He would stand with his arms straight out, **like a ghost** *walking in the night*, claiming that the spirit of nature now flowed from the tree's limbs into his."

(Amy Tan *The Hundred Secret Senses*)

parentheses

● Jane (**once thought to be very beautiful**) is now old.

● A handful of terrorists (**obviously with fewer options available day by day**) started to talk with one another about surrendering.

● She has been enjoying an amazing week after inking a deal for her memoirs (**reportedly seven figures**) with PushPull Press.

Middle Sentence Tertiary Form 10.16:
Middle Sentence – Anecdotal Insertion

Code: 10TP M Insertion

Note: This consists of indirect personal quotations, or narrator or writer or discourse comments.

Anecdotal refers not to a whole story but *to the narrator of a story or writer of an essay who interrupts their narrative or essay with either a personal observation or amplification, or a personal comment, aside, or addition.* Such comments serve to involve the reader more intimately with the author and lend a nuance, tonality, and effective flow to the writing.

An *anecdotal insertion* also lends itself to designating and referring to third-party comments and observations relevant to the text itself. This second type of anecdotal interrupter records or reports indirectly and not verbatim someone's spoken or written words or idea(s).

Quoting someone's exact words as is often done in a story or news article is another type of anecdotal insertion. If the quoted part is split or is put at the beginning of the sentence, often the interrupting part or the part at the end identifies the speaker and can even indicate something of their manner of speaking.

Such constructs are indicative of the presence of the author's unique voice, tone, and style of writing, and serve to engage the reader with the author and keep the reader's attention and focus.

Examples:

10.16   10TP M Insertion

commas

• Someone, **she was sure**, would notice. • There is no way, **you see**, that he could have done it. • The Friday night games, **mark me well**, are always exciting. [anecdotal statement] • Korean spicy soup, **I'll have you know**, is one of my favorite dishes. [writer comment]

quotation marks and comma

- "All children," **she said**, "should get vaccinated." [identifying speaker signal, dialogue in quotation marks] ● "Get a move on," **Mom shouted**, "or you'll be late!" [speaker identification and tone, dialogue in quotation marks]

parenthesis

- Through an oversight **(or else probably, if you think about it, just plain politeness)**, they don't weigh the passengers. (Barbara Kingsolver *The Poisonwood Bible*) [writer comment] ● Things are different now **(aren't** they?) than they ever were before. [anecdotal remark] ● Ronald Reagan was an effective communicator **(some would say just a good storyteller)** as president. [anecdotal remark]

dashes – (another use of the mid-sentence dash – this could have been introduced as a supplemental Form 9.8).

In each of the following, the phrase or clause appearing between the dashes is **an additional and suddenly occurring thought that may have initially been thought irrelevant but suddenly is considered important,** or **a missing fact that just surfaced and is considered essential.** The new thought is considered to be important for purposes of relevancy or clarity or detail, so the thought is immediately spliced into the sentence at the next most suitable pause point. So, we can call this the *suddenly relevant and appearing afterthought insertion*.

Another possibility is that the speaker needs a moment to gather his or her thoughts together, and such a clause as *let me see* or *wait a minute* would be inserted after the beginning of the sentence.

The last possibility is a kind of aside or tipoff or comment by the writer on a more direct level to the reader than the normal narrative writer's point of view (narrative position).

- It was – **let me see** – around the middle of February when I was there. [thinking pause clause] ● Our debt – **let me see** if I can get this right - is ballooning at the rate of $300 billion dollars per year. [thinking pause clause] ● We had set up the sting to catch the traffickers and – **as I found out later that day –** they caught Johnny Jingo at the airport trying to board a private jet. [future event tipoff, writer comment] ● Lincoln was shot in the back of the head on a Friday – **in fact, it was Good Friday –** while he was sitting next to his wife. *(The Wit and Wisdom of Abraham Lincoln* edited by Alex Ayres) [vital information insertion]

third party speech (reporter) – in this case we learn who has said something, what exactly was said, and perhaps something of the manner in which it was said.

● "In our time, **says a twentieth-century Hasidic rabbi,** we are in a coma." (Annie Dillard) ● This small house of Pascal's, **I realized,** was identical in material and design to the house in which he lived. (Barbara Kingsolver *The Poisonwood Bible*) ● The economy had gone into a slump, **they said,** and there was little hope of a short-term recovery."

● "The attempt to reestablish tuatara may provide insights into restocking other reptile populations on islands or in other ecosystems where they've been eliminated," **says Daugherty,** who described the project at last summer's meeting of the Society for Conservation Biology in Victoria, British Columbia. (Christine Mlot *Return of the Tuatara* in *Science News* Vol. 152 1997.11.8)

Primary 10 (TP) Three Places
Sentence Forms – End

10 .17	Word	● The refugee lay on the deck, unconscious. ● I stood there, **stunned**.

Secondary 10 (TP) Three Places
Sentence Forms – End

10 .18	Noun phrase	● He ate his dinner, **broccoli and all**. ● He faced towards Mecca, mind **and soul as one**.
10.19	Prepositional phrase	● The Iraqi family departed in the night, **with only a few possessions**. ● I finally finished my work, **despite the many tasks**.
10 .20	Appositive phrase	● I'd like you to meet Mr. Pak, **my manager**. ● You should climb Mt. Kilimanjaro, **the tallest mountain in Africa**.
10 .21	Verbal phrase	● They decorated the Christmas tree, **adding lights, baubles, and tinsel**. ●I could feel the rain, **falling gently on me**. ● It was a rough trip (**to say the least**).
10 .22	Absolute construction noun + participle	● They walked slowly, **minds filled** *with dreams of a life together.* ● "It snarled, **the sound echoing** *in the darkness."* Crichton Jurassic Park 314

327

Tertiary 10 (TP) Three Places
Sentence Forms – End

10 .23	Adjective phrase	• May shrugged, **indifferent to Al's angry words**. • She smiled, **happy to see her**.
10 .24	Adverb phrase	• I can finish it, **probably by Thursday**. • He moved along the path, **completely hidden from view**.
10 .25	Insertion	• "Everyone will be affected." [quotation] • They want to celebrate in a big way, **I think**. [writer comment] • This will protect the city from future flooding, **she emphasized**. [identifying speaker signal]

END OF SENTENCE

End Sentence Primary Form 10.17:
Word at End of Sentence
Code: 10TP E Word
Examples:

10TP E Word

- The boxer lay on the mat, **unconscious**. ● The Korean middle school student put his head on his desk, **overwhelmed**.

- "Ellie held the radio in her hands, **listening**." (Crichton *Jurassic Park*)

- "Hermione remained with her face lifted up, **abstracted**." (D.H. Lawrence *Women in Love*) ● "He looked at her with a long, slow look, **malevolent, supercilious**." (D.H. Lawrence) ● "The foreigners liked to eat hot and cold things together, very **unhealthy**." (Amy Tan *The Hundred Secret Senses*) ● "She started out and stopped in the doorway, **smiling**." (V.C.Andrews *Ice*)

End Sentence Secondary Form 10.18:
Noun Phase at End of Sentence
Code: 10TP E Noun Phrase
Examples:

10TP E Noun Phrase

- She stood there, **arms** akimbo.   ●Grant drove, *his **foot** to the floor*. (Crichton *Jurassic Park*)   ● The racing car went by, *a deafening blur*. ● "On the Saturday it rained, *a soft drizzling **rain** that held off at times*." (D.H. Lawrence) ● The student struggled to finish the exam, *head in a daze.*   ● The baby tested her new

mobility, *pudgy* **feet** and *tiny* **hands** *all here and there in the air.*

● The afternoon ride home was tortuous, ***pollution** and traffic

jams and bumper to bumper creeping.*   ● The blues signer's

fingers flew and danced over the strings and fret board,

***testimony** to the hours of practice done by her.*

End Sentence Secondary Form 10.19:
Prepositional Phrase at End of Sentence
Code: 10TP E Prepositional Phrase
Examples:

10TP E Prepositional Phrase

●He fought it, **like a lion.**   ● The student waited for the late

bus, **for about 40 minutes.**   ● "One reached up and scratched

his head, **with a five-fingered hand.**" (M. Crichton)   ● "Pete was

calling his name again and again, **with increasing panic.**"   (S. King

Dreamcatcher)   ● "All her suppressed, subconscious fear sprang into

being, **with anguish.**" (D.H. Lawrence *Women in Love*)   ● "Soon they were

chittering all around him, **like excited birds.**" (Crichton *Jurassic Park*)   ●

Sheena was going to perform a five-minute solo act using a silk

red handkerchief and an umbrella as props, **while dancing to**

specific Ilokano folk dance routines.   ● I used to change my

hairstyle, but now I hardly ever change it, **except for hair**

color.

extended phrase

● She spent most of her childhood taking music and dancing lessons, **at a time** *when most children her age were having fun.*

● "And the guy just stood there in his underwear, **like an android** *whose memory circuits have been about three-quarters erased.*" (King *Dreamcatcher*)

● "The Indians were descendents of ancient hunters who migrated from Asia to America across the Bering land bridge some thirty to forty thousand years ago, **about the time** *migrants elsewhere were settling the British Isles.*" (Robert V. Hine and John Mack Faragher *The American West*)   ● "One reason is that black **women** are starved to see themselves portrayed in motion pictures as real people, **with the whole range** *of human emotions.*" (Dorothy Gilliam in *Breathing Easier with a Rare Film* in *The Contemporary Reader* ed. by G.Goshgarian)   ● "In this movie food is on her mind and she forgets all about work, **except for an occasional phone call** *to see how everything is going.*" (bell hooks in Mock Feminism in *The Contemporary Reader* ed. by G.Goshgarian)   ● "'I'm every woman, it's all in me,' Chaka Khan sings, and the chords in the bass modulate optimistically upward, **in a surge of possibility.**" (Holly Brubach *Heroine Worship: the Age of the Female Icon* in *The Contemporary Reader*)

●"Scientists have since unearthed Clovis points and choppers at diggings **from** Montana **to** Mexico, Nova Scotia to Arizona." (Robert V. Hine and John Mack Faragher *The American West*)

variation This form has a clause as the object of a preposition.

●He had to do plenty of physical training, some **of which was**
martial arts.   ●"Our elderly bellhops push us aside and with
mighty huffs finish dragging in our suitcases and duffel bags,
the bottoms **of which are spattered with mud.**" (=*of which the*
bottoms are spattered with mud) (Amy Tan *The Hundred Secret Senses*)   ● "In
one L.A. school district alone, teachers have to gather and
instruct students from 80 different nationalities, just 13% **of**
whom speak English as their first language." (Rolando Flores Acosta in
Seeking Unity in Diversity in *The Contemporary Reader* 6/e)

End Sentence Secondary Form 10.20:
Appositive Phrase at End of Sentence
Code: 10TP E Appositive Phrase
Examples:

10TP E Appositive Phrase

● They hired Belinda, *a top honors cum laude* **graduate** *from*
Buffalo University who was also valedictorian for her class. ●
I met Jake, *the local fire* **chief**. ● This is Sally Strauss, my
co-worker at the bank. ● The arcology in Arizona was
designed by Paolo Soleri, *an Italian-born* **architect** *who came*
to America in the 1950s to apprentice under Frank Lloyd
Wright.   ● On these meridians there are 365 acupuncture
points, **one** *for each day of the year.*   ● I'm pleased to
introduce to you the well-known author of more than three

dozen science fiction stories, **Adrian Bruzinski**.　● She played the role of "*daoma dau*", *the* **role** *of a female who has martial arts skills in a Peking Opera.*　●The concerts will star Li Yundi, *a young but talented Chinese* **pianist** *who won first prize at the 14th International Chopin Competition in Warsaw in 2000.*

● New York State became formally known as the "Empire State", *hence the* **name** *for the Empire State Building.*　●The people might be frightening, but their world would surely be a paradise, *a golden* **land** *somewhere beyond the setting sun.* (Robert V. Hine and John Mack Faragher *The American West*)　● "These times of ours are ordinary times, *a* **slice** *of life like any other.*" (Annie Dillard *For the Time Being*)　●"At noon I stopped for the day and took my recreation by flitting all about with the bees and the butterflies and reveling in the flowers, *those beautiful* **creatures** *that catch the smile of God out of the sky and* **preserve** *it*!" (Mark Twain *Eve's Diary*)

End Sentence Secondary Form 10.21:
　　Verbal Phrase at End of Sentence
Code: 10TP E Verbal Phrase
Examples:

10TP E Verbal Phrase

● Daisies and tulips are so beautiful, **growing** *gracefully in the country fields.*　● "It looked like an ice cream vendor's pushcart, **parked** *incongruously on the badlands."* (Crichton *ibid*) ●

"Columbus called the people of the Caribbean *los Indios,*

mistakenly **thinking** *he had arrived in the East Indies."* (Robert V.

Hine & John Mack Faragher *ibid*)   ● "Within half a century "Indian" had

passed into English, used to refer to all Native Americans,

ridiculously **lumping** *together Aztec militarists, Hopi*

communalists, and Pequot horticulturalists." (*ibid*) ● "But

beyond the misty horizons of dreams was a real world,

throbbing *with human possibility."* (*ibid*)   ● "Previously,

humanity had to rely on solar flow and on wind, water, and

animal power for its sources of energy, **setting upper limits** *to*

the amount of economic activity that could be generated." (Jeremy

Rifkin *The Biotech Century*)   ● Tom finally reached the base camp,

completely **exhausted** *by the descent down the rugged*

mountain. ● "An ice cream tuck overtook them **dinging** *a*

melody and children rushed to it." (Peter Bollington *Salvos*)   ●

"Trawlers, the mega-bulldozers of the sea, drag giant, weighted

nets along the ocean floor, **destroying** *everything in their path.*

(Robert Bateman) ● "The DNA acts as a scaffold for the silver,

enabling *the scientists to make thinner wires than they can*

with conventional techniques." (C.W. in *Grainy wire self-assembles along DNA* in

Science News Vol. 153 1998.4.4)

● The car moved swiftly down the country road, **kicking dust** *in*

every direction and causing many of the hikers to cough and

gag.   ● All of the rehabilitation and flight training rooms are constructed with the raptors' welfare in mind, *each* **equipped** *with adjustable lighting, heating, ventilation, and easy cleaning features.* ● "The hypsy was small dryosaur, seven feet long, **weighing** *about five hundred pounds."* (Crichton *Jurassic Park*) ● "Later I lay in my room, still not thinking about Miss Banner, **refusing** *to give her one piece of my worry or anger or sadness."* (Amy Tan *The Hundred Secret Senses*) ● Thirty-six of the generals were women, **including the Trung sisters' mother.** ● "It loomed in the shadows and corners of our Philadelphia apartment like bats sleeping, **waiting** *to be* nudged, disturbed." (V.C. Andrews *Ice*) ● The huge crowd marched towards the palace, **tired of all the corruption** *and empty promises.* ● "Instead he attacks with a pump fake, **turning a defender's legs** into jelly and then burying a jump shot." (Nelson George in *Rare Jordan* in *The Contemporary Reader* 6/e by Gary Goshgarian) ● "Winter just seemed to be stubborn, **refusing** *to be driven* off." (V.C. Andrews *Ice*)

End Sentence Secondary Form 10.22:
Absolute Construction at End of Sentence
Code: 10TP E Absolute Construction
Examples:

10TP E Absolute Construction

● The dog stood, **tail** *wagging.* ● "The crowd is up, **heads** *weaving for better views."* (Don DeLillo *Underworld*) ● "At the door Dante turned round violently and shouted down the room, *her* cheeks *flushed* and *quivering with rage."* (James Joyce *Portrait of the Artist as a Young Man*) ●"The banks of the river closed in on both sides, *the trees meeting overhead once more.* (Crichton *Jurassic Park*) ● "...he rolled away in flight, *his* **flashlight** *swinging wildly."* (Crichton *Jurassic Park*) ●"The lobby was quiet, *chilly* **fog** *drifting* past **them.** (Crichton in *Jurassic Park*)

● "Some of the hypsilophodonts were chewing, *the* **jaws** *working."* (Crichton *Jurassic Park*) ●"They looked up at the long, low house, dim and glamorous in the wet morning, *its cedar* **trees** *slanting before the windows."* (DH Lawrence *Women in Love*) ● The student dormitory room looked a mess, **books** *and* **papers** *strewn everywhere.* ●"He froze in place, most of his weight thrown forward on his good left leg, **rifle** *raised*, **barrel** *angled* down *that interlacing tunnel of light at a cool thirty-five degrees."* (Stephen King *Dreamcatcher*) ● "Two flickering bugs were zigzagging their way toward each other, *their* **attraction** *looking* haphazard yet predestined." (Amy Tan *The Hundred Secret Senses*) ●"'What do you mean, a date?' I asked, *my* **heart** *thudding like a fist on stone."* (V.C. Andrews *Ice*) ● "She glared at me a moment and then she stepped farther into my room, *her* **eyes** *heating* over, *her* **jaw** *tightening*, *her* **hands** *folding into small fists pressed firmly into her thighs as she hovered over me."* (V.C. Andrews *Ice*) ● "Dad sat back, *his* **smile** *warming again."* (V.C. Andrews *Ice*)

End Sentence Tertiary Form 10.23:
Adjective Phrase at End of Sentence
Code: 10TP E Adjective Phrase
Examples:

10TP E Adjective Phrase

●The place is a Shangri-la, *idyllic and tranquil.*   ● "He listened on the phone and looked at his boss, Daniel Ross, *cold as an undertaker in his dark pinstripe suit.*" (Crichton *Jurassic Park*)   ● "He crouched down between the sheets, *glad of their tepid glow.*" (DH Lawrence *Women in Love*)   ●"In the classroom the last lesson was in progress, *peaceful and still.*"   (D.H. Lawrence *Women in Love*)   ●Maggie shrugged, *indifferent* to Tom's outburst.   ● "The foreigners stood like statues, *unable to speak or move.*"   (Amy Tan *The Hundred Secret Senses*)   ● "That would have been shameful – showing you care more for your sweetheart than for all your family, *living and dead.*" (Amy Tan *The Hundred Secret Senses*)   ● "They were showing him respect because he was a good student, *polite and very ambitious.*" (V.C. Andrews *Ice*)

End Sentence Tertiary Form 10.24:
Adverbial Phrase at End of Sentence
Code: 10TP E Adverb Phrase
Examples:

10TP E Adverb Phrase

● He had to prepare for the opening, *only a month away.*   ● It poured, *all day long.*   ● The commander was certain that the rebels would surrender, sooner or later, *probably within the next few days.*   ● "Our father came in late in the evening, but we were used to that: he stood in the den for a while, leaning against a doorjamb, and then he trudged upstairs, *oddly silent.*" Anna Quindlen *One True Thing*

● "Presently she adds that it was an easy labor, *only twelve hours.*" (Annie Dillard *For the Time Being*)   ● "She couldn't wait to tell my daddy when he came home from work that evening, *a little after ten.*" (V.C. Andrews *Ice*)   ● I don't visit the doctor often, *only when I'm really sick.*   ● The anxious wife waited for the results of her husband's brain tumor operation, *all night long.*   ● She was hurt, *irrevocably damaged beyond words.*

338

End Sentence Tertiary Form 10.25:

Anecdotal Interrupter/Recorder at End of Sentence

Code: 10TP E insertion

Note: This form is used when interspersing a writer's comment directly into a passage or narration. It would be a departure from a more objective viewpoint, and perhaps shows a more personal side of the writer. As well, it is used to report third-party speech – that is, to report a person's exact words to someone else.

Examples: Note that the quote marks normally used to indicate an extracted quotation have been omitted among the following except to show or record someone's direct words.

10TP E Insertion

writer/narrator comment

● Fire is beautiful; some day it will be useful, **I think**. (Mark Twain *Eve's Diary*) [writer comment]   ● The idea was a kind of time travel, and to bring them back alive, **so to speak**.   [writer comment]

● They seemed to like one another, **Bailey sensed**.   (Frances Fyfield *Deep Sleep*) [character observation]

third party speech (recorder)

● The man was detained by police, and then the investigation started, **Han said**. [identifying speaker]   ● Its upgrade is long overdue, **officials said**. [identifying speaker] ● "The economy's in a turmoil," **the financial advisor concluded.** [quotation, identifying speaker] ● They want to celebrate in a big way, **I think**. [writer comment] ● This will protect the city from future flooding, **she emphasized**. [identifying speaker signal]

● "You could have done better," **said Robin bitterly**.

[quotation, identifying speaker] ● *"Could you do better?"* **said Dinsdale lightly.** (Frances Fyfield *Shadow Play*) [quotation, identifying speaker]

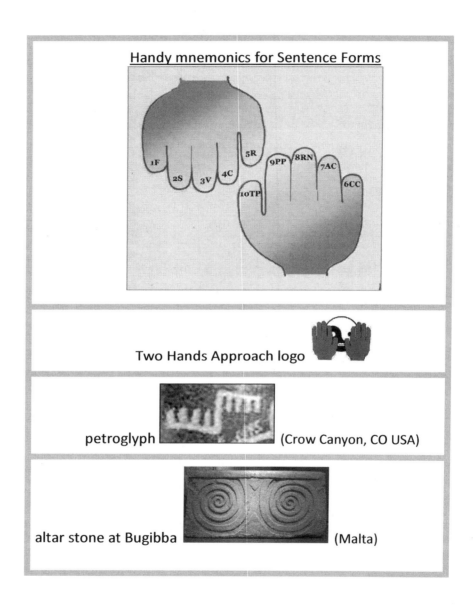

Handy mnemonics for Sentence Forms

Two Hands Approach logo

petroglyph (Crow Canyon, CO USA)

altar stone at Bugibba (Malta)

Short Codes for 10TP Three Places Sentence Forms

The charts on the next two pages presents the 10TP Sentence Forms and their short codes all together according to their placement at the Beginning, Middle, or End of the sentence. Students can use colored pencils to highlight within each of those 3 parts of the charts to indicate whether a Form is of Primary, Secondary, or Tertiary importance and usage.

10 TP Three Places

NUM-BER	SENTENCE FORM LETTER CODE	DESCRIPTION OR FORMULA	SUBFORM NOTATION (NAME OR SHORT CODE)
Beginning of Sentence			
10.1		Word	10TP B word
10.2		Prepositional phrase	10TP B prepositional phrase
10.3	**T**	Verbal phrase	10TP B verbal phrase
10.4	**P**	Noun phrase	10TP B noun phrase
10.5		Absolute construction	10TP B absolute construction
10.6	**B**	Adjective phrase	10TP B adjective phrase
10.7		Adverb phrase	10TP B adverb phrase
Middle of Sentence			
10.8	**T**	Word(s)	10TP M word
10.9		Noun phrase	10TP M noun phrase
10.10	**P**	Appositive phrase	10TP M appositive phrase
10.11		Absolute construction	10TP M absolute construction
10.12	**M**	Adjective phrase	10TP M adjective phrase

10.13	**T**	Adverb phrase	10TP M adverb phrase
10.14	**P**	Prepositional phrase	10TP M prepositional phrase
10.15	**M**	Verbal phrase	10TP M verbal phrase
10.16		Insertion	10TP Insertion
	End of Sentence		
10.17		Word	10TP E word
10.18		Verbal phrase	10TP E verbal phrase
10.19		Appositive phrase	10TP E appositive phrase
10.20	**T**	Absolute construction	10TP E absolute
10.21	**P**	Adjective phrase	10TP E adjective phrase
10.22	**E**	Adverb phrase	10TP E adverb phrase
10.23		Prepositional phrase	10TP E prepositional phrase
10.24		Noun phrase	10TP E noun phrase
10.25		Insertion	10TP E Insertion

SHORT CODE PROCEDURE WHEN INDICATING USE OF **PARENTHESES**

If parentheses are used rather than commas to frame the interruption in the middle or end of a sentence, then add parentheses around the short code for the form inside the parentheses. For example, in

*Cindy **(the youngest of three daughters)** works in a café.*

the interruption is coded – **10TP M (Appositive Phrase).**

from right fist,
flick forefinger
upwards twice

11.1	**ADD** QUESTION	● What should we do? ● What is our purpose? ● Could your assumption be wrong? ● What time are you going?
11.2	**ADD** BEGINNING VERB	● **Add** 270 ml of warm water. ● **Remove** your shoes before entering. ● **Bring** your compass.
11.3	**ADD** BEGINNING CO-ORDINATE CONJUNCTION	● **But** I really had no choice. ● **And** that's that's where I stayed. ● **So** that's it in a nutshell.
11.4	**ADD** INVERSION	● Happy was I. ● Blithe was the singing of the young girls over their test tubes. Aldous Huxley ● In the town where I was born lived a man who sailed the seas. The Beatles ● Only once has the Empire State Building sustained damaged from an aircraft.
11.5	**ADD** AFTER DESCRIPTOR (not separated by a comma)	● The evening **warm and clear**, we went for a walk. ● The new challenge was for minds **open**, spirits **willing**.

11 ADD Additional Forms

We have now described all Sentence Forms that offer a substantial amount of variation within a broader category, yet still retain a common trait with sibling forms. Surprisingly, we end up with the handy total of **10 main Forms**. But, for every general rule, there are exceptions, and in our case we still need one mixed bag of Forms before our collection can be complete.

Any attempt to organize language (or any aspect of Life or Reality) must allow for the **exceptional**, the **different**, the **unexpected**, the **marginal** that do not fit conveniently into prevailing categories. We can call the sub-forms in this group *the Lone Rangers*, since each sub-form bears no resemblance to any of the other sub-forms in the 11th group, and because they *range all over* the place in good writing.

We use the 3-letter abbreviation **ADD** for this assorted collection of forms. It deserves as much attention by the student as each of the previous 10 forms, as the Forms lend themselves to a wide range of creative possibilities when used by the aspiring writer.

 The **mnemonic** for this Form is one of the sign languages ways of signing *11*: from your closed right hand, flick the forefinger (index finger, pointer finger) *twice in quick succession* upwards.

11.1: Additional Form– Question

Code: 11ADD Question

Notes: One of the easiest forms of all. It is the root of all learning and knowledge – providing our initial greeting, and opening window to other cultures. It is our spirit of inquiry and curiosity that will never kill any cat, but might open doors, abolish wars, make new friends.

Examples:

● Who is going to the fair? ● What should we do? ● How will we get there? ● What's on TV? ● Is he really to blame? ● What time should we leave? ● Where is my wallet? ● "What could be more important for the future of our world than that we raise happy and well-adjusted, empowered and empowering children?" (Marianne Williamson *A Woman's Worth*) ● How was your trip? ● Where did we leave off last time? "What else makes sense when all is reduced to what matters?." (Marianne Williamson *A Woman's Worth*)

11.2: Additional Form - Beginning Verb

Code: 11ADD Beginning Verb

Note: This form is used constantly in self-help books. By including more of the verb forms, the pace and movement of the writing is increased, and the tone is more personal, more direct, and more dynamic.

Examples:

●*Look* at this! ●*Take* care! ●*Don't be* late! ●*Put* the dishes in the cabinet when you are finished. ●*Leave* the money with the teacher. ●*Think* before you speak. ●*Wait* a minute! ●*Stop* the ruckus, or everyone will have to go home! ●*Put on* your sweater, or you'll catch a cold! ●*Try* looking in your jacket pocket for your lost keys. ●*Turn* the left knob twice, and then push the green button. ●*Remind* yourself that you are essentially a unique being, amongst billions of unique beings. ● "*Keep* a vigil. *Stay* awake in the garden. *Hold* to the light. *Revere* goodness and integrity and truth." (Marianne Williamson *A Woman's Worth*) ●*Imagine* my surprise when I came home and saw the doorway decorated with balloons! ●*Let's collaborate* and *usher in* a glorious future. ●*Look* before you leap.

11.3: Additional Form - Beginning Coordinate Conjunction

Code: 11ADD Beginning Coordinate Conjunction

Note: Grammarians and purists may shudder at the thought of allowing students to use this form, but professional writers use it all the time, with incredible frequency once you start to observe it. This form also permits a longer moment of reflection following upon the period at the end of the preceding sentence.

The beginning conjunction connects the next sentence to the one before, and sometimes has a tone of surprise or finality.

Examples:

and

1) *And* he never thought about giving her another chance.
2) *And* they applauded with enthusiasm, for the home team had won.
3) *And* there you have it, a complete sentence beginning with "And".
4) *And* sure enough, at the end of the year, he packed up and went to China.
5) "*And* let every other power know that this hemisphere intends to remain master of its own house." (J.F. Kennedy in *Inaugural Address*)
6) "*And* the train raced on over the flat lands and past the Hill of Allen." (James Joyce *Portrait*)
7) *And*, as he was so determined, he hit the ball with all his might.
8) *And* he never thought about giving her another chance.
9) "*And* in any case, he finds he has less interest these days in such things as papers and journals and conventions and colloquia." (Stephen King *ibid*)
10) *And* that's all there is to it!

but

1) *But* you can always choose to go to the canteen instead.

2) *But* what about Melissa, she wanted to go too.

3) *But* this is not the end of the story.

4) *But* if I do not read the magazine review, I will have no idea what the play is about.

5) *"But* you could not have a green rose." (James Joyce *Portrait*)

6) *"But* was there anything around the universe to show where it stopped before the nothing place began?" (*ibid*)

7) *"But* this peaceful revolution of hope cannot become the prey of hostile powers." (J.F. Kennedy *Inaugural Address*)

or

1) *Or* you might try on the red one – I think you'd look good in red, and, besides, you don't have any red clothing at all.

2) *Or* they cut holes in the fences.

3) *Or*, at least when you are going to start talking, get it all out on the table.

4) *"Or* bring me something of alien manufacture next time you're abducted."* Neil deGrasse Tyson on NPR Science talking about *The Pluto Files*

for

1) *For* as soon as you start this system, you will find it getting easier each time.

2) *For*, in view of how little time there is, we must pack our bags and leave quickly and quietly.

3) *"For* man holds in his mortal hands the power to abolish all forms of human poverty and all forms of human life." (J.F. Kennedy *Inaugural Address*)

4) *"For* when the high priest recites the holy name and the blessing, the divine bends down and smites him." (Annie Dillard *ibid*)

so

1) *So* she buried her head in her hands, and wept profusely.
2) *So* that was all we could do.

yet

(1) *Yet* I felt sure that I could trust the newcomers on all accounts.
(2) *Yet* that wasn't the last they would hear of him.

11.4: Additional Form – Inversion of regular order

Code: 11ADD Inversion

Note: Inversion of subject and verb is usually kept for questions and poetry, but certain instances of it are found in modern prose.

Examples:

inversion (distant descriptor-S-MV)

In the following examples, the underlined part is the *inverted and relocated part*, and the ↑ is the part of the sentence from where the inverted part was taken.

  a. <u>Sleek and silver-haired</u> the managers may be ↑, but by and large they tend to be men whose principal concerns involve money. (Waddell)
  b. <u>Young and svelte</u> she was ↑, a mystical presence as fresh as morning dew.
  c. <u>Tired</u> I was ↑ – tired of the pain, tired of the lies, tired of the struggle.

348

inversion (distant descriptor-MV-S)

In the following examples, the <u>underlined parts</u> are the parts that have traded places.

    d. "<u>Sublime</u> is <u>the dominion of the mind over the body</u>, that can make flesh and nerve impregnable, and string the sinews like steel, so that the weak become so mighty." (H. Beecher Stowe *Uncle Tom's Cabin*)

inversion (dir.object-MV-S)

In the following example, the <u>underlined part</u> is the *inverted and relocated part*, and the ↑ is the part of the sentence from where the inverted part was taken.

    e. "<u>The whole other world, wet and remote</u>, he had to himself ↑." (DH Lawrence *ibid*)

inversion (MV-S)

In the following examples, the <u>underlined parts</u> are the parts that have traded places.

    f. <u>Through the blue sky</u> soared <u>the young eagle</u>.
    g. <u>In the cold blue depths</u> moved <u>the whale</u>.
    h. <u>Over the hills and valleys</u> flies <u>a lonely bird</u>.
    i. "<u>There</u> fell from the sky <u>a very bright and beautiful star</u>." (Oscar Wilde *The Star-Child*)
    j. "<u>In front of them, at the corner of the lake, near the road</u>, was <u>a mossy boat-house under a walnut tree</u>." (D.H. Lawrence *ibid*)

split MV with inversion

In these examples, the subject is at the middle or end of the sentence, and the <u>main verb</u> is split.

- k. "*Standing* on the riverbank *were* two dilophosaurs." (= Two dilophosaurs were standing on the river bank.) (Crichton *ibid*)
- l. *Hovering* above my enclave of bedsheets *were* at least two mosquitoes whose buzzing woke me up.
- m. Only once *has* the Empire State Building *sustained* damage from an aircraft.

11.5: Additional Form – The After Descriptor

Code: 11ADD After Descriptor
Note: This is an unusual and infrequently encountered construction, but for that reason is all the more noteworthy when used effectively. In this form, a noun is followed by an adjective or multiple-words-adjective. Usually, one or a series of adjectives follows a noun, with no punctuation in between.

noun after-descriptor

1. His wallet **empty**, he was reduced to begging.
2. She rated the movie **suitable**. (see Form 1F 1.4 F_{obj})
3. The evening **warm and clear**, the neighborhood kids played baseball on the corner lot.
4. They are hooked on keeping their bodies **thin** and weight **down**.
5. My mind a total **blank**, I stood there motionless.
   [occasionally the after–descriptor can be a noun]

7th Century Use of the *Noun Of* Form

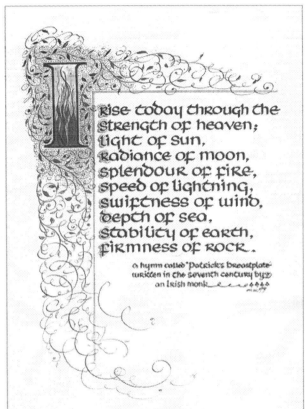

I rise today through the
strength of heaven;
light of sun,
radiance of moon,
splendour of fire,
speed of lightning,
swiftness of wind,
depth of sea,
stability of earth,
firmness of ROCK.

a hymn called "Patrick's breastplate"
written in the seventh century by
an Irish monk

Calligraphy by Muriel Watson

11 (ADD) Additional Forms II

	Additional Forms	Examples
11.6	**ADD** NOUN OF noun + of + noun	Some types of *Noun-of* constructions are commonplace and matter-of-fact: **possession** (*conquest of Peru, voice of Whitney Houston*); **thing container** (*basket of apples, jar of jam*); **animal quantifier** (*herd of cattle, pride of lions*); **human quantifier** (*group of people, a few of us, majority of workers*); **qualitative specifier** (*sign of progress, speed of construction, tone of voice, guarantee of quality*); **material specifier** (*sheet of paper, heart of stone, nerves of steel*). 　　The examples below, however, are what we term ***impact duo Noun of***s. They connect words of power, creating an unlikely but powerful juxtaposition. Often metaphors, *impact duos* appeal to our visual sense.

- **Oceans of sadness**... Richard Marx
- ...the **chimes of freedom** flashing... Bob Dylan
- The baseball game was a **comedy of errors**.
- ...this **hive of activity**... Aldous Huxley
- I was afraid to utter one negative comment or **iota of hesitation.** V.C. Andrews
- I'm dizzy with joy, crying with relief, because I feel the **clarity of peace, the simplicity of trust, the purity of love.** Amy Tan *The Hundred Secret Senses*
- He strives vainly for **crumbs of dignity** as he watches everything he holds dear swept into the **dustbin of history.** Robert J Connors

11ADD Additional Forms (continued)

11.6: Additional – Noun Of
Code: 11ADD Noun of

Notes: We see *Noun Of* constructions in quite a few commonplace areas in English: **possession** (*conquest of Peru, voice of Whitney Houston*); **thing container** (*basket of apples*), **thing partitive** (*piece of paper*); **animal quantifier** (*herd of cattle, pride of lions*); **human quantifier (human partitive)** (*group of people, a few of us, majority of workers*). For the most part, **these types of** *Noun Ofs* **work** *limited* **word magic.**

However, the most important *Noun Of* construction is the ***impact duo Noun Of***. It brings together two words in a rare, often figurative, association; as a result, our imagination is challenged to discover and savor the beauty and power of this new momentary kinship.

We provide examples of each below.

noun-of (possession)

The *noun-of* phrase has a much wider application and usage than to **indicate possession**, though it does that also, with elegance, formality, and dignity. When describing the writings of Charles Dickens or William Shakespeare, we would much rather refer to the *novels of Dickens* or the *sonnets of Shakespeare* than say *Dicken's novels* or *Shakespeare's sonnets*. Likewise, if a person (such as Whitney Houston) has a wonderful voice, we might prefer to say *the amazing voice of Whitney Houston* rather than *Whitney Houston's amazing voice*.

These next examples show a kind of possession of one thing by or over another: *span of time, loss of soul, hand of treason, ground of dreams, change of mind.*

noun-of (container) (1) thing container, (2) thing quantifier

(sometimes called *measure word, classifier,* or *partitive*), **(3) thing composition**

①thing container: *box of cereal, bowl of soup, bottle of wine, basket of apples, vial of pills, jar of honey, pocketful of dreams, barrel of monkeys;*

② thing quantifier (or partitive): *pane of glass, ream of paper, stack of books, kilo of sugar, strand of hair, cube of sugar, slice of bread, brick of cheese, drop of water, bar of soap, lock of hair, fleet of boats, pile of papers, pair of tweezers, blob of paint, wad of banknotes, block of ice, sheet of paper, round of applause, pinch of salt, speck of dirt, pair of jeans, pair of socks, piece of advice, breath of fresh air, shot of liquor, head of lettuce, bunch of bananas;*

③thing composition: *coat of leather, dress of silk, wall of concrete, slab of concrete, block of ice, cloud of dust, gust of wind, . . .*

noun-of (animal quantifier)

Included in this form are all of the unique quantitative nouns that English uses for **collections of animals** (*flock of sheep, a herd of cattle, herd of elephants, litter of pups, pack of wolves, swarm of bees, school of fish, gaggle of geese, colony of ants, etc.*)

noun-of (human quantifier)

Also included are **numeric or quantitative terms that refer to groups of humans**: *lots of people, a few of us, many of the group, some of them, group of students, a handful of people, the people of Guangzhou, school of thought, defenders of wildlife, Council of Europe, President of France, Inns of Court, etc.*

noun-of (place or institution indicator)

Here we include legal titles for institutions and places: *University of Pittsburg, Republic of Ireland, County of York, Bank of China, House of Representatives, Institute of Advanced Physics, Bureau of*

Investigation, Department of Immigration, Museum of Art, School of Esthetics, Institute of Technology, Province of Ontario, ...

noun-of (impact duo)

*Noun Of*s can deal, however, with much more important things than counting and possessing. They bring together two words in a rare, often figurative, association.

Consider: *"A **wave of terror** swept across the city."* The noun-of phrase *wave of terror* conjures up a more powerful image than if we had said *"The terrorists hit the city for a third time."*

A **wave** might be associated with the endlessly repeating, arching, and breaking walls of water rolling in to the shore, or it can be associated with something like a tsunami, while **terror** is a negative, deeply felt emotion that we usually associate with disruption, death, and disorder. As a result, our imagination is challenged to discover and appreciate the connection and symbolic meaning in this fused image.

Upon close observation of text material from both non-fiction and fiction sources, it appears as though we could expand our definition to include gerunds, perhaps more in the second position than the first, and create again a phrase that is memorable.

For example, we could include:

- **noun + of + gerund**
  - (emotional gerund **noun of**): *joy of having fun, joy of making money, fret of having kids, joy of cooking, trauma of losing a parent, fear of losing your investment, pain of breaking up, fear of flying, ...*
  - (technical gerund **noun of**) *art of making pickle, the process of gathering votes, the method of baking bread, repercussions of changing your mind, outcome of wanting to quit your job,...*
- **gerund + of + noun**:
  - outpouring of music, slackening of pace, numbing of feeling, ...

One could also argue that a **noun + of + the + noun** should qualify, as in:

-

- **noun + of + the + noun**
  - shore of the lake, beginning of the week, cusp of the curve, powers of the proletariat, wisdom of the saints, melting pot of the best of all cultures, hands of the sky-god, soup of the day, bulk of the stock market correlation matrix, …

The later grouping could also be expanded to included **Noun + of + a + Noun,** or **Noun + of + some + Noun** (*mind of a child, image of a dying soldier, scent of a woman, enactment of a law, diary of a nobody, torture of some protesters, arrival of some assistance, control of some media, price of some commodities, …*), and so on, and we would have hundreds or even millions of such phrases, many of which have to do with the idea of *possession* or *attachment*, or of the immediate proximity of something, or the nature of something in a certain context.

Since we identify our forms as *basic* ones, and since we do not want to come to a full and final conclusion that the above examples should or should not be included, we leave to the reader to decide the suitability of such phrases in their own writing. It's a **matter of choice**, and the **sense of style** preferred by the writer, and the **richness and degree of imagination** that they wish to employ, or they may even wish to create an **illusion of coolness** or a certain **amount of variety** so that – without any **fear of failure** whatsoever – the writer will feel a **sense of freedom, a taste of delight** about experimenting with these forms, and even experience a **burst of insight** or a **splurge of *creativity*** when pondering what to write next.

So, let there be *porous boundaries* in our **classification of Forms**. The **art of styling sentences** is **the art also of buying time** and of waiting for the **crucible of imagination** to heat up and then for her liquid contents to come pouring forth.

The short voiced word ***of*** is a thin partition, a paper wall, put between two connected giants.[4] Somehow, though, shorn and shrift

---

[4] These days, many young people use an inappropriate phrase that resembles the noun-of. This popular phrase, *kind of*, is used with almost as much frequency as its equally ubiquitous and vaporous partner *like* in casual conversation, as in: *I'm feeling (like)* kind of *tired. You look* kind of *lonely.* The intended meaning here is *rather* or *a bit* or *somewhat*; either of

of non-essential *the* or *a* or other specifiers, the words in the paired phrase resound with all their in its simplicity.

Thus, it is the hunch of the co-authors that the more poetic ***impact duo*** **noun of** will probably be the one that gives the most satisfaction and inspiration to both writers and readers, but that the other "sub-types" of *Noun Of*s should be noticed and used on demand at the appropriate occasion.

Coming up:

We prefaced this section with a calligraphic rendering of a passage from the 8th century that consists of *Noun Of*s. We explained the kinds of *Noun Of*s including the *Impact Duo*. Next there is an extensive chart of sample *Impact Duo*s. No attempt has been made to sort or rank the *Impact Duo*s in the chart. We then provide sample student and professional model sentences exemplifying the many kinds of *Noun Of*s. Finally, we take a look at the imaginative, robust, and surprisingly frequent use of the ***Impact Duo*** *Noun Of* form by two famous literary critics, **Northrop Frye** and **Roland Barthes**.

---

those replacements would be a much better choice of word than *kind of*. **Kind** of is <u>not</u> a **noun-of impact duo**. It is hoped that

11 (ADD) Additional III
Some *Noun Ofs* including *impact duos*

power of words	beacon of hope	sounds of silence
chimes of freedom	pulse of life	ounce of prevention
wail of sorrow	sigh of relief	rule of thumb
brink of extinction	heart of darkness	fit of laughter
tingle of positivism Cintra Wilson	scarcity of food	change of heart
purity of motive	joy of reunion	catalog of misery Ursula LeGuin
voice of authority	pain of separation	bundle of nerves
sorrows of empire Chalmers Johnson	power of attorney	trail of tears
simplicity of design	admission of guilt	tokens of peace Maya Angelou
glory of love	nudge of curiosity	invasion of privacy
ribbon of darkness Marty Robbins	surge of power	veil of silence
breastplate of justice	poison of hate	verge of extinction
mountain range of emotions [solbeam]	jungle of possibilities Thomas Knierim	pangs of consciousness
brink of war	maps of meaning Jordan Peters	flash of inspiration
blanket of fear	fists of hostilities Maya Angelou	expression of gratitude
mote of matter Maya Angelou	nightmares of abuse Maya Angelou	majesty of religion Cintra Wilson
spark of truth	tone of voice	trail of blood
society of equals	ease of access	sprig of hope
shred of evidence	break of dawn	beehive of activity
models of thought	prospects of success	likelihood of defeat
announcement of victory	delusion of grandeur	vote of confidence

358

11.6   ADD *noun of* thing container or partitive

●My new **pack of cards** is on the table. ●Last winter, the Winnipeg family ordered two **truckloads of firewood** from Botany 9 to use in their woodstove. ●Jessie ordered a **round of beer** to share with his friends and associates. ●For Valentine's Day, Charlie had a large **bouquet of flowers** sent to his girlfriend's workplace. ●I bought some **cloves of garlic** to use in the ragoût. ●Where did that **jar of pickles** go that I just bought? ●The law student found that there was a **plethora of cases** that had to be reviewed by the end of the week. ". . . the Administration nevertheless dutifully worked its way through the United Nations, basing its case on a **parcel of lies** and half-truths, . . ." Philip Giraldi at *antiwar.com*

● "**Handful of dust, handful of dust**
  Sums up the richest and poorest of us
  True love makes priceless the worthless
  Whenever it's added to a **handful of dust**"
      (lyrics to *Handful of Dust* by Patty Loveless)

11.6   ADD *noun of* animal quantifier

●The **herd of buffalo** grazed peacefully in the lush green meadow. ●Someone spied a **pod of whales** in the distance and the B.C. tourists got their cameras out, ready for action. ●The **clutch of chicks** ran around like balls of yellow fluff.

11.6 ADD *noun of* human quantifier or partitive

●A large **group of people** assembled in front of the main building. ●A **bevy of beauties** surrounded the Canadian popstar, clamoring for his autograph. ●**Lots of people** came to the wedding. ●A **gaggle of reporters** gathered around the sole survivor. ●A **crowd of civilians** inspected the damage at the police station. ●**Some of you** may remember that I talked about the threats to ancient forests last year. ●The **majority of workers** are in favor of the 4-day work week. ●A **truckload of workers** arrived at the sugarcane field. ●The **cluster of** Chilean mining disaster **survivors** were bused away for medical check-ups.

11.6 ADD Impact Duo *Noun Of*

●China was often considered the **kingdom of bikes**. ●We need new **models of thought**. ●The new software has a definite **ease of operation**. ● "...they tumbled, in a **pile of** immeasurable **giggle**, on the withered turf under the verandah ..." (H.B. Stowe *Uncle Tom's Cabin*) ●The **speed of construction** with which the new apartment went up was remarkable. ● "But, in general, behavioral effects were simply beyond the **reach of understanding**." (Crichton *Jurassic Park*) ●With the **approach of spring**, the pod of blue whales moved up the British Columbian coast. ●"...his comrade marveling much at his foolishness and **softness of heart**." (Oscar

Wilde *The Star-Child*) ● "In this fatal **moment of choice** in which we might begin the patient **architecture of peace** we may also take the last step across the **rim of chaos**." (Thomas Merton) ● "Now I'm drowning in a **river of tears**." (Eric Clapton) ● "And leaders meeting in London must supply **the oxygen of confidence** to today's global economy, to give people in all our countries renewed hope for the future." (UK PM Gordon Brown) ● <u>Book titles</u>: *Empire of Illusion: The End of Literacy and the Triumph of Spectacle* (Chris Hedges), *Frames Of Mind: The Theory Of Multiple Intelligences* (Howard E. Gardner) ● <u>Song, group, album, book titles</u>: *Masters of War* (Bob Dylan), *Eve of Destruction* (Barry McGuire), *Sound of Silence* (Paul Simon), *Mothers of Invention* (Frank Zappa), *Flavors of Entanglement* (Alanis Morissette), *Sultans of Swing* (M. Knopfler, Dire Straits) ● "I'm dizzy with joy, crying with relief, because I feel the **clarity of peace**, the **simplicity of trust**, the **purity of love**." (Amy Tan) ● "**cloak of fiction**" (Peter Carey *The Paris Review Interviews*) ● "A **crest of intention**, a roar **of purpose**, a sluice of slick, purpled body that Lacy quickly lifted into the mother's arms, . . ." (Jodi Picoult *Nineteen Minutes*)

Northrop Frye Notices the *Noun of* Form

We first discovered and elaborated on the *Noun Of* Form and then later found that the Canadian literary critic Northrop Frye had noticed and described one particular variation of the *Noun Of* Form – the *adjective* noun-of *noun*. Below are his observations on this specific instance of a *Noun Of* Form:

> In the twentieth century it was succeeded in favor by another phrase of "the **adjective noun of noun**" type, in which the first noun is usually concrete and the second abstract. Thus: *the pale dawn of longing, the broken collar-bone of silence, the massive eyelids of time, the crimson tree of love.* I have made these up myself, and they are free to any poet who wants them, but on examining a volume of twentieth-century lyrics I find, counting all the variants, thirty-eight phrases of this type in the first five poems.
>
> The fusion of the concrete and abstract is a special case, though a very important one, of a general principle that the technical development of the last century has exposed to critical view. All poetic imagery seems to be founded on metaphor, but in the lyric, where the associative process is strongest and the ready-made descriptive phrases of ordinary prose furthest away, **the unexpected or violent metaphor** that is called *catachresis* **has a peculiar importance. Much more frequently than any other genre does the lyric depend for its main effect on the fresh or surprising image**, a fact which often gives rise to the illusion that such imagery is radically new or unconventional. From Nashe's *Brightness falls from the air* to Dylan Thomas's *A grief ago*, the emotional crux of the lyric has over and over again tended to be this **"sudden glory" of fused metaphor**.

Anatomy of Criticism Princeton University Press 1957 15th ed. [emphasis added]

Frye's observation is an astute and fair, yet inadequate tribute to the powerful, prevalent, and yet larger category of the *Noun of* Form. We have outlined, explained, and exemplified all the sub-types of *noun ofs* with much greater detail. Poets and playwrights have long used this form, and now this **dash of poetry**, this **allusion of inclusion** has crossed over into mainstream non-fiction, and is now a hallmark of good, imaginative writing, as if from a **mill of metaphor**.

Roland Barthes' Frequent Use of *Noun of*s

In his collection of essays and talks entitled *The Rustle of Language*, French post-structuralist, linguist, philosopher, and literary critic **Roland Barthes** shows that he has an affinity, knack, and zest for what we call the *Noun Of sentence* form. The title itself is a direct give-away.

Below we list *some* of the *noun of*s (of both the prosaic and poetic or *impact duo* type) with which he has peppered many of his 45 passages.

burst of ideas, ... fears, delights, desires, oppressions		realm of structure	fragment of desire
delight of reading		society of consumption	lovers of writing
laws of argument		discourse of desire	wellspring of literature
flow of ideas		dawn of linguistics	disorganization of biography
garland of years		rustle of language	indecision of genres
snare of contradictions		retinue of friends	destruction of stereotypes
chain of discourses		power of language	shocks of fashion
offset of circularity		immobility of prattle	progress of discursivity
vanity of meta-language		voices of plurality	odor of language
pith of puns		odor of seriousness	violence of language
division of meanings		rigging of interpretation	space of speech
distribution of genres		experience of limits	energy of exclusion
prestige of method		shudder of meaning	floodgates of time
explosion of tendency		transcendence of egotism	strategies of writing
feats of discourse		scraps of identity	polyphony of pleasures
artifices of writing		man of statements	apocalypse of culture
figures of system		violence of effacement	combat of languages

A page ago, we mentioned that **Northrop Frye** noted this construction, but did not highlight its significance and power; likewise, above, we see that **M. Roland Barthes** uses these forms but has not noticed himself the uniqueness of this form. For the first time in this book, this form is brought to the public eye for the *doors of understanding* it might open, the *curtains of fantasy* it might lift, and the *reservoirs of meaning* that it might reveal.

11 (ADD) Additional Forms IV

	Additional Forms	Examples
11.7	**ADD** ESPECIALLY	● I like fruit, **especially mangoes.** ● I love all reptiles, **especially Australian Bearded Dragons.** ● You should read this story, **especially the last part.**
11.8	**ADD** FRAGMENT	● Another great week. ● Surely not. ● Extraordinary. ● The years of giving. ● Too hard even to try! ● Never! ● Quite the opposite! ● Too much! ● Splendid! ● Awesome! ● A must-see site! http://tr.im/okfrag http://tr.im/crat2
11.9	**ADD** EXCLAMATION	● It rained all the time we were there! ● We won! ● I can hardly believe it! ● Let's hit the road! ● What a voice!
11.10	**ADD** COMPOUND	This involves the use of *compounds* (**more than one**) of **subjects, objects, main verbs, descriptors, and/or prepositions**. Often, the items are put *in parallel constructions*, effectively giving the text and ideas discernible structure and unity.

● Compound (main) verbs
The policeman **listened** and **wrote**.
Log on, open heart, **blog out.** China Daily ezine.chinadaily.com.cn

● Compound subjects
●**Canadians, Koreans**, and **Japanese** participated in the research.

● Compound subjects and and compound (main) verbs
Bruce and **Bjorn played** hard and then **rested**.

● Compound direct objects
Ben sent **postcards** and **letters**.
Jen sent **postcards, email**, and **letters**.

● Compound (main) verbs, one of which has compound direct objects
We **went** to the store, **bought** some **groceries** and a **newspaper**, and **ambled** home.

11 (ADD) Additional Forms ᵥ

	Additional Forms	Examples
	ADD COMPOUND continued	Pay close attention when using compounds. Make sure that parts are treated equally and are arranged properly as to avoid confusion.

11. 10	• <u>Compound distant descriptor</u> He was **young** and **naive**. The plan was **incomplete** and **flawed**. So you **become** 21, **turn** 30, **push** 40, **reach** 50, and **make it** to 60. George Carlin on Aging • <u>Compound (main) verbs with direct objects</u> Tracy **wrote** a poem and **read** it to her granny. • <u>Compound (main) verbs with one direct object</u> Stella **buys** and **re-sells** clay tiles. • <u>Compound indirect objects</u> The teacher told **Jon** and **Jen** their quiz results. • <u>Compound objects of a preposition</u> He spoke in clear **tones** and memorable **phrases**. • <u>Compound relative clause</u> It is clear **that your writing has improved** and **that you still aspire** to your dream of writing a book. • <u>Compound adjectives</u> The **frisky** and **young** puppy played in front of the house. • <u>Compound adverbs</u> The teacher waited **patiently** and **quietly** for the answer.

11.7: Additional - especially

Code: 11ADD especially

Note: This form is a very simple form to master. Keep in mind that it is somewhat informal, so be sure not to overuse it (*especially* by beginning writers!). It must have a comma or dash or parenthesis in front of it. **Do not confuse it with the adverb *especially*** (meaning *considerably*)**,** as in *I was especially tired after the hike.*

Examples:

- Tina likes sweaters – *especially* cashmere ones.

- I love everything about Sumi, *especially* the way she makes me laugh.   • I love the musical style of The Slugs, *especially* how they switch genres several time in a song.

- We are impressed with all that you have done, *especially* your work with the immigrant workers and the poor families in the outlying areas. • Cautious on account of the dark, the bus driver drove very slowly, *especially* around hairpin curves. • There are many mosquitoes, *especially* at night.   • "In her collaborations with scientists, Frankel has learned a great deal about science and about the special needs and constraints of scientific photography, *especially* the necessity for technical accuracy."

(Ivars Peterson in *The Art of Scientific Photography* in Science News Vol 152)   • "His struggle to find the right words, or any words, was clearly visible on his face, **especially in his eyes**." (V.C. Andrews *Ice*)   • "But having been raised in a Korean immigrant family, I saw every day the exacting price and power of language, **especially with my mother**, who was an outsider in an English-only world." (Chang-rae Lee in *Mute in an English-Only World* in The Contemporary Reader 6/e)

11.8: Additional – fragment
Code: 11ADD Fragment
Notes: There will be an outcry against the admissibility of this form to our inventory of forms. We include it because professional writers use it sparingly but effectively in fiction and general documentary works.

Examples:

(1) You may think that he decided to study in the big city. **Not so**.

(2) You may think she has given up. **Never!**

(3) "And there it was on the navicomp screen. **The planet Earth. They were home."** (Grant Naylor *Red Dwarf*)

(4) "Lister rang up 'no sale' on the old-fashioned wrought-iron till, and counted the week's takings. **Fourteen dollars and twenty-five cents. Another great week."** (Grant Naylor *Red Dwarf*)

(5) "The swirling interactions of humanity's three brains, like the shuttling of cups in a shell game, deftly disguise the rules of emotional life and the nature of love. Because people are most aware of the verbal, rational part of their brains, they assume that every part of their mind should be amenable to the pressure of argument and will. **Not so.** Words, good ideas, and logic mean nothing to at least two brains out of three [referring to the reptilian, limbic and cortical brains]. **Much of one's mind does not take orders."** (Thomas Lewis MD, Fari Amini MD, Richard Lannon MD *A General Theory of Love*)

(6) **Not this day or any day.**

(7) **Not with his family's consent.**

(8) **And no sight of relief anytime soon.**

(9) **Memorable and magical.**

(10)   **Extraordinary.**

(11)   **Too challenging even to attempt.**

11.9: Additional – Exclamation

Code: 11ADD Exclamation

Notes: *To exclaim means to cry out or speak suddenly and loudly*, as in a moment of surprise, strong emotion, or protest. An occasional exclamation can elevate a text or passage by bringing near life-like sound to it.

Examples:

● My G-d, we did it!

● "Our substitute for electricity!" (Barbara Kingsolver: *The Poisonwood Bible* 114)

● "Well, that did it!" (*ibid* 129)

● We won the tournament!

● We've almost reached the end of all the Sentence Forms!

11.10: ADDITIONAL – COMPOUND

Code: **11ADD Compound**

Notes: This form could be considered a repeat of $S_{A \text{ and } B}$ or any other of the Series forms – the **careful and balanced use of more than one subject, object, main verb, descriptor, or prepositional phrase**. Strict parallelism says that the look of each element running parallel should be the same; in most cases, this means the elements must be the same Kind of Word. Thus, *"She likes basketball, tennis, and squash."* might be acceptable, whereas *"She likes basketball, swimming, and to chat online with her classmates."* is slightly askew. Depending on your tone, this lack of uniformity might have a certain desired effect, and you can let it stand. For ease of clarity and to bring cohesiveness, continuity, and unity to your sentences, however, standard practice normally requires the consistent use of similar Kinds of Words in both parallel constructions and in series.

EXAMPLES:

- After dinner, I will **finish** the homework *and* **do** some reading.

- He **went** outside *and* **looked** at the sky.

- The car went **down** the street *and* **around** the corner.

- The young bears **wrestled** with each other, **rolled** down the hill, **chased** each through the clearing.

- "A grey, wet wind **hinted** at sleet, **cut** through clothes, **lifted** umbrellas, **attacked** faces." (Frances Fyfield *Deep Sleep*)

- The gypsy rover **rode** over the hill, *and* **down** through the valley so shady...

- **In** your heart and **in** your mind is where I want to be.

- She earned a college **degree** in electrical engineering *and* a master's **degree** in computer science in Canada.

- In this interview, Vanna Karina talks about her **career moves** *and* her **struggles** as a mother.

- "**Phenomena** *could be* rigorously examined, observed, and described *and* **experiments** *could be* made repeatable with exacting **standards** *and* **protocols**, something that was far more difficult to achieve in a **manuscript** *or* **oral** culture." (J.Rifkin *The Biotech Century*)

● "Finally he **squatted** back on his heels *and* **looked** over his work with an earnest, furrowed forehead." (Barbara Kingsolver: *The Poisonwood Bible* 114)

S. Guarrigues

11ADD Additional Forms Short Codes

		11 ADD Additional Forms	
NUMBER	**SENTENCE FORM LETTER CODE**	**DESCRIPTION OR FORMULA**	**SUBFORM NOTATION (NAME OR SHORT CODE)**
11.1	ADD	Question	11ADD Question
11.2		Beginning verb	11ADD Beginning Verb
11.3		Beginning coordinate conjunction	11ADD Beginning Coordinate Conjunction
11.4		Inversion	11ADD Inversion
11.5		Near descriptor Adjective or adverb near descriptor	11ADD Near Descriptor
11.6		Noun of	11ADD Noun of
11.7		Especially	11ADD Especially
11.8		Fragment	11ADD Fragment
11.9		Exclamation	11ADD Exclamation
11.10		Compound	11ADD Compound

When you have written and shared several individual examples of Forms 10 and 11, you should incorporate three to four instances of forms 10 and 11 in a three to four paragraph essay. You should also incorporate a varied selection of earlier sentence forms in the essay, especially one or more examples of Form 9. Once again as in the previous three assignments, you should have a **title** that suggests, focuses, and unifies the main theme of their essay, and *you should **notate and footnote** the sentence forms that you employ.*

Below are some essays by earlier students to serve as models for this assignment.

INDOOR ROCK CLIMBING GYMS **by Destiny Larberg**

Rock climbing has become an increasingly popular sport, but for beginners the great outdoors is not the best place to start.**1** To rock climb outdoors is expensive and not always safe; therefore, more and more people are choosing indoor rock climbing gyms as a starting point.**2**

Indoor rock climbing gyms are now fairly common in large cities around the world.**3** Membership fees are at an affordable price and can be purchased for one year, one month, or even one day at a time.**4** The expensive outdoor anchoring gear is not needed in a gym, and the personal gear (shoes, harness, chalk bag) can be rented on a daily basis for a very low price.**5**

Choosing an indoor rock climbing gym is not only cheaper, but is also far safer than climbing outdoors.**6** There are no rock slides, no inclement weather, no bad anchoring for climbs to worry about.**7** Everything in the gym is safely constructed with varying routes for all skill levels.**8**

Moreover, staff members are always available to give help and answer questions.**9**

For just 20 bucks, you can try out the wonderful sport of rock climbing for a whole day at an indoor rock climbing gym.**10** And don't worry about the weather forecast – an indoor gym is ready for climbing, rain or shine.**11**

Sentence Forms:

1) 6CC But
2) 3V Infinitive; 9PP Expansive Semi-colon; 2S The Pair; 3V Present Participle (2)
3) 3V Present Participle
4) 2S Choice Series
5) 3V Present Participle; 6CC and; 10TP M (Noun Phrase); 2S Triple Force
6) 3V Gerund (2); 3V Present Participle; 6CC But; 4C Not only, but
7) 5R Word; 2S Triple Force; 3V Gerund; 3V Infinitive
8) 3V Present Participle
9) 10TP B Word; 3V Infinitive
10) 10TP B Prepositional Phrase; 3V Gerund; 3V Present Participle
11) 11ADD Beginning Conjunction; 9PP Dash Break; 3V Gerund; 10TP E Adjective Phrase; 2S Choice Series

MY FUTURE OF POSSIBLE POVERTY by Joshua Gatcomb

It was a hot sunny afternoon when I discovered my future – poverty.**1** My latest venture as an entrepreneur was to sell lemonade during the hottest summer on record.**2** Lemon World, the produce giant, had exponentially raised the price of lemons due to the drought.**3** I made the mistake of selling below my cost, losing money on every sale.**4** I would have lost my entire life savings if it had not been for Sarah, my sister.**5**

Once I discovered my *faux pas*, I worked two extra hours a day; Sarah, four extra hours a day.**6** Sarah had three rules (patience, practice, persistence) that kept the business from filing chapter 13 (for bankruptcy).**7**

I think back on those playground days while I am flipping burgers.**8** Money, greed, power – all of these things blinded me.**9** Yes, it was a hot sunny afternoon when I discovered my future: poverty comes to those who fail to count their costs, husband their resources, and work hard and earnestly to progress.**10**

Sentence Forms:

1) 8RN When; 9PP Dash E Word
2) 3V Infinitive
3) 10TP M Appositive
4) 3V Gerund; 3V Present Participle
5) 7AC If; 10 TP E Appositive
6) 7AC Once; 9PP Stylish Semicolon
7) 10 TP M (Appositives); 2S Triple Force; 8RN That; 3V Gerund; 10TP E (Prepositional Phrase)
8) 7AC While
9) 2S Triple Force; 9PP Dash B Wrap-up
10) 10TP B Word; 7AC When; 9PP Explanation Colon; 8RN Who; 3V Infinitive (2); 2S Standard Series; 2S The Pair

A CITY OF DREAMS by Trucquynh Hua

Everyone has at least one dream, one goal, and one hobby.**1** I always dream of visiting new places and trying new things, so travel is one of my hobbies.**2** In my opinion, traveling should be fun and relaxing, as well as provide new learning opportunities.**3** I discovered three amazing vacation destinations – Paris, Berlin, and Amsterdam – during my European tours.**4**

Paris is my favorite city: it has many interesting and historical sites; there are many wonderful restaurants with amazing and delicious food; it is also a fashion capital of the world.**5** Paris is the largest city in France as well as its capital; furthermore, it is considered to be one of the greatest cities in the world.**6** The Eiffel Tower, the Cathedral of Notre Dame, the Louvre, and the Arc de Triomphe – all are famous Paris landmarks.**7** The most distinctive symbol of Paris is the Eiffel Tower. From the third-level of this magnificent structure, it is possible to see all across the lovely city.**8** After witnessing the ironwork of the tower, one may then wish to visit the famous Gothic Cathedral of Paris, Notre Dame.**9** This gorgeous cathedral is a repository of French art and history; moreover, it represents the geographical and spiritual heart of France.**10** Another must-see attraction in Paris is the Louvre – the world's most impressive and largest art museum.**11** Most of the Louvre's collections come from six countries: French paintings and sculptures; Egyptian antiquities; Greek antiquities; Italian paintings and sculptures; Dutch paintings; and Islamic arts.**12** This famous museum contains more than 350,000 priceless objects, including the Mona Lisa and the Venus de Milo.**13** Moving from indoors to outdoors, one can enjoy the beautiful glass pyramids (Pei's Pyramids) outside of the Louvre.**14**

From the Louvre, one can stroll down the Champs-Elysées – one of the world's most famous avenues – to see the Arc de Triomphe.**15** It is Napoleon's triumphal arch; in addition, in the center of the arch flickers the eternal flame on the Tomb of the Unknown Soldier, a victim of War World I buried on 11 November 1920.**16**

After pleasing the eyes with Paris's famous landmarks, one needs to please the stomach with some delicious Parisian food.**17** Good food and restaurants are easy to find in Paris.**18** A very popular appetizer and French delicacy is *escargot* which is merely just snails.**19** There is a popular chicken entrée called *coq au vin*.**20** One of the delicious desserts found in Paris is *crème brûlée*; it is like chocolate pudding and brown sugar, and it is very rich and creamy.**21** France is also renowned for its pastries. They have the best in the world!**22** Paris also has many elegant and formal restaurants if that is what one prefers.**23** In addition, there are many casual sidewalk cafés and restaurants with food that is both fast and cheap.**24**

Besides distinguished as well as delicious food, Paris is no doubt the fashion capital of the world.**25** The city has many famous designer clothing stores: Gucci, Versace, Valentino, Louis Vuitton, Prada, Chanel, and Christian Dior.**26** Beautiful supermodels come to Paris to do fashion shows and photo shoots.**27** Fashion shows mainly consist of models walking down a runway while showing off high fashion clothing.**28** Most people who attend fashion shows are people of high society.**29** An average Parisian will not wear designer clothing. Only the rich and the famous can afford designer clothing; furthermore, they always want to be wearing the latest fashions.**30** Fashion is a big part of French culture.

Overall, Paris is certainly one of the most beautiful and exciting cities in the world.**31** There are many interesting and historical sites in this fabulous city.**32** It has great food and restaurants.**33** And it is the place to go for the best names in the fashion industry.**34** I hope to come back to Paris – a city of dreams – in the near future.**35**

Sentence Forms:

1) 5R Word; 2S Standard Series
2) 3V Gerund (2); 2S The Pair; 6CC So
3) 10TP B Prepositional Phrase; 2S The Pair; 4C As Well As; 3V Present Participle
4) 9PP Dash M Appositives; 2S Standard Series
5) 9PP Explanation Colon; 9PP Trio Semicolon; 2S The Pair (2)
6) 4C As well as; 9PP Expansive Semicolon
7) 9PP Dash B Wrap-up; 2S Standard Series extended
8) 10TP B Prepositional Phrase; 3V Infinitive
9) 10TP B Prepositional Phrase; 3V Gerund; 3V Infinitive; 10TP E Appositive
10) 9PP Expansive Semicolon; 2S The Pair (2)
11) 9PP Dash E Appositive; 2S The Pair
12) 9PP Numeric Precursor Colon; 9PP Difficult Semicolon Long Items In List; 2S The Pair (2)
13) 10TP E Verbal Phrase; 2S The Pair
14) 10TP B Verbal Phrase; 4C From To; 10TP M (Appositive)
15) 10TP B Prepositional Phrase; 9PP Dash M Appositive; 3V Infinitive
16) 9PP Expansive Semicolon; 10 TP E Appositive Phrase; 3V Past Participle
17) 10TP B Prepositional Phrase; 3V Gerund; 3V Infinitive
18) 2S The Pair; 3V Infinitive
19) 2S The Pair; 8RN Which
20) 3V Past Participle
21) 9PP Complicated Semicolon; 2S The Pair (2)
22) 11ADD Exclamation
23) 2S The Pair; 7AC If; 8RN What

24) 10TP B Prepositional Phrase; 2S The Pair (2);
    8RN That
25) 10TP B Prepositional Phrase; 3V Past Participle;
    4C As Well As
26) 9PP List Colon
27) 3V Infinitive; 2S The Pair
28) 3V Present Participle; 3V Gerund;
29) 8RN Who
30) 2S The Pair; 9PP Expansive Colon; 3V Infinitive
31) 10TP B Word; 2S The Pair
32) 2S The Pair
33) 2S The Pair
34) 11ADD Beginning conjunction; 2S The Pair
35) 9PP Dash M Appositive Phrase

MORE STUFF by Melinda Robertson

Fifteen years ago when my husband and I got married, we were like most young couples, in that we had no stuff.**1** The term "no stuff" means that we did not have the basic tangible objects needed to maintain a home.**2** We didn't have furniture, dishes, linens – all of the things that most reasonable people expect to see in a home – nor did we have the money to buy them.**3** It was rough for a while, but it was fun.**4** We slept on the floor (with our clothes on because we didn't have any blankets) and ate (sitting on the floor) off of paper plates.**5** We didn't have a TV, so we did what most newlyweds do to amuse themselves – a lot.**6** However, as the saying goes, all things change with time and, in our case, with the acquisition of 'stuff'.**7**

It all began innocently enough, when we didn't have any stuff: we bought it, because we needed it.**8** Unfortunately, because we didn't have a lot of money, it was cheap stuff.**9** Over time, we replaced the cheap stuff, with something more expensive.**10** As my husband and I have gotten older, fatter, and wiser, we've outgrown, discarded, and even sold some of our stuff.**11** We've even bought new stuff to replace the perfectly good stuff that we *already have,* but aren't using, because we put it in storage before we moved to Japan.**12** (Which means that we are double-stuffed.)**13** Now, we're beginning to buy larger, more luxurious, built-to-stand-the-test–of-time type of stuff.**14** And, with every new purchase, we promise ourselves that we're going to keep it forever and ever – until we both die – and will it to an unsuspecting family member.**15**

In fact, we now have so much stuff that we don't have anywhere to put anything, and no more room to grow.**16** As a military family, we change duty stations and move to a different city, state, or country about every three years — and it has become a nightmare.**17** It's a hassle to move when you have so much stuff.**18** It took the moving company three whole days to box up our household goods and pack it into crates, so that it could be shipped from California to Japan.**19** Once it arrived in Japan, it took one day for the moving company to unload the crates and put the boxes in our new house, and three whole weeks for my husband and I to unpack the boxes and organize everything.**20** At times like that, you wonder how you managed to collect so much stuff, and you fantasize about getting rid of it.**21** After all, there was a time when we didn't have anything except each other, and it wasn't so terrible.**22**

Don't get me wrong, having "stuff" is great.**23** All this "stuff" means that we have the necessities and luxuries of life, that in the beginning we did without.**24** For instance, nowadays, my husband and I own three cars – two of which are in Japan with us, and one (brand new) in long term storage back in California.**25** That makes our days much easier when we have to carpool to work, coordinate grocery shopping trips around the bus schedule, and keep a taxi service on speed dial obsolete.**26** We now have nice furniture, plenty of dishes, a TV in every room, and enough towels and blankets to supply a small army.**27** I'm very grateful for all of the things that we have, and I feel that my husband and I have been blessed.**28** I just think that we could probably *de-junk* a little and get rid of some of the burdensome stuff.**29**

Sentence Forms:

1) 10TP B Noun Phrase; 7AC When; 10TP E Prepositional Phrase; 8RN That
2) 8RN That; 3V Past Participle; 3V Infinitive

3) 2S Triple Force; 9PP Dash M Appositive Phrase; 8RN That; 3V Infinitive (2); 6CC Nor
4) 6CC But
5) 10TP M (Prepositional Phrase); 7AC Because; 10TP M (Verbal Phrase)
6) 6CC So; 8RN What; 3V Infinitive; 9PP Dash E Word
7) 10TP B Word; 7AC As; 10TP M Prepositional Phrase
8) 7AC When; 9PP Explanation Colon; 7AC Because
9) 10TP B Word' 7AC Because
10) 10TP B Prepositional Phrase; 10TP E Prepositional Phrase; 11ADD After Descriptor
11) 7AC As; 2S The Pair; 2S Standard Series (2)
12) 3V Infinitive; 8RN That; 6CC But; 7AC Because; 7AC Before
13) 11ADD (Fragment); 8RN That
14) 10TP B Word; 3V Infinitive; 2S Triple Force
15) 11ADD Beginning Conjunction; 10TP B Prepositional Phrase; 8RN That; 3V Infinitive; 9PP Dash M Adverbial Clause (supplemental); 3V Present Participle
16) 10TP B Prepositional Phrase; 8RN That; 3V Infinitive (2); 6CC And
17) 10TP B Prepositional Phrase; 2S Choice Series; 9PP Dash Break
18) 3V Infinitive; 7AC When
19) 3V Present Participle; 3V Infinitive; 2S The Pair; 7AC So That (supplemental); 4C From to
20) 7AC Once; 3V Present Participle; 3V Infinitive (2); 2S The Pair (4)
21) 10TP B Prepositional Phrase; 8RN How; 6CC And; 3V Gerund
22) 10TP B Prepositional Phrase; 7AC When; 6CC And
23) 11ADD Beginning Verb; 3V Gerund
24) 2S The Pair; 8RN That (2)
25) 10TP B Prepositional Phrase; 10TP B Word; 2S The Pair; 9PP Dash E Adjective Phrases (numeric); 10TP M (Adjective Phrase)
26) 7AC When; 3V Infinitive; 2S Standard Series
27) 11ADD Noun of; 2S Standard Series extended; 3V Infinitive

COMMON SENSE by Betty Warren

I remember growing up.**1** If you did something stupid, you were held accountable.**2** We were all raised – or should have been – to be responsible for our own actions, or at the very least to display an iota of common sense on occasion.**3** Clearly, this is no longer the case.**4**

The perfect example: Several school districts throughout the United States have banned tag, chase, and touch football.**5** Why?**6** Sadly, children are no longer required to be responsible for what they do on a playground.**7** Instead of being sent to the principal (as was done in my day), hiring a lawyer now seems to be the standard.**8** Not only does this apply to schools, but it unfortunately applies to literally everything we do and everywhere we go.**9** Under the ruse of protecting our children, we are unwittingly creating a society of an extremely litigious nature**10**.

The point I am trying to make is that nobody has to be responsible for what they do anymore, and our children are learning this from a young age.**11** There must be teams of lawyers on stand-by, just waiting for people to call and report that they have done something reckless or irresponsible, and need to know who they can sue for that.**12** Don't believe me?**13** Just go home and start reading the warning labels on everything that you own.**14** As crazy as some of them might sound, be assured that they are there because someone, at sometime, has committed these insane acts and has sued someone for their own stupidity.**15** Instead of teaching our kids how to call a lawyer, maybe we need to get back to the basics, and teach them a little common sense.**16**

Sentence Forms:

1) 3V Gerund
2) 7AC If
3) 3V Infinitive (2); 9PP Dash M Anecdotal Interrupter; 2S Choices Series

4) 10TP B Word
5) 11ADD Fragment; 9PP Explanation Colon; 2S Standard Series
6) 11ADD Question
7) 10TP B Word; 3V Infinitive; 8RN What
8) 10TP Prepositional Phrase; 3V Gerund (2); 10TP M (AC As Clause); 3V Infinitive
9) 4C Not Only, But; 2S The Pair
10) 10TP B Prepositional Phrase; 3V Gerund
11) 8RN Missing That; 3V Infinitive; 8RN That; 8RN What; 6CC And
12) 10TP E Adverbial Phrase; 3V Infinitive; 2S The Pair; 8RN That; 11ADD After Descriptor (2); 8RN Missing That; 8RN Who
13) 11ADD Question
14) 11ADD Beginning Verb; 10TP B Word; 11ADD Compound; 3V Gerund; 3v Present Participle; 8RN That;
15) 7AC As; 8RN That; 7AC Because; 10TP M Prepositional Phrase; 11ADD Compound
16) 10TP B Prepositional Phrase; 3V Gerund; 8RN How; 3V Infinitive (2); 11ADD Compound

DANNY DANDRUFF by April Turner

Who is that one person in school you will always remember?**1** Everyone has one. Is it the school athlete, head cheerleader or that funny, weird person that everyone knew but no one talked to?**2** I remember my person. His name was Daniel Randolph. Everyone knew Daniel as Danny: Danny "Dandruff" Randolph.**3** Danny was a pretty normal kid; indeed, he wanted to fit in like everyone else.**4** But Danny had one small problem – dandruff.**5** He tried everything: Head & Shoulders, medication, and a priest.**6** Nothing Danny tried worked.**7** Looking back I sometimes feel bad: making fun of him, when it was clear he couldn't help his problem.**8** I even remember our high school prom and how we ruined it for him.**9**

Danny was a scrawny, weak, little boy.**10** He didn't have many friends, although he was very friendly to everyone.**11** We didn't care how nice he was.**12** All we cared about was the fact that he had dandruff.**13** And I don't mean a little bit of dandruff!**14** It was out of control, and it was everywhere: in his hair, on his eyebrows, and on his clothes.**15** Sometimes, I would sit in class and just stare at it.**16** It truly amazed me, for it was not possible to have so much dandruff.**17** One time I actually thought I saw more appearing.**18** Right there in class, right before my eyes.**19**

Danny tried to do something about the dandruff, but it didn't matter to us.**20** We saw him with the big, white bottle of Head & Shoulders in the show room, after gym class.**21** We saw the pamphlets, explaining the use and aide effects of the medication issued to him by doctors.**22** We even knew that he went to the town priest praying that it would just go away.**23** But it did not go away; instead, it lingered on – seeming to grow bigger and stronger, thicker and whiter every day.**24**

Everyone was sure Danny had outgrown the problem by high school, or that is what we all hoped.**25** The first day of school promptly ended that rumor.**26** The next four years went on without change. Before we knew it, senior prom was just around the corner.**27** It was the talk of the school. Everyone was going crazy trying to figure out what to wear, who to take, and how to get there.**28** No one stopped to wonder if Danny was even going, until the prom nominations came out.**29** I almost fainted: Danny Randolph nominated as prom king.**30** It was absurd.**31** Who would do such a crazy thing?**32**

Inevitably, prom night came.**33** When the votes were counted, no one could believe their ears – "Dandruff Randolph" prom king.**34** He was more surprised than anyone. Randolph walked to the stage with a look of awe on his face.**35** He had finally been accepted – after all these years.**36** We clapped and cheered, as they placed the crown upon his head.**37**

I wasn't sure whether I was clapping at how comical the whole ordeal was, or if I was genuinely happy for him.**38** I don't think anyone knew.**39** But before we knew it, the joke was played.**40** Instead of glitter and confetti, a bucket of white powdery flakes had been poured all over Daniel Randolph.**41** We were in shock. The whole Gymnasium went silent – and then immediately erupted into laughter.**42**

Looking back, I am ashamed of how cruel we once were as kids.**43** "Daniel Randolph, King of Dandruff," we chanted the rest of our high school days.**44** I sometimes wanted to stand up for him, although there were other times I wanted to join in.**45** I don't know if I would change anything about the past, but I do feel guilty every time I think about that night at our senior prom.**46** What was I to do?**47** "Danny Dandruff" looked hilarious up there covered in those powdered flakes.**48** I don't think they knew how much it would hurt him.**49** We all kind of thought he was used to the teasing by then.**50** After all, he was a symbol at our school; we gave him a motto and everything: "Randolph and dandruff – you can't have one without the other".**51** The prom nomination and the bucket were like the closing to a chapter in our lives that we would always remember.**52** It was our way of saying goodbye and saying, in our immaturely insensitive and even cruel way, have a nice life to a friend that we would never forget and might never see again.**53**

Sentence Forms:

1) 11ADD Question; 8RN Missing That
2) 11ADD Question; 2S Choice Series; 2S Compact Duo; 8RN That; 6CC But
3) 9PP Explanation Colon
4) 9PP Expansive Semicolon; 3V Infinitive
5) 11ADD Beginning Conjunction; 9PP Dash E Word
6) 9PP List Colon; 2S Standard Series
7) 8RN Missing That
8) 10TP B Verbal Phrase present participle; 9PP Explanation Colon; 3V Gerund; 7AC When
9) 8RN How; 11ADD Compound
10) 2S Triple Force
11) 7AC Although
12) 8RN How
13) 8RN Missing That; 8RN That
14) 11ADD Beginning Conjunction; 11ADD Exclamation
15) 6CC And; 9PP Explanation Colon; 2S Standard Series
16) 10TP B Word; 2S The Pair (or 11ADD Compound)
17) 6CC For; 3V Infinitive
18) 10TP B Noun Phrase; 8RN Missing That; 3V Present Participle

19) 1ADD Fragment; 5R Keyword
20) 3V Infinitive; 6CC But
21) 2S Compact Duo; 10TP E Prepositional Phrase
22) 10TP E Verbal Phrase present participle; 2S The Pair; 3V Past Participle
23) 8RN That (2); 3V Present Participle
24) 9PP Expansive Semicolon; 10TP Dash E Present Participle; 3V Infinitive; 2S Rhythmical Pairs
25) 8RN Missing That; 6CC Or; 8RN What
26) 11ADD Noun Of
27) 7AC Before
28) 3V Present Participle; 3V Infinitive (3); 8RN What; 2S Standard Series
29) 3V Infinitive; 8RN If supplemental; 7AC Until
30) 9PP Explanation Colon; 3V Past Participle
31) 1F Descriptor
32) 11ADD Question
33) 10TP B Word
34) 7AC When; 10TP E Noun Phrase
35) 11ADD Noun of
36) 10TP Dash Break
37) 2S The Pair; 7AC As
38) 8RN Whether supplemental; 8RN How; 8RN If supplemental
39) 8RN Missing That
40) 11ADD Beginning Conjunction; 7AC Before
41) 10TP B Prepositional Phrase; 2S The Pair
42) 9PP Dash Break
43) 10TP B Verbal Phrase present participle; 8RN How; 11ADD Inversion
44) 10TP B Noun Phrase; 10TP M Appositive
45) 3V Infinitive (2); 7AC Although
46) 8RN If supplemental; 6CC But; 8RN Missing That
47) 11ADD Question; 3V Infinitive
48) 3V Past Participle (2)
49) 8RN Missing That; 8RN How
50) 8RN Missing That; 3V Gerund
51) 10TP B Prepositional Phrase; 9PP Association Semicolon; 9PP Explanation Colon; 2S The Pair; 9PP Dash B List WrapUp variation
52) 2S The Pair; 3V Gerund; 8RN That

53) 3V Gerund (2); 5R Keyword; 11ADD Compound;
    10TP M Prepositional Phrase; 2S The Pair; 8RN
    Missing That; 11ADD Compound

SPORTS, LAUNDRY, AND TRAVEL by E.H. Ha

I enjoy playing sports, doing laundry, and travelling.**1**

Playing sports makes me feel happy and more energetic.**2** So, I want to do them every day, but sometimes I don't have enough time, especially nowadays.**3** I used to play basketball regularly, but now I am too busy.**4** For example, tomorrow I must take exams in two subjects, and then I must give a class presentation on Monday .**5**

After playing sports, I like to take a shower and do laundry.**6**

Doing my laundry and then seeing wet, clean clothes, I feel fresh.**7** I feel cleansed, renewed, energetic again and happy.**8**

As well as sports and doing laundry, I like to travel.**9** On the one hand, I enjoy travelling to other places in the world; on the other hand, I explore local sites and scenes on my bicycle.**10** Usually, I don't have any special plans, and I never know when I'll start when I travel.**11** However, when the day is right and I feel like going outside, I just start – going anywhere, any place.**12**

During my trip, sometimes I feel freedom, sometimes loneliness, and sometimes I feel thrilled.**13**

For example, once I couldn't find an inn.**14** Did you know that some small villages don't have any inns?**15** So, I had to go to another village over the hills and along very long, narrow paths (no lights, no people) late at night.**16** At that time, I felt freedom, loneliness, thrills, and I sang a song, very loudly.**17**

And I felt exhilarated, comfortable with myself, rising to the challenge of darkness, uncertainty, and the unknown.**18**

Sports, doing laundry, and travel are three activities that engage my interests and feelings, and suit my temperament and personality.**19**

Sentence Forms:

1) 3V Gerund (3); 2S Standard Series
2) 3V Gerund; 2S The Pair
3) 10TP B Word; 3V Infinitive; 6CC But; 11ADD Especially
4) 3V Infinitive; 6CC But
5) 10TP B Prepositional Phrase; 6CC And
6) 10TP B Prepositional Phrase; 3V Gerund; 3V Infinitive;11ADD Compound infinitive with their objects
7) 3V Present Participle (2); 11ADD Compound participles with their objects; 2S Compact Duo
8) 2S Triple Force; 11ADD Compound adjectives
9) 4C As well as; 10TP B Correlative Phrase; 3V Infinitive
10) 10TP B Prepositional Phrase; 3V Gerund; 4C On the one hand; on the other hand supplemental; 9PP Opposition Semicolon; 2S The Pair [alliteration]
11) 10TP B Word; 6CC And; 8RN When; 7AC When
12) 10TP B Word; 7AC When; 3V Gerund; 9PP Dash E Verbal Phrase present participle
13) 10TP B Prepositional Phrase; 5R Keyword; 2S Standard Series
14) 10TP B Prepositional Phrase
15) 8RN That; 11ADD Question
16) 10TP B Word; 3V Infinitive; 11ADD Compound prepositional phrase; 2S Compact Duo; 10TP M (Compact Duo); 5R Word
17) 10TP B Prepositional Phrase; 2S Triple Force; 6CC And; 10TP E Adverb Phrase; [alliteration]
18) 11ADD Beginning Conjunction; 2S Triple Force; 2S Standard Series
19) 2S Standard Series; 8RN That; 2S The Pair (2)

FINDING YOUR OWN CHEESE by Melissa Hatfield

When a scientist raises a mouse, they must teach it, care for it, and feed it (lots of cheese).**1** After several years of this, however, the scientist will put the mouse to the ultimate test: finding its own cheese.**2** The scientist will conduct this experiment by placing the mouse in a maze, putting some cheese at the end, and then setting it free.**3** Now, without any help, the mouse must find its own way through the maze, find the cheese, and feed itself.**4** If the experiment is successful, the scientist – with a sense of hesitation – will be able to release the mouse to live on its own.**5** With the skills and knowledge the scientist taught it, the mouse will be able to go on and lead a productive life.**6**

Parents are just like the scientist, and we as children are just like the mouse.**7** Think about it: parents first care for, teach, and feed us (sometimes even with lots of cheese).**8** After several years of this and after many obstacles and challenges (they seem to create them just for us), they make us face the ultimate test: finding our own way through life.**9** Although they don't place us in an actual maze or place cheese at the very end, they do kick us out of the house at a certain age and just like the mouse – without any help – they expect us to make our own decisions and our own money.**10** They also expect us to find our own dreams and certainly to find our own cheese (so we no longer have to eat theirs).**11** If this experiment proves successful, the parents – with lots of joy and happiness – will set their children free.**12**

Quickly, the parents then lock the doors behind them and throw a party.**13** So, the next time you speak to your parents, and they give you a hard time about how you run your life, just say: "Mom and Dad, weren't you the ones who wanted me to find my own cheese?"**14**

Sentence Forms:

1) 7AC When; 2S Standard Series; 10TP E (Noun Phrase noun of)
2) 10TP B Prepositional Phrase; 10TP M Word; 9PP Explanation Colon; 3V Gerund
3) 2S Standard Series; 3V Gerunds (3)
4) 10 TP B Word; 10TP B Prepositional Phrase; 2S Standard Series
5) 7AC If; 9PP Dash M Prepositional Phrase extended; 11ADD Noun of; 3V Infinitive (2)
6) 10TP B Prepositional Phrase; 2S The Pair; 8RN Missing That; 3V Infinitive (2); 2S The Pair
7) 6CC And   [figure of speech – similes developing into an analogy]

8) 11ADD Beginning Verb; 9PP Explanation Colon; 2S Standard Series; 10TP E (Adverb Phrase)
9) 10TP B Prepositional Phrase (2); 2S The Pair; 10TP M (Insertion Writer Comment); 9PP Explanation Colon
10) 7AC Although; 11ADD Compound verb (2); 9PP Dash M Prepositional Phrase; 3V Infinitive; 2S The Pair
11) 11ADD Compound infinitive; 3V Infinitive (3); 10TP E (Insertion Writer Comment)
12) 7AC If; 10TP Dash M Prepositional Phrase; 2S The Pair
13) 10TP B Word; 11ADD Compound verb
14) 10TP B Word; 6CC And; 8RN How; 10TP E Insertion Quotation; 2S The Pair; 8RN Who; 3V Infinitive

Exam #1:
FORM-SPECIFIC EXAM
(Specified Forms Used, Notated, Footnoted)

After you have finished the 4 required writing assignments, the time has arrived to write an in-class exam. However, this exam does not come at the midpoint of the course, but almost at the end.

In this exam, you will be given 1.5 to 2.5 hours to complete an essay with a focused title, using required, specified Sentence Forms. At the beginning of the exam class, you and your classmates may nominate 2 topics of your own choice and the teacher will nominate 3 other topics for a total of 5 topics. You must choose 1 of the 5 topics as the theme of your composition, giving your essay a **more focused, original title**.

*This form-specific exam requires you to **use, notate, and footnote** specified Sentence Forms*. The teacher will give you the specified mix of required Sentence Forms to use in your composition. You do not have to use every form required, but should use most of them.

Below is a sample list of required Sentence Forms that a teacher might specify for this exam, followed by actual examples of essays written by students in class for the form-specific exam.

- 2 of 2S Series
- 3 of 3V Verbals
- 2 of 4C Correlative
- 1 of 5R Repetition
- 2 of 6CC Coordinating Conjunction

389

- 4 of 7AC Adverbial Conjunction
- 2 of 9PP Colon
- 2 of 9PP Dash
- 2 of 9PP Semicolon
- 2 of 10TP Three Places
- 1 of 11ADD Additional

You should be allowed to consult your charts or books or notes to assist you in writing the essay as well as notating and footnoting the sentence forms.

LOSING THE NOTES by Matt Ormita

Music is men's highest art form, perhaps men's highest achievement, and what is so amazing is that it is not tangible.**1** Music fills the world with color, beauty, emotion.**2** Inspiration, sadness, anger – all this and more can be generated just by listening to one minute of sound.**3** It's so fascinating.

What I find so magnificent about music is that it can take you into a time warp.**4** Driving to school one day, I turned on the radio and Groove Theory was playing.**5** All of a sudden, all of these memories from freshmen year came back to me.**6** I could remember my friends – some were still my friends and some no longer – dancing around in the lunchroom and singing the exact tune that was playing in my car at that moment.**7** Dozens of memories came back to me within a minute's time, and I had my own little video yearbook playing in my mind.**8** I sat in my car watching it play back, and I laughed, screamed, and cried all at the same time.**9**

I love older music: there was just more happiness and hope to it.**10** In today's music, there just seems to be anger and more anger.**11** Our society today is based on negativity. This has spawned off more furious styles of music: rap, hip-hop, grunge rock.**12** Look at our generation – we reflect our music perfectly.**13** We have no direction, no guidance, no inner confidence.**14** We commend kids that swear at their elders and steal from honest workers; however, we laugh at kids who help an old lady across the street.**15** Society needs a change, and perhaps it should start with the music.**16** What happened to the good old 60's when hippies smoked pot and sang songs of love and peace and harmony?**17** There's one thing that generation had that our generation lacks – hope.**18** There's no longer a hope for change or for something better.**19** There is just a realization of what is.**20**

This is just my own personal opinion: When the arts go down, so too will the quality of life.**21** And again, in my own personal opinion, the music has collapsed in quality.**22** It all sounds the same: There are no different textures; there are no really different styles; there is no real beauty.**23** The longer our generation lets the destruction continue, the more life will remain stagnant.**24** So let's bring it back to what it was all about in the beginning – beauty, color, emotion.**25**

Sentence Forms:

1) 10TP M Adverb Phrase; 8RN What; 8RN That
2) 2S Triple Force
3) 9PP Dash B List Wrap-Up; 3V Gerund; 11ADD Noun of
4) 8RN What; 8RN That
5) 3V Present Participle; 6CC And (comma omitted for if clauses are short)
6) 10TP B Adverb Phrase
7) 9PP Dash M Noun Phrase, 2S The Pair; 5R Word; 3V Present Participle (2); 8RN That
8) 11ADD Noun of; 6CC And
9) 3V Present Participle; 6CC And; 2S Standard Series
10) 9PP Explanation Colon; 2S The Pair
11) 10TP B Prepositional Phrase; 3V Infinitive; 2S The Pair; 5R Keyword
12) 9PP Explanation Colon
13) 11ADD Beginning Word; 9PP Explanation Colon
14) 5R Word; 2S Triple Force
15) 8RN That; 11ADD Compound verb; 9PP Expansive Semicolon; 8RN Who
16) 6CC And
17) 11ADD Question; 7AC When; 2S Lyrical Series
18) 8RN That (2); 9PP Dash E Word
19) 2S Choice Series
20) 8RN What

The Jazz Improv Solo   by Aaron Marshall

Charlie Parker, Dizzy Gillespie, John Coltrane – all are jazz legends known for their improv solos.**1** For a jazz musician, playing a solo on the spot is more than playing random notes and making it sound good.**2** There are basic techniques that a musician must learn.**3** The improv solo is much like a piece of writing: it should have a beginning, middle, and end.**4** There should be a guiding thesis (or unifying mood or tone to the music), supporting ideas (or a melody in the music), and facts (or the series of notes that comprise the piece).**5** And, of course, the musician should appeal to the audience, express his or her own feelings, and enjoy playing the music.**6**

The intro – like writing – should usually state the "thesis" and mood of the solo.**7** The musical thesis can be derived from a choral refrain, an excerpt from a popular song, a melodic string put together by the musician, or a composite of more than one of these.**8** The thesis is what the rest of the solo will be based on.**9** If the thesis is played in a certain key, the rest of the solo should be played in the same key.**10**

There is one major feature to one's solo – individuality.**11** The middle is considered the meat – the foundation – of the solo.**12** This part of the solo is where the player gets to include his or her own style and individuality as well as state their ideas and feelings, including variations of the thesis, harmonic notes, and the occasional color note (a note that sticks out from the rest, yet seems to give the melodic phrase "color").**13** And you must always keep the solo moving.**14**

Once the solo has stated its thesis and ideas, the only thing left is the conclusion.**15** How do you conclude a solo?**16** Usually, you sum it up with a restatement of the thesis.**17** Finally, fade out or restart the original song, letting the rest of your accompanying musicians know that you are finished and have made your point.**18** Remember to play what you feel, and playing improv will begin to seem not only a lot easier but also a lot more fun once you keep these steps in mind.**19**

Sentence Forms:

1) 9PP Dash B Wrap-up; 2S Triple Force; 3V Past Participle
2) 10TP B Prepositional Phrase; 3V Gerund (3);
3) 8RN That
4) 9PP Explanation Colon; 2S Standard Series
5) 2S Standard Series; 3V Present Participle (2); 10TP M (Noun Phrase) (3); 8RN That; 11ADD Noun of
6) 11ADD Beginning Conjunction; 2S Standard Series
7) 9PP Dash M Prepositional Phrase; 2S The Pair
8) 2S Choice Series extended; 3V Past Participle
9) 8RN What
10) 7AC If
11) 1F There is; 9PP Dash E Word
12) 9PP Dash M Appositive
13) 8RN Where; 3V Infinitive (2); 2S Choice; 2S The Pair (2); 4C As well as; 10TP E Verbal Phrase Present Participle; 2S Standard Series; 10TP E (Appositive Phrase); 8RN That; 6CC Yet
14) 11ADD Beginning Conjunction; 3V Present Participle
15) 7AC Once; 2S The Pair; 3V Past Participle
16) 11ADD Question
17) 10TP B Word
18) 10TP B Word; 11ADD Beginning Verb; 2S Choice; 10TP E Verbal Phrase; 3V Present Participle; 8RN That; 11ADD Compound verb
19) 11ADD Beginning Verb; 3V Infinitive (2); 8RN What; 6CC And; 3V Gerund; 4C Not only, but; 7AC Once

FAMILY by Nicole Alexander

Family is very important in one's life; family contributes the most to one's character.**1** Although there are many different kinds of relationships within families, all the members of a family should love each other.**2**

A mother's relationship with her children is warm, caring, protective.**3** Though she has wants and needs and desires, she is willing to give up some of her time for her children.**4** The mother is the hen; her children, the baby chicks under her wing.**5**

The father's relationship with the mother is romantic and caring and compassionate.**6** Before they made the commitment to each other to have a family, they had to make sure that they were right for each other.**7** They did not have to be together, but because of the love and faith of a successful marriage, they decided to spend the rest of their lives together.**8**

As the parents of the family show their love for each other, the children inadvertently learn from them.**9** In the future, they may also have successful marriages, but until then, they will often fight amongst themselves.**10** Children are young; children are inexperienced; children are often loud.**11** They will harass each other, and they will hit each other constantly; all the while they will be yelling and screaming.**12** So, in the beginning, it seems that siblings will never get along, let alone be friends, but later on they will begin to mature and laugh at the havoc they caused.**13**

The trials and tribulations of a family are many, but the end results are rewarding.**14**

Sentence Forms:

1) 9PP Association Semicolon
2) 7AC Although
3) 2S Triple Force
4) 7AC Though; 2S Lyrical Series; 3V Infinitive
5) 9PP Stylish Semicolon [figure of speech – metaphor]
6) 2S Lyrical Series
7) 7AC Before; 3V Infinitive (2); 8RN That
8) 3V Infinitive (2); 6CC But; 10TP B or M Prepositional Phrase; 2S The Pair

9) 7AC As
10) 10TP B Prepositional Phrase; 6CC But; 10TP B or M Prepositional Phrase
11) 5R Keyword; 9PP Trio Semicolon
12) 9PP Complicated Semicolon; 11ADD Compound Verb
13) 10TP B Word; 10TP B Prepositional Phrase; 8RN That; 2S Compact Duo [verbs]; 6CC But; 3V Infinitive (2); 8RN Missing That
14) 2S The Pair; 6CC But

MY HUSBAND'S SUMMER WARDROBE   by Melinda Robertson

I've always considered my husband's obsession with his summer wardrobe to be an anomaly.**1** He has a very individualistic sense of fashion – which is not always consistent with the current decade, his age group, socio-economic status, or any other established societal 'norms'.**2** Anyone under the age of sixty that can wear knee-high football socks with sandals, faded t-shirts with giant holes, and short pants with permanent grass stains – in public with no sense of embarrassment – should be considered devoid of any fashion sense.**3**

His clothing may appear to have been put on indiscriminately; however, all of his outfits have been planned well in advance of any summer outings.**4** At the beginning of the season (to eliminate time spent selecting the perfect outfit for any planned outings), he purchases the most monochromatic clothing that he can find – provided that it coordinates with his idea of fashion.**5** Shoes, shorts, shirts – all these items must be either khaki, drab olive, or black; if they do not qualify as part of these color categories, he will not buy them.**6**

Not only is he concerned with color, but with style and function according to his own unique conception.**7** His shorts must fit into his fashion code exactly: they must have two back pockets with flaps, and four front pockets.**8** His shorts must also have the 'zip on legs' option, so they may be converted to pants, and – most important of all – they must not be too long.**9** His shirts are the easiest to pick out; they must have a 'cool' design that is non-offensive.**10** His shirts must also be long enough to cover the waistband of his shorts, so that if he bends over, his butt crack won't show.**11**

Shopping with my husband for his summer wardrobe can be tiring.**12** Hopefully, the fashion experts will one day make "robot animals" to assist the adult male in his shopping as well as accompany him.**13** Until then, I will continue to suffer through every summer season. **14**

Sentence Forms:

1) 3V Infinitive
2) 11ADD Noun of; 8RN Which; 2S Choices Series; 3V Past Participle
3) 8RN That; 11ADD Compound Noun Phrases in a List; 3V Past Participle; 10TP M Prepositional Phrase extended; 11ADD Noun of
4) 9PP Expansive Colon
5) 10TP B Prepositional phrase extended; 10TP B (Verbal Phrase Infinitive); 9PP Dash Break; 3V Past Participle
6) 9PP B List Wrap-Up; 4C Either or; 9PP Association Semicolon; 7AC If
7) 4CC Not only, but; 2S The Pair
8) 9PP Explanation Semicolon
9) 6CC So; 6CC And; 9PP Dash M Adjective Phrase
10) 9PP Association Semicolon; 8RN That
11) 3V Infinitive; 7AC So that supplemental; 7AC If
12) 3V Gerund
13) 10TP B Word; 3V Infinitive; 4C As well as; 3V Infinitive Missing to
14) 10 TP B Prepositional Phrase; 3V Infinitive

GONE FISHING by Jimmy Currie

Life can be hard at times and a person needs some way of relieving stress.**1** I have tried them all, but the one thing that works best for me is fishing.**2** I remember catching my very first fish, just like it was yesterday.**3** That fish started tugging, pulling, jerking me all over the place.**4** Since that day I have had a passion for fishing and the joy that it brings.**5** A day spent behind the rod leaves me felling refreshed and ready for the curves life has in store.**6**

I travel around all the time with fishing supplies in my car.**7** You never know when you may come across a good fishing hole.**8** Rivers, lakes, streams – these are the places where I like fishing the most.**9** My favorite fish – bass, cat, and brim – are all found in rivers and streams.**10** However, lakes provide excellent varieties of fish also.**11** Fishing rods are my choice for fishing in lakes; poles are my choice of fishing in rivers and streams.**12** Earthworms and grasshoppers, crickets and minnows, lures and liver are all types of fish bait.**13** If you are lucky enough to have a boat, you get the best fishing from rivers, lakes, or streams.**14**

Fishing allows me to spend quality time with friends and family.**15** My family – as much as I like having them around – are not good fishermen at all.**16** I spend more of my time baiting their hooks rather than fishing.**17** Pretty soon someone will catch a fish: this starts the competition.**18** For the rest of the day, everyone's goal is to catch a bigger one.**19**

Casting out every time, not knowing what you will catch, brings everybody excitement.**20** Sometimes, I like to fish alone to have peace and quiet.**21** Any problem that I may be having usually can be worked out on the banks of a river.**22**

You never know how long you are going to be away when you go fishing, so pack a lunch.**23** Even though fishing relieves my stress, one other thing keeps me coming book: the one that got away.**24**

Sentence Forms:

1) 3V Gerund
2) 6CC But; 8RN That; 3V Gerund
3) 3V Gerund; 7AC As If supplemental
4) 2S Triple Force
5) 10TP B Prepositional Phrase; 3V Gerund; 2S The Pair; 8RN That
6) 3V Past Participle; 3V Present Participle; 2S The Pair; 8RN Missing That
7) 3V Present Participle
8) 8RN When; 3V Present Participle
9) 9PP Dash List Wrap-Up; 7AC Where; 3V Gerund
10) 9PP Dash M List Appositives in Standard Series; 2S The Pair
11) 10TP B Word; 11ADD Noun of
12) 3V Present Participle; 3V Gerund (2); 9PP Association Semicolon; 2S The Pair
13) 2S The Pair (3); 2S Triple Force
14) 7AC If; 2V Infinitive; 3V Gerund; 2S Choices Series

15) 3V Gerund; 3V Infinitive; 2S The Pair
16) 9PP Dash M AC Clause supplemental; 3V Gerund
17) 4C Rather than; 3V Present Participle (2)
18) 9PP Explanation Colon
19) 10 TP B Prepositional Phrase extended; 3V Infinitive
20) 3V Gerund; 3V Present Participle; 8RN What
21) 10TP B Word; 3V Infinitive (2); 2S The Pair
22) 8RN That
23) 8RN How; 3V Infinitive; 7AC When; 6CC So
24) 7AC Even Though; 3V Gerund; 9PP Explanation Colon; 8RN That

RESTORING TRUCKS AND SPEEDING DOWN THE ROAD by Chris Page

Although the restoration of cars takes a lot of time and patience, the thrill of speeding down the road is well worth the time spent.**1**

My hobby started one day in the backyard as my father began rebuilding the engine in his newly purchased 1965 Chevy truck.**2** I didn't know much about cars at the time, and I was only old enough to hand my dad tools, but I managed to ask a few questions.**3** Before I knew it, I was right beside him, getting greasy and grimy.**4** The more that I helped him, the more I seemed to learn.**5** With every new learning experience, I grew more interested and knew what I wanted when I turned sixteen.**6**

Finally, the day came.**7** I turned sixteen and got my license.**8** My dad gave me that 1965 Chevy truck that we spent many days together, rebuilding.**9** It had been five years, five long years since we first worked on this truck together.**10** Spending much of my time and effort in the restoration of this truck, I had little time to do anything else.**11** If I was not in school, if I was not working, if the sun was still in the sky, I was working on the truck.**12** Since I had worked so hard on the truck, my dad decided to surprise me.**13** He bought all the parts that I had wanted to make my truck a hotrod.**14**

All I could think about was what I would fix first, for this is what I had always dreamed.**15** The time I had waited for all week had finally arrived – the weekend.**16** It was cold outside, but that would not stop my eagerness and enthusiasm to start working.**17** The camshaft, the carburetor, the manifold – these were all the parts that needed to be removed and replaced.**18**

The day finally came when all the parts had been replaced, and it was time to go out for a test drive.**19** There is nothing more thrilling than to pull out onto the road, push the accelerator to the floor, and feel the power in the engine being released.**20** The tires start to smoke, the engine reaches its peak, and then you shift into second.**21** By the time you start slowing down, you are going well over 120 m.p.h.**22**

It took me many years to realize the satisfaction of that moment on the road.**23** Although it has been several years since I have been able to work on cars, my passion to restore trucks and cars will always be there, and I long for the day when I will once again be able to speed down the road.**24**

Sentence Forms:

1) 7AC Although; 2S The Pair; 3V Gerund; 3V Past Participle
2) 7AC As; 3V Gerund; 3V Past Participle
3) 6CC And; 6CC But; 3V Infinitive (2)
4) 7AC Before; 3V Present Participle; 2S The Pair
5) 4C The more, the more; 8RN That; 8RN Missing that; 3V Infinitive
6) 10TP B Prepositional Phrase; 11ADD Compound verb; 8RN What; 7AC When
7) 10TP B Word
8) 11ADD Compound verb
9) 8RN That; 10TP E Word
10) 5R Repetition Keyword; 7AC Since; 10TP E Noun Phrase
11) 10TP B Verbal Phrase; 2S The Pair; 3V Infinitive
12) 5R Adverbial Conjunction
13) 7AC Since; 3V Infinitive
14) 8RN That; 3V Infinitive
15) 8RN What (2); 6CC For
16) 8RN Missing that; 9PP E Word
17) 6CC But; 2S The Pair; 3V Infinitive; 3v Gerund

18) 2S Triple Force; 9PP Dash B Wrap-up; 8RN
That; 11ADD Compound Infinitive
19) 7AC When; 6CC And; 3V Infinitive
20) 11ADD Compound Infinitive; 2S Standard
Series; 3V Present Participle
21) 3V Infinitive; 2S Standard Series
22) 10TP B Prepositional Phrase; 8RN Missing that;
3V Gerund
23) 3V Infinitive
24) 7C Although; 7AC Since; 3V Infinitive (2); 2S
The Pair; 6CC And; 7AC When

FASHION PERSONALITIES **by April Turner**

The clothes we wear say more about us than we think.**1**
I have come to learn that a person's personality and
wardrobe go hand-in-hand.**2** You cannot judge a person
solely on a first impression; rather, it takes a long time.**3** It
takes several weeks of observation to make a sound
judgment: weeks of seeing the person, weeks of watching the
person, weeks of studying his or her dress pattern.**4** You will
– 9 times out of 10 – find three main personality types: those
who dress to fit in, those who dress to stand out, and those
who dress whichever way they please.**5**

Do you know someone who only wears the latest
fashions?**6** He wouldn't be caught dead in a pair of "Air
Jordans" more than 6 months old. Every piece of clothing he
owns is name brand: Nautica, Nike, Polo. **7** He doesn't own a
shirt that cost him less than $30.00.**8** He will only wear
clothes that he knows are in style, as long as baggy pants
and big shirts will bring popularity.**9**

Then there is the shy, stand-offish person. You will only
find him in the back of the room or to the side of any
crowd.**10** This guy most likely has a basic wardrobe,
because he doesn't want to wear anything that may draw
attention to himself.**11** He owns about seven pairs of jeans –
all blue. He likes to wear white or black shirts, but never a
bright color.**12**

Finally, there is my favorite. This person wears anything
that catches his eye.**13** He knows what he likes and goes for
it.**14** He is not out to impress, for he does not worry about

401

what others think.**15** He likes to wear name brands, but he loves a good bargain.**16** He dresses how he feels.**17** If he is in a good mood, he looks nice, whereas you may catch him on a bad day and not even recognize him.**18** This person is outgoing; however, he can sometimes be moody.**19** He is happy and content with himself; he has confidence in himself and in his preferences and taste in clothes.**20** He chooses and wears clothes that reflect his character and personality.**21**

Sentence Forms:

1) 8RN Missing that; 7AC Than supplemental
2) 3VInfinitive; 8RN That; 2S The Pair
3) 9PP Expansive Semicolon
4) 11ADD Noun of; 3V Infinitive; 9PP Explanation Colon; 5R Keyword; 3V Gerund
5) 10TP M Adverb Phrase; 9PP List Colon; 8RN Who (3); 3V Infinitive (2); 8RN Missing that
6) 11ADD Question
7) 8RN Missing that; 9PP List Colon
8) 8RN That
9) 8RN That; 7AC As long as supplementary; 2S The Pair
10) 2S Choices Series
11) 7AC Because; 3V Infinitive; 8RN That
12) 9PP Dash E Adjective Phrase
13) 8RN That
14) 8RN What; 11ADD Compound Verb
15) 3V Infinitive; 6CC For; 8RN What
16) 3V Infinitive; 6CC But
17) 8RN How
18) 7AC If; 7AC Whereas supplemental; 11ADD Compound verb
19) 9PP Expansive Semicolon
20) 2S The Pair (2); 9PP Association Semicolon
21) 11ADD Compound verb; 8RN That; 2S The Pair

GERMAN SHEPHERD by PFC Johnson, N.

While I was young, my mother, acting as both parents, bought a dog.**1** The dog was a puppy at the time, but was everything a boy could want in a friend: playful, thoughtful, always there, willing to do anything, and would listen to you longer than anyone (aside from a nosy high school counselor).**2** This dog, a German Shepherd, was the closest thing to a sibling to me, a friend to me, and even, in a sense, a parent to me.**3**

Sassy, the name of my puppy, watched over me and kept me company, protecting me from danger, for I lived in a rough neighborhood.**4** Because my mother worked all night and slept all day, I was alone most of the time with nothing but my thoughts and my dog to entertain me.**5** Sassy was the one thing I needed to get though my childhood: she was the stepping stone to my happiness.**6**

Having a dog like Sassy was one of the best things that ever occurred in my life; but all good things must come to an end (and the greatest sometimes come to a screeching halt, leaving you with the feeling of being stabbed in the chest with a 2x4).**7** So, with Sassy locked in the backseat, we made our way to the animal clinic: she was going to be "put to sleep".**8** We were moving across the country, and we could not bring her along.**9** We could have given her to another family, but there were a few problems: she was getting old, she was going blind, and she had a broken leg that had never fully healed.**10** Our only choice was a choice too difficult for a 12-year-old boy – me – to deal with.**11**

After that heart-wrenching drama, and after my mother and I settled in our new house, we bought new animals of different types and genders.**12** But nothing could ever replace my German shepherd, Sassy.**13** As long as I live, I will never forget what that animal taught me, and where I might be if she had not come into my life.**14**

Sentence Forms:

1) 7AC While; 10TP M Verbal Phrase Present Participle
2) 6CC But (assumed subject); 8RN Missing that; 9PP Explanation Colon; 2S Standard Series extended; 10TP E (Prepositional Phrase)

403

3) 10TP M Appositive (2); 2S Standard Series; 10TP M Prepositional Phrase
4) 10TP M Appositive; 11ADD Compound Verb; 3V Present Participle; 6CC For
5) 7AC Because; 11ADD Compound Verb
6) 8RN Missing that; 3V Infinitive; 9PP Explanation Colon; literary device alliteration
7) 3V Gerund (2); 8RN That; 9PP Association Semicolon; 10TP E (Anecdotal Insertion); 3V Present Participle (2)
8) 10TP B Word; 10TP B Prepositional Phrase; 3V Past Participle; 9PP Explanation Colon
9) 6CC And
10) 6CC But; 9PP List Colon; 5R Word; 8RN That
11) 9PP Dash M Appositive; 3V Infinitive
12) 10TP B Prepositional Phrase; 7AC After; 11ADD Compound Prepositional Phrase; 2S The Pair
13) 11ADD Beginning Conjunction; 10TPE Appositive
14) 7AC As long as supplemental; 8RN What; 8RN Where; 7AC If

THE LAST PLAY OF THE GAME

by William Gonzales

Everyone on the team, who were seniors, knew the significance of this play.**1** It was the fourth quarter of Sam Rayburn High School vs. Aldene Nimitz High School; there were twenty-six seconds left in the game.**2** The score was 17 to 12 in Aldene's favor; however, we still had a chance, if we could only get four yards on this fourth down play.**3** This play meant more than just winning or losing a football game: it was the culmination of our adolescent lives.**4**

The seniors on the field were all thinking the same thing. We realized that this was possibly not only the last play of the football season, but it could also so be the last play and day of high school, of our innocence, of our youth.**5** Visions of the past appeared; our whole lives loomed before us.**6** After what seemed to be an eternal time out, we were in the huddle.**7**

Signals were flashed from the sidelines to our quarterback; the play was called.**8** I was to run a short slant pattern. I knew the pass would not go to me; however, the pass would go to another player, no mediocre pass catcher but an all-state receiver.**9** Everyone knew what they had to do, as we broke our huddle and stepped to the line.**10**

We lined up in formation as soldiers would, which is exactly what we were – soldiers (after all we had just been through a war).**11** We watched the enemy while our minds raced, raced through memories, raced through visions of success, raced through visions of defeat.**12** Brett, our quarterback, began yelling his commands; he yelled red, a code for when to react and begin the play.**13** It was time.

The play began – time to go to work.**14** Brett was in trouble; the enemy was blitzing; he had no one to throw to.**15** Suddenly, our eyes made contact, and he was able to lob a pass to me.**16** The ball hung in the air for an eternity. I thought if I could just catch it, if I could just get the first down, if I could just get out of bounds, then we had a chance.**17** The ball found my hands, but the clock ended the game before I could get out of bounds.**18** Then in a blink, high school and our youth and everything we had been were over.**19**

Sentence Forms:

1) 10TP M Clausal Interruption supplemental
2) 9PP Association Semicolon
3) 9PP Expansive Semicolon; 7AC If
4) 3V Gerund (2); 2S Choice Series; 9PP Explanation Colon
5) 4C Not Only, But; 2S The Pair; 5R Word
6) 9PP Association Semicolon
7) 8RN What
8) 9PP Association Semicolon
9) 9PP Expansive Semicolon; 10TP E Appositive Phrase (2); 4C Not only, but (variation)
10) 8RN What; 7AC As; 11ADD Compound Verb
11) 8RN Which; 8RN What; 10TP E Word; 10TP E (Clause) supplemental
12) 7AC While; 5R Keyword; 11ADD Noun of (2)
13) 10TP M Appositive; 3V Gerund; 10TP E Appositive Phrase; 8RN When; 3V Infinitive; 11ADD Compound Verbal Infinitive Missing to
14) 9PP Dash Break; 3V Infinitive
15) 9PP Trio Semicolon; 3V Infinitive
16) 10TP M Word; 6CC And; 3V Infinitive
17) 5R Adverbial Conjunction
18) 6CC But; 7AC Before
19) 10TP B Adverb Phrase; 2S Lyrical Series; 8RN Missing that

WINTER IN MAINE by Joshua Gatromb

There are only three seasons in Maine – winter, June, and July.**1** This joke is intended to make you realize the truth: Maine has the harshest, longest, and most intense winter in the United States.**2** I left the state vowing never to return, just because of the winter.**3** Some may argue that the sports and recreation associated with snow and winter are beneficial to the state: They are wrong.**4**

Being on the coast, being in the northeast, being at the epicenter of two converging weather fronts – all these things contribute to the harsh Maine winters.**5** The lack of sunlight is a major contributor to seasonal depression.**6** The above average number of cold weather injuries and deaths has led to a decline in population.**7** The benefits, a dismally small number, are not enough to counterbalance the detriments.**8**

On a frozen riverbed, in the month of April, is where I learned to ice skate.**9** The cold, frigid air still turns your nose red long after the calendar declares its spring.**10** Amazingly, snow has been reported to fall on July 4.**11** It is hard to imagine what a long winter can do to your psyche if you have not spent seventeen days in a row, at home, away from school, because the frozen pipes busted from the cold.**12** A Maine winter can literally last over six months.

Not only are the winters long, but they are also intense.**13** A continuous snowstorm, lasting twenty-three days, dumped 6'10" [208.3 cm] of snow one year.**14** The wind caused snowdrifts so high that people had to climb out their second story windows, and snowmobiles were the only mode of transportation.**15** The air is freezing, the water is freezing, and yes, the blanket-infested bed is freezing.**16** It takes a hearty Nordic Viking to brave the intensity of a Maine winter and live to tell the tale.**17**

Having experienced the harshest, longest, and most intense of winters, I have no affinity for the cold.**18** No individual that has lived in Maine can argue these points, and no individual that has not lived in Maine can understand them.**19** I may never get to experience a Maine winter again, if I am lucky, but I will never forget them.**20**

Sentence Forms:

1) 9PP Dash E List
2) 9PP Explanation Colon
3) 3V Present Participle; 3V Infinitive; 10TP E Prepositional or Adverb Phrase
4) 8RN That; 2S The Pair (2); 9PP Explanation Colon
5) 5R Keyword; 3V Gerund (3); 3V Present Participle; 9PP Dash B Wrap-Up
6) 11ADD Noun of
7) 2S The Pair
8) 10TP M Appositive Phrase

9) 10TP B Prepositional Phrase; 10TP M Prepositional Phrase; 8RN Where; 3V Infinitive
10) 2S Compact Duo; 7AC After
11) 10TP B Word; 3V Infinitive
12) 3V Infinitive; 8RN What; 7AC If; 7AC Because; 10TP M Prepositional Phrase; 10TP M Adverb Phrase
13) 4C Not Only, But
14) 10TP M Verbal Phrase Present Participle
15) 8RN That; 6CC And; 11ADD Noun of
16) 5R Keyword; 2S Standard Series
17) 3V Infinitive; 3V Infinitive Missing to
18) 3V Present Participle; 2S Standard Series
19) 8RN That (2); 5R Keyword
20) 3V Infinitive; 7AC If; 6CC But

EXAM #2:
FREE-FORM EXAM
(NO SPECIFIED FORMS, NO NOTATION, AT-WILL USE OF FORMS)

In the Free-Form Exam, you are given 1.5 to 2.5 hours to write an essay on one of 5 possible subjects. **You are *not* required to notate, and footnote any specified Sentence Forms**. You are *not* given any specific mix of Forms to include and do *not* have to notate and footnote at all. Your use of the Forms learned is entirely of your own choosing.

The aim of the examination is simply to see how effectively and gracefully you can write in a specified, reasonable period of time. The 5 subjects given for the final exam can either be nominated by you and your classmates the night before the exam and then the final subject chosen on the day of the exam itself. Or, if your teacher prefers, the 5 initial topics may be chosen from the following list the night or class before the exam and then the actual final topic chosen by you and your classmates on the day of the exam itself: *Music, Family, Vacations, Work, Hobbies, Animals, Friends, Memories, Clothes, Movies, Travel, Entertainment, Food, Seasons, Holidays, Life Lessons, and Sports.* The subjects were chosen because of their general familiarity to most people and therefore the ease with which you should be able to write about them.

What follows are some examples of final examinations written by previous students.

Extraordinary Travel

BY MATTHEW GARVIN

What comes to mind when you hear the word *travel*? Most of us would think of foreign countries or faraway lands where adventures occur only in the movies. Others may think of long, boring car rides from point A to point B – with nothing much in between worth taking the time to look at. Still, to some of us, the word *travel* brings to mind such topics as vacation or time-off. People reminisce of fun times with the family at Disney World or week-long camping trips to places where time was forgotten.

The truth is, travel includes all of these. Many people are constantly going from one place to another. Whether it be for business or pleasure, people today have seen and experienced much more of the world than their ancestors ever dreamed of seeing. I myself have done a great deal of traveling, mostly between the ages of five and twelve. I have been to many places that others would have considered impossible to visit.

For instance, when I was seven years old, my sister and I took an unannounced trip to Mars. Yes, you heard me – Mars. The capabilities of our backyard jungle gym far exceeded any technology NASA possessed at the time. As I piloted the spacecraft through devastating solar winds and unpredictable meteor shows, my sister operated the controls and monitored the instruments. Thoughtfully, she also brought supplies to eat and drink just in case we would be away for longer than expected. After completing a successful landing and walking around on the surface, we collected a few rocks and returned home. Upon our arrival back on Earth, we were confronted with an angry mom. Much to our surprise, we had missed dinner.

"I knew we were gone a while," my sister exclaimed.

After a little explaining, mom finally understood our adventure. She was glad we were home where we belonged, and safe. She did, however, make us promise to tell her before we planned on taking future expeditions. Perhaps she wanted to come along.

Another trip I took happened when I was in the fifth grade. Our science teacher assigned each student in the class a report on a kind of animal. The animals I chose were dinosaurs. After checking out a few titles from the school library, I went home to begin reading. Before too much time went by, my eyes were getting frustrated following all the words on the page. Since I really didn't feel like writing much anyway, I grabbed the family camcorder and decided to have some fun.

There was an enormous cardboard box in the storage room that my mother declared off limits. In a few minutes, I would learn why. My mother was concealing a top secret time machine. I was extremely excited, so I started to check it out. I couldn't believe my own mother would keep such a thing a secret. Knowing full well that I wasn't supposed to be playing around with it, I decided a quick look wouldn't hurt anybody, as long as no one found out. So I took a peek inside. As I was on my tippy toes straining to see, something slipped from under me and I went tumbling to the bottom. All of a sudden it started shaking wildly and making all kinds of strange noises.

"Oh, great, I'm dead," I thought. "Mom's surely gonna hear about this."

My first instinct was to get out and pretend nothing happened. As I hoisted myself over the top, I was the most surprised I've ever been in my entire life. I looked around, noticing that I wasn't in the house anymore. There were giant Tyrannosaurs and Brontosaurs all around. A Pterodactyl swooped down and almost took my head off! Literally scared out of my pants, I fell back down inside the machine and passed out. Next thing I know, my mom was downstairs wondering why the room was in shambles and there were little plastic figurines all over the floor. I pleaded with her and explained that I didn't know. I wasn't ever one for crying out loud. However, I had somehow been transported back to Jurassic Park. Though my mom hardly believed me, I insisted she watch the video; the film was all there was to back up my unbelievable story. Unfortunately, in the midst of all the action, I forgot to press the play button. The only proof I had from my trip was a sore butt and a deadline to clean up the mess.

One of the last places I went that I remember vividly was to the Super Bowl. My friends and I were planning a big party Super Bowl Sunday at my house. We were well-prepared: we stocked chips, dip, pretzels, cheese, peanuts, chocolate, and enough

Mountain Dew for the entire neighborhood. Before long the game had started and the 49ers were slaughtering the NY Giants by three whole touchdowns! Then, unexpectedly, something happened to the TV. There was no picture, no sound, no Super Bowl. Disappointed beyond compare, my buddies and I went outside for some air. At once we noticed some kids down the street playing football in the old wheat field. So we took off – heading for the action. Since we couldn't watch the game, and they obviously weren't watching it either, we proposed a challenge: our "49ers" against their "Giants". Willingly, they agreed, and we were now engaged in our own Super Bowl. The crowd ranted and raved at my 40-yard touchdown pass to John Taylor. They cheered again as Ricky Waters ran for a 22-yard touchdown. With the setting of the sun, our game was soon over. San Francisco won 56 to 21. We later learned that our TV had a fried circuit, and a new one would arrive next week. Too bad, but I was already looking forward to next season.

These are just a few of the exciting places and things I've had the opportunity to do or see throughout my life. Many people think that to travel the country or visit foreign lands or explore the unknown, you need lots of money and equipment. You must plan your events to conform to the allotted time and prepare for the unexpected. This is not true. All you need is a comfy chair or a warm bed, or a nice shady spot outdoors under a tree. Oh, I almost forgot something – don't leave behind your imagination.

The Joy, Challenge, Discipline, and Achievement of Being on a Swim Team BY Shana Dymeck

Ever since I was a little girl, I have always loved to swim. My grandparents have a pool – an indoor pool – where I swim every day. My family calls me Aqualungs because I can stay under water for a long time. My mom throws coins in the deep end; I dive down to get them, and I don't come up until I have all of them. Nobody in my family can stay under water for long, whereas I can stay under water for a minute and a half.

I remember when I was in the ninth grade, and there was an announcement for the swim team sign-ups. I was so fat, so inexperienced, so out-of-shape, that I really did not want to join. I decided to go anyway, so I could see who else wanted to join. I went to the meeting; I stayed for half an hour, but nobody I knew showed up. I left and walked back to my homeroom. Disappointed that none of my friends signed up, I sat at my desk and stared at the brick wall. I went home that day and called my friend Amy. I asked her why she wasn't at the meeting. She told me, because she was joining the diving team, she didn't need to be there. That made me feel a lot better. Then I called my friend Erica and asked her why she had not joined, and she told me it was because she had signed up the day before. Upon hearing this, I was really motivated.

The first day of practice was just the initial getting to know my teammates. The next day, we were in the pool, swimming laps. The first day of practice killed me. I think I swam more that night than I did my whole life. As the days turned into weeks and weeks to months, I could see a change in my strokes and breathing techniques. I began swimming faster and more accurately. My flip turns became easier, and I could do them in less time. I was really improving.

By the time our first meet rolled around, I felt I was ready to do my best. My coach put me in the 100yd backstroke. I was so nervous. I entered the pool; I heard the scorekeeper telling us to take our marks; I heard the horn,

413

and I was off. All I remember is that I was talking to myself through the stroke: "kick, kick, kick, kick." As soon as I saw the flags, I counted "1, 2, 3, 4, flip." By this time I had only a few more laps to go. My heart was pumping; my adrenaline was racing. I could see my teammates cheering me on, "GO, GO, GO!"

I knew I was close to finishing. I saw the flags and counted to 5 as I took each stroke. Finally, I finished; I felt the time pad and knew I did well. I looked up at the scoreboard and saw that I had come in second. A female from the opposite team had finished one-tenth of a second before I did. That didn't bother me though; it was my first race. Many more meets came, and I improved more and more.

By the time the swimming season was over, I had improved my time by 26 seconds. I was really proud of myself, and others appreciated what I had accomplished. We had a banquet, and my coach presented me with the most improved swimmer award. It made me feel so good. I knew I had accomplished something great.

Now, every time I get a chance to swim, I don't hesitate to go. It always brings back memories of my swim team experiences. Swimming – what a fun sport!

KIDS TODAY BY ALICIA ALLEN

Today's kids are a terror. Every day you see kids fighting, cursing and gambling, yet we are often encouraged by the ingenuity and quick-thinking skills that modern youth possess. Sometimes we may overlook their personalities because of what we see and hear, but we as adults don't understand their points of view, nor bother to ask. Many parents these days – and even those who do not have children of their won – say that children are unruly and undisciplined compared to when they were growing up, yet they fail to realize that there is no one to blame but themselves. Parents must realize that discipline begins at home and not in the classroom, while it is certainly not learned on the streets. Many believe that these same kids do not appreciate where they come from or even at times respect their parents and that may seem true to some, but as times change and evolve so do people and the way we view families and the ever-changing environment around us.

Kids seem to be constantly put down for the bad and negative effects they have on society, but we fail to see the good things they do as well. Perhaps, we will always have kids doing drugs or committing crimes, but we also have more and more kids graduating from colleges and becoming professionals. And many people these days strive to bring this world into the next century with better technology and innovations to make life better for their future kids.

I believe we, as a society, are underestimating the potential of children these days. Compared to the 1920s when children were seen mainly as labor and not heard at all, we have come a long way to the age of the independent, curious, and outspoken children of today. Kids these days have the tools and technology that people in the early 1900s never dreamed about. For example, we have gone from an environment full of disease we could never cure to a place where diseases can be controlled. This knowledge allows kids of today an edge never dreamed of before, and it's only getting better as time moves forward.

Violence among kids always seems to be a hot topic in society today. Kids didn't have the access to guns or lethal weapons many years ago, but these are the changes that come with a changing society. We must always remember that we take the good with the bad, and we must look at the entire picture to form an overall fair view and opinion. I believe that violence will always be an issue, and when we look at kids in the future, we will be saying the same things about them then that we do today.

A lot of parents and people also like to analyze the rates of kids having kids these days, and parents always say it was never like that when they were growing up. They also must look at the way that we have evolved in terms of sexual safety, and how we have prepared these kids for parenthood and the options they have today compared to say 20 years ago. The main point is that these kids have more options than they did in the past. Whether or not they choose to exercise them is their responsibility and choice, and their choice alone.

Finally, kids are viewed as children for too long in my opinion. This has not seemed to change from past times to now. People always underestimate kids and try to plan their lives too much for them. I don't see this as very different from the past. Parents and role models always try to sculpt children into what they see and want them to be, but we must all realize that there comes a point when a kid is no longer just a kid, but has become a grown young person.

BUILDING CHARACTER THROUGH WORK **BY RITA CHUNG**

It was a Friday evening, and my mom had the sudden craving for a quart of Baskin Robbin's Jamoca Almond Fudge ice cream. Of course, I volunteered to pick some up for her. As I reached the Baskin Robbin's front door, I noticed a sign posted on the glass window. The one thing that I was looking for had finally appeared right in front of my eyes. That sign contained the words that I had been hoping to read since the beginning of my senior year: "Now Hiring!"

I had never had a job before; at least, not a genuine job that paid the minimum wage. I lacked experience, and I never had the experience of taking orders from someone who was neither my parents nor a school administrator. This was, indeed, a challenge and a change. However, I was prepared for anything that might to be thrown my way. I bought the quart of Jamoca Almond Fudge and asked the cashier about the hiring sign. He informed me that the interviews were going to be Saturday afternoon and to come any time between the hours of 2-4 p.m. I thanked him, left the store, and anxiously waited for the next day to arrive.

As I entered Baskin Robbin's again the next day, I was confident, poised, and ready for anything. I was told to sit down and wait patiently for the manager to arrive. While doing that, I noticed a room full of people replicating the same actions as myself. Apparently, they were my competition. Was I afraid of competition? No. Was I intimidated by the competition? Yes, somewhat.

I was the first person to be interviewed by the manager. She was blunt and straightforward. I answered all her questions as honestly as possible; I became more intimidated by her than the competition. Surprisingly, the interview only lasted about 15 minutes, though it felt more like an eternity with infinity added on. Without hesitation, she hired me and shook my hand with approval. I was astonished.

During subsequent times at the store, when I was scooping rock hard ice cream, producing numerous sundaes, and making overly priced shakes and smoothies, I had many encounters with the nearby community. Indeed, I learned how to deal with obnoxious customers, annoying children and their even more annoying parents, and the daily deeds of being a cashier, a janitor, and a convincing sales person, who always encouraged customers to "upgrade" their scoop of ice cream for a dollar more. It was marvelous. I loved my job with a passion, and I soon got the chance to feel that exhilarating sense of obtaining a hard earned paycheck as well as having Uncle Sam's greedy hands swiping half of it for state taxes. Oh, what a joy it was, indubitably. Eventually, after I graduated from high school, and summer was coming to an end, I had to leave behind Baskin Robbin's and the wonderful people there. I had a new job to tend to: The United States Navy.

I had no idea what I was getting myself into as I stepped off the plane at Great Lakes, Illinois. As I went through basic training, I was constantly told by my division officer that enduring boot camp was the easiest job I could undertake; after all, I was provided with three meals a day, a bed, urinating facilities, and an intense workout or two. I even learned how to iron, starch, and fold my underwear properly. And for all of that, I was getting paid. My division officer was correct; but at times, I must admit, even a hardy paycheck couldn't brighten the many somber days I endured there.

Naturally, I passed basic training, went on to complete "A" school in the Information Systems of Technology (IT) field, and am now working as an IT in Korea.

The hours are long and unproductive at times; the job is tedious, redundant, and boring as well. However, the attributes that I acquired during my days at Baskin Robbins helped me conquer any task that was given to me in the Navy. I had already learned to tolerate those who ranked above me and who had the ultimate effect on my paycheck. I had already learned to appreciate and respect my colleagues, and I had learned to separate work and play, business and pleasure.

Having a job prior to the Navy taught me to be understanding and think through rough situations and that performing your job right will always get you through anything. The things that I've learned from my first job as a talented ice cream scooper, to my current job as an IT, can never be taken away from me. I've earned my merits, whether they are official or not, and I am grateful to have gone through a variety of jobs that have impacted me one way or another. Work allows you to grow, to interact with an assortment of people, and it builds moral character that will be instilled in you throughout your life.

THE VACATION FROM HELL   BY ANDRE COUNCIL

It was the summer of 1992. I had just graduated from high school, and it was time to party. We decided to take a long overdue vacation to Nags Head, NC. I had never been there before, but my friends assured me it would be the time of my life – they didn't lie about that one.

We packed our bags, filled the cooler, and journeyed off to North Carolina. The trip was so full of chaos and craziness, full of drinking, and flirting with women. We rented a minivan, and two hours into the ride we heard a rumbling noise coming from the tire. It was unbelievable. Before we could even get halfway there, we were fixing a flat tire. The job normally takes about 10-15 minutes to complete, but because we were so drunk, it must have taken us 45 minutes.

The tire was fixed, and we were on our way (still drinking of course). Jeff, who was driving, was not drinking; you see he was the type of person who behaved inebriated even when he was sober. All of sudden we heard sirens; the police were behind us because we were going well above the posted speed limit.

As we pulled over, we hurriedly put all the alcohol out of sight. The officer pulled up and asked if Jeff knew how fast he had been going. Jeff's response was a big mistake: he told the officer he didn't know and didn't care. (His exact words being "Dude I don't give a f*#$$.") The police officer immediately ordered Jeff out of the van and read him his rights. And then his partner also ordered all of us out of the van. "But sir we are going to Nags Head for a week's vacation," I pleaded. But now the search was on and he was sure to find the alcohol. We were all under age and under a lot of pressure at this point. We were told that we had no choice but to come down to the station and face our charges.

The charges were drinking under age, having an open container of alcohol in a vehicle, and Jeff's reckless driving charge. We had no choice but to call our parents, face the charges brought against us, miss our vacation, and spend a week in jail.

Needless to say, we were pretty upset at the fact that our vacation was history, that we were in jail in the middle of nowhere, and that there was no way we were ever going to be able to get to Nags Head. So there we were – looking like idiots – all because of immaturity.

SKYDIVING BY HEE GON YANG

Let me tell you what it feels like to fly: to soar through the air like the birds. In my opinion, there is no other feeling like it in the world. I don't know why I am attracted to it, but it draws me toward it. You see I got hooked on skydiving a few years ago when my friends introduced me to the sport. The anticipation of the freefall grips you like a vice. I think I love the sport because it defies the law of gravity; it breaks every law of nature. The anxious moments waiting for the flight into space, the rapid acceleration of the freefall, and the knowledge that I am defying nature are what make it so exciting.

It all starts in a classroom where the basics of skydiving are taught. The instructor teaches – in detail – every aspect of the art of freefall. The importance of safety and timing as well as of the form and style of the freefall are heavily stressed. This only adds to the excitement. After the classroom instructions, you must attempt a few dry runs on ground. Dry runs allow you to get familiar with the equipment and identify mistakes before you attempt the real thing.

I don't think any amount of instructions prepare anyone for the real thing: like learning to fly an airplane strictly in a simulator. The whirl of the propeller, the smell of jet fuel, the roar of planes taking off signifies it is time to do the real thing. The air rushing through the open plane only adds to the anticipation of actually freefalling. Once the plane reaches the proper altitude, the jumpmaster signals for everyone to start jumping. Once you debark, the instant adrenaline rush hits you like a brick. Once terminal velocity is reached, it feels like you are suspended in air; it must be what birds are feeling. The feeling lasts but seconds. If only briefly, I get to soar with the birds.

Our Family Trip to Florida by Melissa Hatfield

Family vacations at my house always started out at two o'clock in the morning as all six of us filed into our family van. Our father always went over his list for the trip and checked for the following items: food, luggage, money, four kids and one wife. After this, all was accounted for, and we were ready to go. This time we headed out for Orlando, Florida, and since we lived in Virginia Beach at the time, you can imagine easily what a long trip it was.

It took us an entire day just to get there, with my little brother Danny asking our mother if we were there yet twenty million times. My mother would respond suggesting that we play a fun car game. This is when Danny learned that he should just be quiet. I would have rather sat in silence or listened to my CD player. My other little brother Andrew was only two, so he couldn't play, but my sister Lara would, and even though my dad was driving, he knew better than to say no. After countless hours of hearing them play I-spy, find-that-license-plate, and the memory game, we finally arrived at our vacation spot.

The first task to complete was to get all of our stuff into the hotel room. Not only did we all bring about six pieces of luggage each, but our hotel room was always on the top floor. After this chore, my sibling and I would be full of energy and ready to go and do something fun, but our parents would be too tired from the long drive. All they would want to do was sleep.

When the next day came, our vacation began. My mother woke us all up at six in the morning, so that we wouldn't miss the free hotel breakfast (that always seemed to end at eight o'clock) after which we would start our day. Every day was always something different: a new amusement park, a new sightseeing place, or a new tourist attraction.

After two complete weeks of this, we would all be left so tired, so exhausted, so ready to go home, we would actually take the long trip back home feeling that we needed an additional vacation to recover from our family vacation.

THE SECOND CHILD   BY DEVINE DAVIS

I always believed once you have a second child, you could never love him as much as your first, yet I was wrong – in a way. I remember it as if it was yesterday, traveling to Saarbrucken, Germany, where he was born, to meet him and his foster parent. I was told his short history. He had two siblings who were already taken away: *Rech* and *Schiuchtern*, when translated to English, meant *pretty* and *shy*. Meanwhile, his own birth name was *Gewalttatig*, which meant *rowdy*. That should have been warning enough for my husband and I, yet when I saw his beautiful, big, brown eyes, it was love at first sight, and we told his foster mother "yes", we would take him. The next big step was the trip back to the United States.

"King William" – his new name – was plastered all over his shot records, birth certificate, and any other important documents that were needed in order to make his first trip to his new home in the United States as smooth as possible. As the months passed, my baby was not only rowdy, but also very active! He crawled all over the place and sometimes even ignored me when I called his name to come; instead, he crawled to strangers begging to be picked up. Whenever we all took family walks together, everyone always stopped to compliment King, for he and his sister always wore matching outfits. Although my daughter was young at the time, she never showed an ounce of jealousy towards him; instead, she always referred to him as her little "*budder*". Time passed, and their relationship only grew stronger.

Every year he grew older, but he always looked the same – same hair, same eyes, same size. I am so familiar with the stares I receive: in restaurants, video stores, and even restrooms! I am aware that King doesn't look like the rest of his family. But photographers, when they took pictures of our family, were so stunned with the way the family looked, they regularly asked my daughter "Where did you get your little brother from?", and she proudly replied "Germany!" The noisy photographers smiled and continued on with their task. My family members have become accustomed to the stares, questions, and whispers; they only make us stronger and more confident.

My daughter is now 5½, and to this day she remembers when we brought King into our family; regardless of his appearance and his nature, she loved him like a big sister should. Every June 23rd we celebrate King's birthday, and this past June, even though I was here in Korea, my husband and daughter made sure they had his cake ready with candles – his age in human years. And even though he is a dog, he loves to wear his birthday hat and lick the icing off the cake. He acts like a typical 7 year old (in human terms) – like a boy to me!

> Writing, then, rarely involves the spontaneous production of language; instead, we write and rewrite, revise and edit, arranging and rearranging words. . . . That's why it makes sense to speak of writing as a craft: writers begin with the raw material of language and shape it until it expresses something of ourselves – our experiences, observations, and feelings, our ideas and convictions.
>
> Nora Bacon
>
> *The Well-Crafted Sentence: a writer's guide to style* (2009)

Pursing Semester 2 of the Writing Course

Students have now acquired an understanding of the Form features and Form options available in the English Sentence. Our system covers most if not all of such Forms found in Sentences in this first semester of writing instruction.

Students can further improve their writing skills by pursuing the second semester of our 1-year course in writing instruction. A process essay, an essay on the paragraph, a narrative essay, an expository essay, a descriptive essay, and an autobiographical essay form the bulk of the writing assignments for Semester 2.

Students can pursue the second semester of the full 1-year course using our method of teaching writing as laid out in the second volume of our original, 2-volume set entitled *The Two Hands Approach to the English Language: A Symphonic Assemblage.* It provides model professional essays and numerous model student essays – most of them with the Forms used, notated, and footnoted – to support each of the essay types, and it also covers Poetry and more effective methods of Reading. See **symphonicassemblage.org**.

A more economical choice is *New Angle on Writing (Semester 2).* This is a much slimmer edition of the Volume II book described above, but provides the essential charts and model student compositions from the essay writing section of the larger book, a course outline, plus a review of the Sentence Forms taught in that book. See the title page of the shorter book on the next page. To purchase it, visit **newangleonwriting.org**.

Below is a snapshot of the title page for the companion and recommended next book for use in the 1-year writing course, *New Angle on Writing (Semester 2).*

Selected Bibliography

A much larger bibliography (than the selected bibliography below) of all the books we consulted for our 2 volume study of the English language, *The Two Hands Approach to the English Language: A Symphonic Assemblage,* is given at the end of Volume II.

(1)   Bacon, Nora. *The Well-Crafted Sentence: a writer's guide to style.* Boston: Bedford/St.Martins, 2009.

(2)   Barzun, Jacques. *Simple & Direct: a rhetoric for writers, 4th ed.* New York: Harper, 1975, 2001.

(3)   Beaufort, Anne. *College Writing and Beyond: A New Framework for University Writing Instruction.* Logan, Utah: Utah State University Press, 2007.

(4)   Beaufort, Anne. *Writing in the Real World: Making the transition from school to work.* New York: Teachers College Press (Columbia University), 1999,

(5)   Berlin, James A. *Rhetoric and Reality: Writing Instruction in American Colleges 1900-1985.* Carbondale: Southern Illinois UP, 1987.

(6)   Berlin, James A. *Writing Instruction in 19th Century American Colleges.* Carbondale: Southern Illinois UP, 1984.

(7)   Bishop, Wendy, Deborah Coxwell Teague. *Finding Our Way: A Writing Teacher's Sourcebook.* Boston: Houghton Mifflin, 2005.

(8)   Blumenthal, Joseph C. *English 2600 with Writing Applications: A Programmed Course in Grammar and Usage.* New York: Wordworth Publishing, 1994.

(9)   Boice, Robert. *Professors as Writers: a self-help guide to productive writing.* Stillwater OK: New Forums Press Inc. 1990.

(10) Brown, H. Douglas. *Teaching by Principles: an interactive approach to language pedagogy.* Englewood Cliffs NJ: Prentice Hall, 1994.

(11) Britton, James. *Language and Learning.* 2nd ed. Portsmouth, NH: Boynton/Cook, 1993.

(12) Britton, James, et al. *The Development of Writing Abilities 11 to 18.* London: Macmillan, 1975.

(13) Carroll, Joyce Armstrong, Edward E. Wilson. *Acts of Teaching: How to Teach Writing.* Englewood, CO: Teacher Ideas Press, 1993.

(14) Casagrande, June. *It was the best of sentences, it was the worst of sentences.* Berkeley: Ten Speed Press, 2010.

(15) Christensen, Francis. *Notes Toward a New Rhetoric: 6 Essays for Teachers*. New York: Harper, 1967.

(16) Clark, Roy Peter. *The Glamour of Grammar: a guide to the magic and mystery of practical English*. New York: Little, Brown and Company, 2010.

(17) Connors, Robert J. *Selected Essays of Robert J. Connors*. Ed. by Lisa Ede and Andrea A. Lunsford. Urbana, Illinois: Bedford/St. Martins, 2003.

(18) Connors, Robert J. *The Erasure of the Sentence*. From *College Composition and Composition* 52.1 (2000: 96-128)

(19) Corbett, Edward P.J., Nancy Myers, and Gary Tate. *The Writing Teacher's Sourcebook. 4th edition*. New York: Oxford University Press, 2000.

(20) Crowley, Sharon. *Composition in the University: Historical and Polemic Essays*. Pittsburgh: Univ. of Pittsburgh Press, 1998.

(21) Delbanco, Nicholas. *The Sincerest Form: Writing Fiction by Imitation*. New York: McGraw-Hill, 2004.

(22) Elbow, Peter. *Everyone Can Write: Essays Toward a Hopeful Theory of Writing and Teaching Writing*. New York: Oxford University Press, 2000.

(23) Fish, Stanley. *How to Write a Sentence: and how to read one*. New York: HarperCollins, 2011.

(24) Glaser, Joe. *Understanding Style: practical ways to improve your writing*. New York: Oxford University Press. 1999.

(25) Haek, Byron. *A Counter-History of Composition*. Pittsburgh: University of Pittsburgh Press, 2007.

(26) Kinneavy, James. *A Theory of Discourse*. Englewood Cliffs, NJ: Prentice-Hall, 1971.

(27) MacNeil, Robert. *Listening to our Language*. English Journal, Oct. 1988.

(28) Miller, Susan (ed.). *The Norton Book of Composition Studies*. New York: W.W. Norton & Co.,2009.

(29) Moffett, James. *Detecting Growth in Language*. Portsmouth NH: Boyton/Cook Heinemann, 1992.

(30) Moffett, James. *Teaching the Universe of Discourse*. New York: Boynton/Cook, 1987.

(31) North, Stephen M. *The Making of Knowledge in Composition: Portrait of an emerging field*. Portsmouth NH: Boyton/Cook Heinemann, 2000.

(32) O'Reilly, Mary. *The Peaceable Classroom*. New York: Boynton/Cook, 1993.

(33) Ohmann, Richard. *English in America: A Radical View of the Profession*. New York: Oxford University Press, 1976.

(34) Pellegrino, Victor C. *A Writer's Guide to Powerful Paragraphs: 30 Ways Organize and Write Effective Paragraphs.* Wailuku, Hawaii: Maui ar Thoughts Co., 1993.

(35) Pellegrino, Victor C. *A Writer's Guide to Transitional Words and Expressions.* Wailuku, Hawaii: Maui ar Thoughts Co., 1987.

(36) Perl, Sondra, ed. *Landmark Essays on Writing Process.* Davis, CA, USA: Hermagoras Press, 1994.

(37) Roen, Duane, Veronica Pantoja, Lauren Yena, Susan K. Miller, Eri Waggoner. *Strategies for Teaching First-Year Composition.* Urbana IL: National Council of Teachers of English, 2002.

(38) Russell, David R. *Writing in the Academic Disciplines, 1870-1990: a curricular history.* Carbondale, Souther Illinois UP, 1991.

(39) Scholes, Robert. *The Rise and Fall of English: Reconstructing a discipline.* New Haven: Yale University Press, 1998.

(40) Strong, William. *Sentence Combining: a composing book* (3rd ed.) New York: McGraw-Hill, 1994, 1983.

(41) Strong, William. *Writer's Toolbox: a sentence-combining workshop.* New York: McGraw-Hill, 1996.

(42) Tate, Gary, Amy Rupiper, and Kurt Schick. *A Guide to Composition Pedagogies.* New York: Oxford University Press, 2001.

(43) Tate, Gary, Edward P.J. Corbett, and Nancy Myers. *The Writing Teacher's Sourcebook.* 3rd ed. New York: Oxford University Press, 1994.

(44) Trimble, John R. *Writing with Style: Conversations on the Art of Writing.* Englecliffs, New Jersey: Prentice-Hall, Inc., 1975.

(45) Villanueva, Victor Jr. (ed.). *Cross-Talk in Comp Theory: A Reader.* Urbana, Illinois: National Council of Teachers of English, 1997.

(46) Von Hallberg, Robert. *Canons.* Chicago: University of Chicago Press, 1984.

(47) Waddell, Maria L., Robert M. Esch, and Roberta R. Walker. *The Art of Styling Sentences: 20 Patterns for Success.* 3rd ed. Hauppauge, NY: Barron's Educational Service, 1993.

(48) Yagoda, Ben. *The Sound on the Page: Style and Voice in Writing.* New York: Harper, 2005.

Valuable Writing Websites:

1) Harvard Guides for Writing http://is.gd/hAiOu

2) UMUC Online Guide to Writing and Research http://is.gd/hAj4i

Biographical Notes on the Authors

Richard Dowling, M.A.

Richard Dowling is an associate professor with the Asian Division of the University of Maryland University College, where he has taught English Composition, History, and Government courses in Asia for 20 years – including Guam, Japan, and Australia for 20 years, with 15 of those years in South Korea. He received a B.A. in History and Philosophy from Wheeling University in 1966, and an M.A. in History from Duquesne University in 1968. He also completed two years of doctoral work in History at the University of Connecticut from 1968 to 1970. Subsequently, he received a B.S. in English from the State University of New York in 1990, and a permanent certificate to teach both English and Social Studies in grade 7-12 from the State of New York in1991.

In 2008, he published his first book *The Youth and Maturity of Humanity: Interpreting American, Modern, and Impending Global History as One Story*. The book is available online.

He introduced the *New Angle on Writing* in a preliminary form (*The Two Hands Approach*) at the KOTESOL conference in Daegu, South Korea in October 2000 and again in a talk at a KOTESOL meeting in the spring of 2010.

He has taught this Approach for over 12 years.

Stephen D. Watson, M.Ed.

Stephen Watson has taught English at universities in Gumi and Daegu, South Korea and in Guangzhou, China for more than 9 years. Prior to that, he taught high school mathematics in Canada, Tanzania, and Guyana. He also participated in the Arcosanti arcology project in Arizona, and he contributed to greenbelt afforestation at Auroville in Tamil Nadu, India. He has B.Ed. and B.A. degrees from Queen's University in Kingston, Ontario, Canada. He completed his M.Ed. in Teaching Second Languages from the University of Southern Queensland, Australia in 2002.

He has written and illustrated a children's book entitled *Moss, the Bike-Riding Mosquito*, published in 2008 and available online.

He has also produced 4 musical CDs with songs under the artist name stedawa. He plays guitar and sings all the songs on the 4 CDs, most of which were written by him; additionally, he puts fine poems by other writers to music. The 4 CDs are available online with the following titles: "*in it for the long haul*", "*Peoples of the World – A New Day*", "*Burst onto the Scene*", and "*Symphony of Song*".

He taught an earlier version of this book in Gumi, South Korea and Guangzhou, China.

Made in the USA
Lexington, KY
31 March 2013